Empirical Analysis of Determinants, Distribution and Dynamics of Poverty

Göttinger Studien zur Entwicklungsökonomik
Göttingen Studies in Development Economics
Herausgegeben von/ Edited by Hermann Sautter und/and Stephan Klasen

Bd./Vol. 19

PETER LANG
Frankfurt am Main · Berlin · Bern · Bruxelles · New York · Oxford · Wien

Kenneth Harttgen

Empirical Analysis of Determinants, Distribution and Dynamics of Poverty

PETER LANG
Internationaler Verlag der Wissenschaften

Bibliographic Information published by the Deutsche Nationalbibliothek
The Deutsche Nationalbibliothek lists this publication in the Deutsche Nationalbibliografie; detailed bibliographic data is available in the internet at <http://www.d-nb.de>.

Zugl.: Göttingen, Univ., Diss., 2007

Gratefully acknowledging the support of the
Ibero-Amerika-Institut für Wirtschaftsforschung, Göttingen.

Cover illustration by courtesy of the
Ibero-Amerika-Institut für Wirtschaftsforschung, Göttingen.

D 7
ISSN 1439-3395
ISBN 978-3-631-57398-3

www.peterlang.de

für Oma und Opa

Editor's Preface

The reduction of poverty and inequality in its many dimensions remains the key objective of development policy. This has been emphasized, for example, by the Millennium Development Goals agreed to by the world community in 2000. While some regions and countries have been made considerable progress towards the achievement of the goals, many countries are lagging behind. This is particularly the case in Sub Saharan Africa where there continues to be many knowledge gaps about what policies are needed to reach the goals. Without a better understanding of the interdependencies of poverty dimensions and their determinants it is very difficult to generate any reliable policy interventions.

This thesis contributes to analyzing unresolved important issues in the fight against poverty by examining the correlations, determinants, and dynamics of several dimensions of poverty. In the first essay, Kenneth Harttgen examines the interdependencies and determinants of child mortality and child undernutrition in several countries in Sub-Saharan Africa and South Asia using representative microdata sets. In particular, he analyzes the question why child mortality is considerable higher in Africa than in South Asia although the incidence of child undernutrition is higher in South Asia than in Africa. Harttgen shows that differences in the determinants of both phenomena partly explain this puzzle. The overall poor health care system in African countries strongly contributes to the high rates of child mortality in this region whereas the relatively low nutritional status of mothers contributes to the high rates of child undernutrition in South Asia.

In the second essay Harttgen takes a closer look at how the HIV/AIDS epidemic affects childrens' welfare. Unlike many studies using aggregated data to study the effects of HIV/AIDS on outcomes of human well-being, the author uses household survey data at the micro level and focuses on the direct effect of the epidemic and also on the potential indirect socio-economic effects on children living in HIV/AIDS-affected households. By applying several econometric methodologies, a special focus of this essay is on studying the impact of HIV/AIDS on child mortality, undernutrition, and school enrollment. He shows that HIV/AIDS have a considerable negative impact on the welfare of children.

The third essay is concerned with the measurement of pro-poor growth, i.e. with an analysis of how progress in income and non-income indicators of well-being is distributed over the population. The question whether the poor have benefited more from poverty reduction and economic growth than the non-poor is of particular policy relevance to reduce poverty and reach the Millennium Development Goals. Since existing measures of pro-poor growth rely only on the monetary dimension of poverty, Harttgen addresses an important gap in the literature by extending the existing toolbox of measuring pro-poor growth to the non-monetary dimensions of poverty. This new approach is then applied to study pro-poor growth in income and non-income dimensions in Bolivia in the 1990s.

In the fourth essay, Harttgen picks up another important question in the analysis of poverty and analyzes how shocks affect the poverty risk of households. In recent years, the literature has began to focus on the so-called vulnerability to poverty, i.e. the risk a household to fall into poverty in the future. The risk of falling into poverty is also an important factor for the households' current status of well-being. However, mostly due to data constrains empirical studies are still rare. The author overcomes this problem and proposes an accurate and intuitive method to empirically assess the impact of shocks at the household and at the community level on households' vulnerability to poverty. Applying this approach to Madagascar, he comes to the conclusion that whereas household-level shocks play a much more important role for urban households' vulnerability, vulnerability of households in rural areas is mainly driven by shocks at the community level.

Kenneth Harttgen thus addresses a number of highly topical issues discussed in the ongoing literature on poverty and inequality in developing countries. Harttgen also provides very important new insights for our understanding of poverty dynamics in its many dimensions. Apart from the analysis of the determinants of poverty in its socio-economic dimension, the thesis sheds more light on the dynamic dimensions of poverty reduction across the population and on poverty risk over time. With his analysis, Harttgen provides a valuable contribution to the economic literature on the empirical analysis of poverty in general, and on child mortality, undernutrition, HIV/AIDS, pro-poor growth and vulnerability to poverty in particular.

Prof. Stephan Klasen, Phd.
Göttingen, June 2007

Author's Preface

An expert is a man who has made all the mistakes which can be made in a very narrow field.
Nils Bohr, 1885-1962

At least I tried hard to make really all of them and learned much about the trial and error principle.

Writing a doctoral thesis for me was a little bit like climbing a mountain. The focus on the summit, it seems to be that it does not come closer at all and each step forward is slow and exhausting. But as soon as the summit is reached, any struggle is forgotten instantly, and there is no doubt of doing it again.

The last three years have been a very special time in my life and writing my doctoral thesis has had a substantial impact on me. When I started to write this thesis, I did not really know what the content would be. But after a somewhat cumbersome start, I got involved in some other projects at work, which provided me with many new insights and ideas to really take off. Working at the Department of Economics at the University of Göttingen endowed me with a lot of freedom both for many different work experiences and for many time intensive activities off the job, which I really appreciated. Besides the academical experience, I have also learned many things that had nothing to do with my thesis but which were very important for my personal development. In particular, working on and struggling with my thesis have shown me the limits of my intellectual abilities very often but, at the same time, exactly this brought me forward. The most important thing I have learned during that time is that I got a very sensiblelized feeling to what I can and, most notably, what I can learn, which is a very valuable skill for me, also for all other upcoming challenges in my life. In sum, I have really had a good time with many more ups than downs, which I do not want to miss at all.

However, I would not have been able to finish this thesis without the great help and support of many colleagues and friends, to whom I would like to express my thanks with this preface. First of all, I would like to thank my supervisor Prof. Stephan Klasen for accepting me as a doctoral student and giving me the chance to write my thesis and for motivating me over the last three years. He gave me great input and ideas (and I am still fascinating that he knew always an answer to whatever I have asked him). I am also thankful to Prof. Stephan Klasen for the good boss he was, who gave me so much freedom at work and who entrusted me with a lot of responsibility when working with him (even when Mark was involved). I am also very grateful to J.Prof. Michael Grimm who, first of all, became a good friend over the last three years. He supported me whenever needed and always gave very helpful comments to my research. Working for him and with him was always very pleasurable and I have learned quite a lot about the empirical analysis of poverty from him.

Turning to the Department of Economics at the University of Göttingen, I am also very thankful to many of my colleagues. Without their great support I certainly would not have made it this far. At the department, I met three persons who have accompanied my work and my life over the last three years and who have become of particular importance to me. I would like to express my sincere thanks to my co-authors Isabel Günther, Melanie Grosse, and Mark Misselhorn. Your help and support was of really unpayable value to finish this thesis, but your friendship is of very much more value to me. ¡Muchas Gracias!

Thinking about finishing this thesis reminds me eminently of Kai Stukenbrock. Working at the department of Economics, he accompanied me from my very beginning of my study of economics (without him, I probably would have even quit after one semester). He believed in me and encouraged me to write this thesis. Furthermore, I would also like to thank Silke Woltermann and Matthias Witt for their continuing support and friendship.

I am also very grateful to my friends outside of the University, who supported me in many ways. My special thank goes to Wibke Saathoff who takes care of me and who proofed to become an irreplaceable part in my life. And nobody knows me better than my best friend Gregor Iwanoff, who always supports me in any ways (above all in non-economic things) and who is always there when I need him.

Furthermore, I would like to express a very big thanks to all other people who helped me directly and indirectly with my thesis and who I forgot to explicitly mention here.

Finally, the biggest and ultimate thank goes to my great family, especially to my parents. They never questioned my doing and always trusted in me (which really must have been a tremendous challenge for them). Without their persistent support (not only financially) and their great care, I would never have been able to write this thesis.

Kenneth Harttgen
Göttingen, March 2007

Contents

List of Tables

List of Figures

List of Abbreviations

ACC	United Nations Administrative Committee on Coordination
AIDS	Acquired Immunodeficiency Syndrome
BCG	Tuberculosis vaccine
BMI	Body Mass Index
CHIM	Change in Mean
CI	Confidence Interval
CIAF	Composite Index of Anthropometric Failure
CIPREE	Centre Interuniversitaire sur le Risque, les Politiques Economiques et l'Emploi
CISAF	Composite Index of Severe Anthropometric Failure
CMH	Commission on Macro-economics and Health
Cov	Covariance
CPI	Consumer Price Index
CWI	Composite Welfare Index
DAC	Development Assistance Committee
DHS	Demographic and Health Survey
DIAL	Developpement Institutions and Analyses de Long terme
DPT	Diphterie
DPRU	Development Policy Research Unit
ECH	Encuesta Continua de Hogares
Ed	Editor
EIH	Encuesta Integrada de Hogares
EPM	Enquete Aupres Des Menages
FAO	Food and Agriculture Organization
FCND	Food Consumption and Nutrition Division
FGT	Foster Greer Thorebecke
GIC	Growth Incidence Curve
HIV	Human Immunodeficiency Virus
IAE	Ibero America Institute für Economic Research
IAEN	International AIDS Economics Network
ICRISAT	International Crops Research Institute for Semi-Arid Tropics

IFPRI	International Food Policy Research Institute
IMF	International Monetary Fund
INE	Instituto Nacional de Estadística
ISER	Institute for Social and Economic Research
Lhs	Left hand scaled
LSMS	Living Standard Measurement Surveys
MGD	Millennium Development Goals
Nd	Not defined
NIGIC	Non Income Growth Incidence Curve
No	Number
Obs	Observations
ODI	Overseas Development Institute
OECD	Organization for Economic Cooperation and Development
OLS	Ordinary Least Squares
PPCH	Pro-Poor Change
PPGR	Pro-Poor Growth Rate
PPP	Purchasing Power Parity
SARA	Support for Analysis and Research in Africa
SCN	United Nations Sub-Committee on Nutrition
SMERU	Social Monitoring and Early Response Unit
SSA	Sub-Saharan Africa
Std	Standard Deviation
TV	Television
UN	United Nations
UNAIDS	United Nations Programme on HIV/AIDS
UNDP	United Nations Development Programme
UNICEF	United Nations Childrens' Fund
USD	United States Dollar
Var	Variance
Vol	Volume
WHO	World Health Organization
WIDER	World Institute for Development Economics Research

Introduction and Overview

We have the means and the capacity to deal with our problems, if only we can find the political will.
Kofi Annan

At the beginning of the new century, extreme poverty persists in many regions of the developing world, hampering economic growth and human development. Moreover, poverty is often accompanied by high inequality between countries and within countries between population groups. Overcoming poverty and inequality in their many dimensions remains one of the biggest human development challenges of the new century for economists and politicians both in developing and developed countries. The success in addressing the challenge of poverty reduction requires national and multinational response. The most prominent example of this collective fight against poverty are the Millennium Development Goals (MDG), committed by the United Nations (UN) in the year 2000, which consist of eight goals that should be reached until the year 2015.[1] The formulation of appropriate policy interventions and policy measures for poverty reduction requires a well-grounded empirical analysis of the country specific determinants of poverty and inequality.

Empirical Analysis of Poverty

The empirical analysis of poverty seeks to measure the magnitude of poverty in its many dimensions. From a more analytical perspective, it allows to examine and understand the factors that determine poverty. From a policy perspective, it allows to deduce appropriate policy interventions and measures for poverty reduction. In

[1]In particular, goal 1 is to eradicate extreme poverty and hunger, goal 2 is to achieve universal primary education, goal 3 is to promote gender equality and empower women, goal 4 is to reduce child mortality, goal 5 is to improve maternal health, goal 6 is to combat HIV/AIDS, malaria and other diseases, goal 7 is to ensure environmental sustainability and goal 8 is to develop a global partnership for development. Each of the eight goals breaks down to 18 quantifiable targets (UN, 2005).

addition, it allows the monitoring of progress in poverty and inequality reduction, poverty trends, and effectiveness of policy interventions.

In order to understand the determinants and threats of poverty and its distribution between and within countries, it is necessary to know its dimensions and the channels through which poverty and inequality affect human well-being. Various definitions and concepts exist for measuring human well-being and poverty. Traditionally, measures of well-being are based on money-metric indicators. Improvements in human well-being are associated with a rise in average incomes or consumption levels per capita, or with a decreasing number of people below a specific poverty line, which is defined as the minimum threshold to satisfy the daily basic needs and which separates the poor from the non-poor.

Besides monetary poverty, i.e. low levels of income and expenditure, people also suffer from several other dimensions of poverty, which have to be taken into account both when measuring poverty and when deducing policy implications for poverty reduction. For example, many households and individuals suffer from malnourishment, infectious diseases, and have very poor access to public social infrastructure like health care systems, piped drinking water, sanitation and education.

In this context, Sen (1987) focusses on the multidimensionality of poverty and defines human well-being in terms of functionings and capabilities, where functionings are achievements of human well-being and capabilities the ability to achieve these functionings. As money-metric indicators of poverty reflect only the ability to achieve functionings, they serve only as indirect measure of the standard of living, whereas direct measures are, for example, the status and access to health and education, which are two fundamental outcomes of human well-being and important factors for economic development (see e.g. Schultz, 1999; Strauss and Duncan, 1998).

Certainly, higher income or expenditures levels would improve a persons' or households' position in some non-monetary dimensions of poverty. But at the same time, an increase in income is not a guarantee for an improvement in the non-income dimensions of poverty. While a large number of studies find a positive correlation between income and non-income dimensions of poverty, the measurement of direct outcomes of human well-being and of its distribution has the advantage that it does not require the adoption of any hypotheses about this correlation.

In recent years, the multidimensionality of poverty has been widely accepted and applied in the empirical analysis of poverty (see e.g. World Bank, 2000; Bourguignon and Chakravarty, 2002). The explicit inclusion of non-monetary indicators and among the MDGs reflects that these indicators are fundamental dimensions of human well-being (Cornia et al., 2007).

Recent Development in Poverty Reduction

Today, more than half of the time period to reach the MDGs has passed. During the last decade, many regions, particular in East and South Asia, have experienced large economic and social progress towards the achievement of the goals by 2015 and many household and individuals have moved out of poverty. Besides reduction in monetary poverty, progress has also been made concerning the other goals, for example, an overall increasing rate of primary education, an improvement of maternal health, and decreasing infection rates of HIV/AIDS.

It is important to emphasize that the MDGs are understood and interpreted as country specific goals to avoid that progress of countries with large populations such as India or China is not interpreted as an overall success towards the achievements of the goals, as long as many other countries are not meeting the goals. Particularly, the persistent shortfalls in many indicators of poverty in Sub-Saharan African countries show the importance of country-specific poverty assessments and measures to foster progress towards the MDGs.

Besides improvements towards reduction in poverty and inequality, there are still large shortcomings in many poverty indicators. For some goals, only limited improvements have been achieved. Also, inequality between and within countries remains a major concern. Wide disparities in progress remain between regions and countries, and within countries between population sub-groups, i.e. between urban and rural areas, where the latter areas considerably lacks behind all targets in almost all Sub-Saharan African countries. For example, whereas countries in South Asia and Latin America have made a lot of progress towards the goal of reducing the share of people suffering from hunger, many other regions and countries remain well short of the targets, particularly in Sub-Saharan Africa, where many countries are still stuck in a poverty trap. Furthermore, whereas child mortality rates decrease in nearly all developing regions, it remains very high in Sub-Saharan Africa, where about twice as many children die before reaching the age of five as compared to the average of all developing countries. The situation is even more alarming concerning the HIV/AIDS epidemic and its consequences on human well-being and economic development. Although rates of new infections have started to decline in many countries in recent years, the number of AIDS deaths is still very high and still decreasing life expectancy. Given this situation, it is currently not very likely that some countries, especially in Sub-Saharan Africa, reach the goals.

The heterogenous situation regarding the improvements towards the MDGs and the persisting shortcomings in some indicators, especially in Sub-Saharan Africa, has resulted in an animated debate in the literature of development economics and among policy makers on the pace of improvements and convergence in levels of human well-being and on the required policies to reach the MDGs. From a research perspective, several conceptual and methodological issues arise both in monitoring progress towards poverty reduction and in analyzing country-specific determinants of poverty in its many dimensions. Given the current situation in poverty reduction and its distribution between and within countries, there is still much effort needed in the empirical analysis of poverty to foster and accelerate human development.

This thesis contributes to some of these open issues and questions in the empirical analysis of poverty. It contains four essays, which will be introduced below in more detail, each of them concerned with the analysis of poverty dimensions that are in line with the MDGs. In particular, these essays are concerned with spatial disparities of the outcomes and determinants of poverty, the interdependencies of dimensions of poverty, the distribution of progress in human development over the population and with the dynamics of poverty over time. Based on cross-country comparisons, the thesis does not consider only on average outcomes and determinants of different indicators of human well-being but examines also their distribution between and within countries. The thesis takes account of the global spread of poverty. It considers from all developing regions, namely Bolivia from Latin America and Bangladesh and India from South Asia. At the same time, the thesis acknowledges the strong concentration of poverty in its many dimensions in Sub-Saharan Africa and, therefore, includes country studies for Burkina Faso, Cameroon, Ghana, Kenya, Madagascar, Mali, Uganda, and Zimbabwe.

The aim of the thesis is to provide new insights into the analysis of poverty that contribute to a better understanding of determinants of poverty dimensions and which helps to bring forward the research towards poverty reduction.

Empirical Analysis of Determinants and Interdependencies of Poverty

Poverty and changes in poverty are determined by various household, individual socio-economic and demographic characteristics as well as by various environmental factors. **Essay 1**, which is based on joint work with Mark Misselhorn, is concerned both with the regional differences and the interdependencies of the outcomes and determinants of two of the most important factors of human well-being, namely child mortality (MDG 4) and child undernutrition (MDG 1) in South Asia and Sub-Saharan Africa.

Child mortality and undernutrition remain still on a high level both in South Asia and Sub-Saharan Africa. Arguing that child mortality and undernutrition are highly correlated, i.e that a bad nutritional status of the child strongly increases the childs' mortality risk (see e.g. Pelletier et al., 1995), a puzzle arises when comparing the two regions regarding the outcomes of both phenomena. Anthropometric outcomes of children are considerably better (but still on a very low level) in Sub-Saharan Africa than in South Asia. In contrast to the severe anthropometric failure in South Asia, Sub-Saharan African countries suffer from relatively high rates of child mortality (see e.g. Klasen, 2007; Ramalingaswami et al., 1996). This regional puzzle of child mortality and undernutrition between both regions is called the South Asia - Sub-Saharan Africa Enigma. To shed more light on this puzzle and the underlying reasons is of particular relevance. First, it would allow a much more detailed assessment of what is needed to reduce child mortality and undernutrition in these two regions. Second, it could show how strong the MDG to reduce child mortality and the MDG to reduce hunger are correlated and whether it is really sufficient to reduce undernutrition in order to reach the goal of reducing child mortality. Approaches using macro-data have not been able to explain the South Asia - Sub-Saharan Africa Enigma appropriately, however, and less attention has been paid so far to the analysis of determinants and child mortality based on micro-data, i.e population based household survey data.

Essay 1 analyzes the determinants of child mortality as well as of child undernutrition based on large-scale Demographic and Health Surveys (DHS) data for a sample of five developing countries in South Asia and Sub-Saharan Africa, namely Bangladesh, India, Uganda, Mali, and Zimbabwe. In particular, **Essay 1** investigates the effects of a set of individual, household and cluster socio-economic characteristics both on child mortality and undernutrition based on the analytical framework proposed by Mosley and Chen (1984).

The aim of the paper is helping to explain the South Asia - Sub-Saharan Africa Enigma. To achieve this, first, **Essay 1** analyzes the relationships between child mortality and undernutrition. The aim of this analysis is, first, to identify determinants that affect child mortality and undernutrition in different ways, which would help to explain the South Asia Sub-Sahara Africa Enigma. Second, analyzing the determinants of child mortality and undernutrition, **Essay 1** concentrates on region-specific and country-specific differences both in the outcomes and determinants of both phenomena. This allows one to identify major differences that drive the puzzle of child mortality and undernutrition in the two regions and between countries.

The main result of **Essay 1** is the identification of several determinants that differ significantly from each other regarding their impact on child mortality and undernutrition, with respect to the two regions of South Asia and Sub-Saharan Africa, and also with respect to countries within the two regions. Whereas the access to health infrastructure is relatively more important ro reduce the risk of child mortality than the reduce the risk of undernutrition, the nutritional status of the mother, which is worse in South Asia than in Sub-Saharan Africa, has a much higher impact on child undernutrition than on child mortality, which can partly explain the Enigma.

Empirical Analysis the Impact of HIV/AIDS on Childrens' Welfare

Essay 2 also considers the interdependencies among poverty dimensions and analyzes the effects of the HIV/AIDS epidemic on childrens' welfare outcomes. In particular, **Essay 2** analyzes how HIV infected household members affect the mortality risk, nutritional status, and the probability of school enrollment of children in four countries in Sub-Saharan Africa, namely Burkina Faso, Cameroon, Ghana, and Kenya.

As described above, the fight against the HIV/AIDS epidemic and its consequences remains one of the biggest challenges for policy makers and researchers both in developing and developed countries. The region that is most strongly affected by the epidemic is Sub-Saharan Africa, exhibiting also relatively poor socio-economic indicators. The HIV/AIDS epidemic dramatically increases mortality rates among young adults in many developing countries, which may also have severe negative consequences for the surviving household members. Especially, children living in HIV/AIDS-affected households bear the heaviest burden of the epidemic. Besides direct vertical transmission through mother-to-child-transmission, HIV/AIDS potentially worsens the childrens' welfare indirectly through its socio-economic impact of reduced capacities of parents to care for their children.

Although a large body of literature exists that analyzes the effects of HIV/AIDS on the economic development based on aggregated macro-data, only very limited research on the socio-economic impact of HIV/AIDS has been done using household survey data, mostly due to the very limited availability of data on HIV/AIDS at the individual level. **Essay 2** contributes to the literature by analyzing the direct and indirect effects of HIV infected mothers or her male partners on child mortality, undernutrition, and school enrollment at the micro-level using large scale Demographic and Health Surveys (DHS) including information about the individual HIV infection status. So far, no such analysis has been undertaken using large-scale household survey data to investigate the relationship of childrens' welfare and the HIV status of parents who were alive at the time of the survey.

The aim of **Essay 2** is to shed more light on the effects of the HIV/AIDS epidemic on the welfare of children and to identify effects that go beyond the effect of vertical transmission, showing the socio-economic impact on children living in HIV/AIDS affected households. This question is of particular relevance because if HIV/AIDS lowers the ability of households to invest in their children through its socio-economic impact, i.e. if it lowers future human capital. Appropriate policy interventions are necessary, therefore, to improve the childrens' future welfare perspectives. The results show that the main channel through which HIV/AIDS affects the child mortality risk is mother-to-child-transmission, but there are also indirect effects of the HIV status on the welfare of the children. Whereas no socio-economic effect of the HIV status of the mother or her partner is found for child undernutrition, a negative relationship between the HIV status of the mother and school enrollment is found in Burkina Faso and Ghana indicating also indirect impacts of HIV/AIDS on childrens' welfare.

Empirical Analysis of the Distribution of Non-Monetary Poverty Reduction

The debate of the distribution and convergence in levels of human development between countries and within countries has been given growing attention in recent years. While much progress has been made in the literature in measuring monetary poverty, there is still much effort needed to improve the measurement of other dimensions of poverty, particularly when it comes to the analysis of how progress in non-monetary dimensions of poverty is distributed across the population.

In recent years, a fast growing field of literature in developing economics emerged that is concerned with the question of 'pro poor growth', i.e. how economic growth is distributed over the population. In particular, the question is whether the poor benefit from economic growth and if yes, to what extent (see e.g. Klasen, 2004), which is of particular policy relevance for achieving poverty reduction and for reaching the MDGs.

In order to track progress on MDG 1 and explicitly link growth, inequality, and poverty reduction, several measures of pro-poor growth have been proposed in the literature and have been used in applied academic and policy work (see e.g. Son, 2003). However, current concepts and measurements of pro-poor growth are entirely focussed on money-metric indicators of well-being, and are, therefore, focussed on MDG 1. While the multidimensionality of poverty is currently well recognized when measuring the magnitude of poverty, less attention has been paid to the question how progress in social indicators of poverty are distributed across the population. It, therefore, neglects non-monetary dimensions of well-being. The question whether the poor can benefit from progress in non-monetary poverty indicators is of considerable importance because growth in monetary indicators of well-being does not necessarily lead to improvements in other dimensions of poverty, i.e. MDG 2-6.

Essay 3, which is based on joint work with Melanie Grosse and Stephan Klasen, takes into account this question and introduces the multidimensionality of poverty into the measurement of pro-poor growth by applying the growth incidence curve (Ravallion and Chen, 2003) to non-income indicators such as education, mortality, vaccinations, nutritional status, and a multidimensional well-being measure. With this approach, one can determine whether improvements in non-income indicators were pro-poor in an absolute and relative sense. Moreover, this extension allows the assessment of the linkage between progress in monetary and non-monetary dimensions of poverty which is an important extension to traditional incidence analysis, and furthermore allows an explicit assessment of the linkage between progress in MDG 1 and MDGs 2-6.

Essay 3 illustrates this approach empirically for Bolivia between 1989 and 1998 and find that growth was relatively pro-poor in the non-income dimension of poverty but results for the non-income dimensions are less clear when the poor are ranked by income.

Empirical Analysis of Poverty Dynamics in Africa

Many households in developing countries face high income risks. In particular, many households are frequently hit by severe climatic, economic, and other household- or individual-specific shocks resulting in high consumption volatility. The risk of falling into poverty tomorrow has important implications for the decision-making process of households, i.e. it constrains the household to lower investments (e.g. in human capital) and, therefore, is also a factor for the households' current status of well-being. However, the MDGs and the most established poverty measurements, e.g. the FGT poverty measures (Foster et al., 1984) represent only a static snap-shot of poverty, which does not take into account the households' general poverty risk, or, in other words, its vulnerability to poverty.

To overcome these shortcomings of traditional poverty assessments, which only present a static and *ex post* picture of households' welfare, the empirical literature has paid more and more attention to the analysis of vulnerability to poverty, which estimates the *ex ante* welfare of households taking into account the dynamic dimension of poverty (see e.g. Calvo and Dercon, 2005).

Whereas it is not possible to observe the probability of falling into poverty in the future, one can analyze the dynamics of income and consumption data and estimate the vulnerability to poverty. However, although several measurements to analyze vulnerability to poverty have recently been proposed, empirical studies are still rare as the data requirements for these measurements are often not met by the surveys that are available for developing countries. For the analysis of the *ex ante* poverty risk, longitudinal household survey data that follow variations in income or consumption for households over time would be ideal, but which are rarely available in developing countries. In addition, reliable data on shocks is very often completely missing.

Essay 4, which is based on a joint work with Isabel Günther, combines the issues of *ex ante* versus *ex post* poverty measurement and the problem of limited availability of longitudinal data. **Essay 4** proposes a simple method to empirically assess the impact of idiosyncratic (e.g. illness or unemployment) and covariate (e.g. climatic shocks) shocks on households' vulnerability to poverty, which can be used in a wide context as the method relies on commonly available living standard measurement surveys.

Essay 4 illustrates the approach using data from Madagascar and shows that whereas covariate and idiosyncratic shocks have both a substantial impact on rural households' vulnerability, urban households' vulnerability is largely determined by idiosyncratic shocks.

The Appendices following **Essay 4** contain additional country specific information on the data sets and results of the respective empirical analysis. The Bibliography for all parts is also located at the end of the thesis.

Essay 1

A Regional Puzzle of Child Mortality and Undernutrition

Abstract: While undernutrition among children is very pervasive both in Sub-Saharan Africa and South Asia, child mortality is rather low in South Asia. In contrast to that, Sub-Saharan African countries suffer by far the worst from high rates of child mortality. This different pattern of child mortality and undernutrition in both regions is well known, but approaches using aggregated macro-data have not been able to explain it appropriately. In this paper, we analyze the determinants of child mortality as well as child undernutrition based on DHS data sets for a sample of five developing countries in South Asia and Sub-Saharan Africa. We investigate the effects of individual, household, and cluster socio-economic characteristics using a multilevel model approach and examine their respective influences on both phenomena. The results show significant differences in outcomes of child mortality and undernutrition and in their respective determinants between the two regions and between countries. Whereas the access to health infrastructure is more important for child mortality than for undernutrition, the nutritional status of the mother, which is worse in South Asia than in Sub-Saharan Africa, has a much higher impact on child undernutrition than on child mortality.

---

based on joint work with Mark Konrad Misselhorn.

1.1 Introduction

1.1.1 Child Mortality and Undernutrition

Despite the overall decline in the prevalence of undernutrition and child mortality in developing countries, both phenomena are still at unacceptably high levels and, therefore, remain big challenges in the fight against lacking capabilities and reaching the MDGs. Concerning the childrens' anthropometric failure, the WHO (2002) estimated that almost 27 percent (168 million) of children under five years of age are underweight. And looking at the threat of child mortality, nearly 11 million children died in the year 2003 before reaching the age of five. Around 98 percent of the deaths occur in developing countries (UN, 2005). Several papers have studied the socio-economic determinants of child mortality and undernutrition. Examples for empirical studies of child mortality are Subbaro and Rany (1995), Pritchett and Summers (1996), Ssewanyana and Younger (2004), and for undernutrition Gillespie et al (1996), Osmani (1997), and more recently Smith and Haddad (2000). As stated in numerous studies in this field, one of the major causes of child mortality is undernutrition itself. Most studies cite this result by referring to a study by Pelletier et al. (1995), which finds that more than 50 percent of child mortality is attributable to mild, moderate, and severe undernutrition. In addition, a study of Pelletier et al. (2002) measures the effect of malnutrition on changes in child mortality for 59 developing countries using aggregate longitudinal data from 1966 to 1996, finding that reducing malnutrition by 5 percent could reduce under-five child mortality by 30 percent. Although, intuitively it seems to be clear that being malnourished increases the risk of child mortality, considerable doubts concerning the closeness of the relationship exist.

1.1.2 The South Asia - Sub-Saharan Africa Enigma

Assuming a close relationship between child mortality and undernutrition, two glaring puzzles exist when the two regions of South Asia and Sub-Saharan Africa are compared. The first puzzle is the so called South Asian Enigma. The anthropometric outcomes are considerably better in Sub-Saharan Africa than in South Asia. Almost half of the children in South Asia are malnourished. Compared to Sub-Saharan Africa the anthropometric shortfall is almost 70 percent higher in South Asia (WHO, 2005), despite higher per capita calorie availability and better provision of health care, water, and sanitation (Ramalingaswami et al., 1996; Osmani, 1997; Svedberg, 2002). The second puzzle concerns the existing child mortality reversals between these two regions (Svedberg, 2000; Klasen, 2003, 2007). In contrast to the severe anthropometric failure in South Asia, Sub-Saharan African countries suffer by far the worst from high rates of child mortality. In Sub-Saharan

Africa, 174 children out of 1000 die before reaching the age of five, while 97 die in South Asia (UNICEF, 2004). Together, these two puzzles can then be defined as the South Asia - Sub-Saharan Africa Enigma of anthropometric failure and mortality reversals.

Various possible explanations for the Enigma exists. First, the level of income poverty is a obvious and major cause both for child mortality and undernutrition, but this cannot explain the regional differences as the average incidence of poverty is quite similar in the two regions. Second, the high magnitude of undernutrition is a result of how undernutrition is measured. For example, Klasen (2003, 2007) argues that the US-based reference standard for international comparison of undernutrition proposed by the WHO (1995) leads to an overestimation of undernutrition in South Asia. This overestimation could be due to different genetic potential in growth between the population in these two regions. The high level of undernutrition in South Asia might then appear because of genetic differences in height and weight, i.e. that children in South Asia are genetically shorter and/or lighter compared to the reference population and are, therefore, spuriously considered as malnourished. But even if this is the case, this could explain only a part of the large differences in the anthropometric outcomes between South Asia and Sub-Saharan Africa. However, also the use of the new reference standard by the WHO (WHO, 2006) that is based on child growth data from six different developed and developing countries[1] that takes explicitly into account the growth potential of children by selecting children from well-doing households, has not been able to solve the Enigma. In particular, using the new reference standard only leads to an upward shift in the level of anthropometric measures compared to the old reference standard, but it does not provide any changes in the ratio of the outcomes of anthropometric measures between South Asia and Sub-Saharan Africa (see also Klasen, 2007). Besides, several authors have demonstrated evidence that no real genetic differences exist between childrens' growth paths below the age of five in South Asia (see e.g. Gopalan, 1992; Eveleth and Tanner, 1990; Svedberg, 2000; Svedberg, 2002), which suggests that these differences are caused by other factors, although a final conclusion concerning the influence of genetic factors on childrens' growth paths is not yet possible. Third, the relative higher rates of child mortality in Sub-Saharan Africa than in South Asia can partly be explained through the fact that Sub-Saharan Africa is much more affected by diseases, among other things also due to climatic reasons. In addition, the high incidence of HIV/AIDS and Malaria can potentially explain a part of the Enigma, but a further assessment of this effect is strongly constraint by data availability.[2] Fourth, the primary health care provision and other public services are possible ex-

[1]Brazil, Oman, Ghana, India, USA, and Norway.

[2]See Essay 2 for an analysis of HIV/AIDS on child mortality and undernutrition.

planations, which is less adequately provided in Sub-Saharan Africa (Svedberg, 1999; Ramalingaswami et al., 1996). Fifth, a further explanation is that the same determinants of child mortality and undernutrition may have different impacts in the two regions or that both phenomena are not as closely related as generally assumed (see e.g. Seckler, 1982; Messer, 1986).[3]

Explaining the different relationships of child mortality and undernutrition between these two forms of deprivation within a country and also between countries and regions has important policy implications, as it supports a much more detailed assessment of required policy interventions to fight child mortality and undernutrition in order to reach the MDGs. But approaches using aggregated macro-data have not been able to explain this regional puzzle appropriately. So far, we find no attempts to explain the South Asia - Sub-Saharan Africa Enigma from a microeconomic perspective that have analyzed the socio-economic determinants simultaneously for child mortality and undernutrition with the focus on their differences and similarities using micro-data.

This paper analyzes the regional puzzle of child mortality and undernutrition between South Asia and Sub-Saharan Africa. The aim of the paper is helping to explain the South Asia - Sub-Saharan Africa Enigma using micro-data. To achieve this, we address three main issues concerning the explanation of the Enigma. First, we analyze the relationship between child mortality and undernutrition. We simultaneously try to find socio-economic determinants that affect child mortality and undernutrition. In particular, we try to find out, which determinants drive undernutrition as well as child mortality in a similar way and what factors have differing effects on both phenomena. Identifying determinants that drive both phenomena in a different way can than help to explain the Enigma. Second, analyzing the determinants of child mortality and undernutrition, we concentrate also on region-specific differences both in the outcomes and determinants of both phenomena. This allows us to identify major differences that drives the puzzle of child mortality and undernutrition in the two regions. Third, we also focuss on country-specific differences. Especially, if countries differ in the outcomes of socio-economic characteristics that have different impacts on child mortality and undernutrition. In addition to these three issues, we argue that socio-economic characteristics at the community level (e.g. infrastructure) play an important role both for child mortality and undernutrition, but standard regression models do not allow to incorporate these higher-level information appropriately. Therefore, in contrast to most cross-country studies that investigate the determinants of child mortality and undernutrition, we introduce the methodology of multilevel mod-

[3]In particular, the assumed small relationship between child mortality and undernutrition goes back to the so-called 'small but healthy' hypothesis, which claims that populations adapt to different physical and socio-economic environments and that individuals can adapt to lower levels of energy and protein intakes without suffering from functional deteriorations (Seckler, 1982).

elling into our analysis that explicitly takes into account the hierarchical structure of the Demographic and Health Survey (DHS) data sets. This will also help to provide information about differences in the outcome variables due to differences in community characteristics, especially about the provision of infrastructure service. We investigate the effects of individual, household, and cluster socio-economic characteristics on anthropometric shortfalls and child mortality to examine their respective influences and relationships on both phenomena and to capture both within and between community effects in a single model. For the empirical analysis we use several nationally representative DHS data for a sample of five developing countries in South Asia and Sub-Saharan Africa.

The results show determinants of child mortality and undernutrition that differ significantly from each other. Access to health infrastructure is more important for child mortality, whereas individual characteristics like wealth and educational and nutritional characteristics of mothers play a larger role for anthropometric shortfalls. Although very similar patterns in the determinants of each phenomenon are discernable, we find large differences in the magnitude of the coefficients. However, regressions using a combined data set including all five countries and dummies for the two regions show that there are still significant differences between the two regions that remain unexplained. Both region dummies as well as numerous interaction effects are significant. Therefore, given the underlying data and the proposed methodology, the South Asia - Sub-Saharan Africa Enigma cannot be fully solved by different levels in access to health facilities, education, wealth, and status of women alone. The results suggest that unobserved characteristics (e.g. HIV/AIDS) on the one hand and the measurement of undernutrition on the other hand might also play an important role to explain the Enigma.

The paper is structured as follows. After the given problem statement and an overview about the existing literature on measuring child mortality and child undernutrition and the differences in their outcomes in South Asia and Sub-Saharan Africa, Section 1.2 explains the empirical method of multilevel models and specifies our model. Section 1.3 presents the data sources. In Section 1.3.2, first descriptive statistics show the different patterns of child mortality and undernutrition within and between the analyzed countries. Second, in Section 1.3.3, we provide estimation results of the multilevel analysis. Third and finally, we simulate changes in the outcome variables for changes in selected covariates. Section 1.4 concludes.

1.2 Methodology

1.2.1 Multilevel Analysis

Many population based household surveys in economics have a clustered or hierarchical data structure, where a hierarchy consists of units grouped at different levels. For instance, individuals (level 1) are nested within households (level 2), households are nested within communities (level 3), and communities are nested within states and countries. Standard regression models have problems dealing with the hierarchical data structure, even if we only include variables at level one (i.e. the child level), since they assume independent and normally distributed errors with a constant variance. But analyzing variables from different levels without taking into account the hierarchical data structure might lead to misleading estimation results, because one faces the problem of heteroscedasticity. The individual observations in hierarchical data structure are not completely independent, and the results of the analysis can be affected by this clustered structure of the underlying data. To put it differently, households in the same community are more homogenous than households in different communities. In particular, in the case of child undernutrition this means that the anthropometric outcomes in different communities might be independent from each other, but that outcomes within a community are not independent, especially when children live in the same household. This leads to a violation of the assumption of independent errors, i.e. the assumption of homoscedasticity, which has consequences for the estimation results. The estimated coefficients are unbiased but not efficient because the standard errors are negatively biased, which leads to misleading significance inference. What is typically done in the empirical literature is to regress an independent variable at the lowest level on a set of explanatory variables available for any other level by disaggregating all higher level variables to the individual level. This is done, for example, by assigning each individual in the same community the same value of the community variable. But this leads to the problem of inefficient estimation results mentioned before.[4]

In this analysis, we want to study whether mortality rates and undernutrition rates differ between several individual and household characteristics that vary from community to community, on the basis of clustered household surveys. Furthermore, we are concerned with understanding the factors associated with variations between regions, countries, and within a country between communities. This means that we want to analyze the impact of community characteristics on the two outcome variables, e.g. the access to health facilities, and how much of the

[4]One can also think of aggregating the variables of the individual level to a higher level and do the analysis on the higher level. However, in many cases this leads to a loss of the within-group information we are interested in.

between-community variation is explained by community explanatory variables. Instead of relying upon the use of standard regression models, a more adequate way to take into account the hierarchical data structure is the methodology of multilevel modelling. A multilevel model is concerned with the analysis of the relationship between variables that are measured at different hierarchical levels (Hox, 2002).[5] The aim of a multilevel model is to take explicitly into account this data structure and to determine the direct effect of the individual and the group explanatory variables. Methodological work on analyzing multilevel models was done, for instance, by Bryk and Raudenbush (1992), Goldstein (1999, 1987), and more recently by Hox (2002), who gives an illustrative introduction to multilevel models with an application to educational data.[6]

Multilevel models correct for the bias in the parameter estimates resulting from the clustered data structure, because in a multilevel model each level is represented by it own sub-model, which expresses the relationship among explanatory variables within that level. This possibility leads to several advantages using multilevel modelling. First, it provides statistically efficient estimates of the regression coefficients by providing correct standard errors, confidence intervals, and significance tests (Goldstein, 1999). Second, cross-level effects and cross-level interactions, i.e. the relationship of variables at different levels, can be analyzed. This means, measuring covariates at each level provides the possibility to analyze the extent to which differences in child mortality and undernutrition between communities are due to community factors like access to health facilities or due to factors at the individual level like gender. Third, estimates of the variances and covariances at each level of the model allows to decompose the total variance in the outcome variable into fractions for each level.[7] In the so-called variance component models, the error term is divided into two parts, the group component and the individual component. This allows the assessment of the variation that is due to differences at the group-level and due to differences at the individual level.[8]

[5] For a description on multilevel analysis, see also Section 4.5.2 in Essay 4.

[6] The first multilevel analysis in social sciences was done by Aitkin et al. (1981). He analyzed the impact of the teaching style on progress in reading capabilities of children in primary schools in Great Britain using traditional multiple regression techniques shown by Bennett (1976). When the data is analyzed only with the individual children as the units of the analysis without recognizing that they are groups within classes, the results were statistically significant. When the grouping of children in classes is taken into account, then the significant differences between teaching styles found before disappear.

[7] For a more detailed description of the variance decomposition in multilevel analysis, see Section 4.5.2 in Essay 4.

[8] For instance, Pebley et al. (1996) investigate the receipt of vaccinations of children in Guatemala with variables at the individual, at the household, and at the community level. When controlling for the observed variables, they found that the variance due to households is five times higher than due to communities.

1.2.2 The Basic Multilevel Model

In a multilevel model, the dependent variable is located at the lowest level, in our case the individual (child) level. Following Hox (2002), the basic multilevel model with two different levels can be described as follows. Suppose that we have $j = 1, ..., J$ level 2 units (i.e. communities), where there are $i = 1, ..., n_j$ level 1 units (i.e. children). Then, we can speak of child i being nested within community j. To analyze the outcome variable, we can set up the regression equation as follows:

$$Y_{ij} = \beta_{0j} + \beta_{1j} X_{ij} + e_{ij} \tag{1.1}$$

with β_0 as the intercept and β_1 as the slope, defined as the expected change in the dependent variable with an increase in the individual variable X of one unit.[9] The difference to standard regression models is that equation 1.1 contains two subscripts, one referring to the individual i and one to the community level j. The clustered data structure and the within- and between-community variations are now taken into account by assuming that each community has a different intercept β_{0j} and a different slope β_{1j}. Then, the explanatory variables at the second level Z can be introduced into the model. For this, the coefficients β_{0j} and β_{1j} are themselves given in a regression model as dependent variables via two regression equations with the level two variables as the independent explanatory variables:

$$\beta_{0j} = \gamma_{00} + \gamma_{01} Z_j + u_{0j} \tag{1.2}$$

$$\beta_{1j} = \gamma_{10} + \gamma_{11} Z_j + u_{1j}. \tag{1.3}$$

Equations 1.2 and 1.3 explain the variations between communities, because the intercept β_{0j} and the slope β_{1j} depend on the community variables in community j. For example, Equation 1.2 predicts the average anthropometric outcome of the child at the level 2 variable Z in community j. Equation 1.3 states that the slope β_{1j} between the anthropometric outcome (Y) and level-1 variable (X), i.e. gender, depends on the level-2 variable (Z), i.e. access to health. The error terms u_{0j} and u_{1j} are level-2 residuals.[10]

The combined model can now be expressed by one single regression equation by substituting Equations 1.2 and 1.3 into Equation 1.1:

$$Y_{ij} = \gamma_{00} + \gamma_{10} X_{ij} + \gamma_{01} Z_j + \gamma_{11} X_{ij} Z_j + (u_{1j} X_{ij} + u_{0j} + e_{ij}). \tag{1.4}$$

[9] We assume that the errors e_{ij} have a mean of zero so that $E(e_{ij}) = 0$ and a variance $var(e_{ij}) = \sigma_e^2$ so that $e_{ij} \sim N(0, \sigma_e^2)$.

[10] The residuals u_{0j} and u_{1j} are also assumed to have mean of zero so that $E(u_{oj}) = E(u_{1j}) = 0$. It is also assumed that the variance is defined as $var(u_{oj}) = \sigma_{u_0}^2$, $var(u_{1j}) = \sigma_{u_1}^2$, and the covariance as $cov(u_{oj}, u_{1j}) = \sigma_{u_{01}}$. A positive value of the covariance between β_0 and β_1 indicates that communities with high means tend also to have positive slopes.

In Equation 1.4, the first part can be defined as the deterministic part referring to the fixed coefficients, which means that coefficients do not vary across level. The part of Equation 1.4 expressed in parentheses can be defined as the stochastic part, containing the random error terms. The term $X_{ij}Z_j$ is an interaction term analyzing the cross-level interaction.[11]

The stochastic part in Equation 1.4 again demonstrates the problem of dependent errors. In contrast to standard ordinary least squares (OLS) regression, the error term in 1.4 contains one individual component e_{ij} and a group or community component $u_{0j} + u_{1j}X_{ij}$. The individual error component e_{ij} is independent across all individuals. In contrast, the community level errors u_{0j} and u_{1j} are independent between communities, but dependent within each community, because the components are the same for every child i in community j. These dependencies lead to unequal variances of the error terms, which results into heteroscedasticity, because $u_{0j} + u_{1j}X_{ij}$ depend on u_{0j} and u_{1j}, which vary across communities, and on X_{ij}, which vary across children.

1.2.3 Model Specification

In our multilevel analysis, we set up a 2-level model to identify, which socio-economic characteristics determine child mortality and undernutrition and to explain the South Asia - Sub-Saharan Africa Enigma. Level 1 includes both individual and household variables, level 2 is the cluster level. We do not differentiate between the individual (child) level and the household level, because there are no real differences between individual and the household information, since there are only a very few households with more than three young children in the data.[12]

The empirical analysis proceeds in 6 basic steps. First, we run several regression model types to get a benchmark for our two outcome variables and to explain the differences between the multilevel approach and standard regression models. For child mortality, we run a logit regression. For stunting, we also run a logit regression on a dummy whether the child is stunted and an OLS regression on the stunting z-scores.[13] Second, to build up the multilevel model, we start by including all explanatory variables of level 1 into the model, which means that the

[11] As OLS estimations techniques are inappropriate to deal with the within level-2 dependencies, the multilevel analysis is based on an iterative maximum likelihood estimation (Mason et al., 1983; Goldstein, 1987; Bryk and Raudenbsuh, 1992). An advantage of the maximum likelihood method is that it provides estimates that are asymptotically efficient and consistent (for a detailed description of maximum likelihood estimation technique, see e.g. Eliason (1993)).

[12] When setting up a multilevel model, Mass and Hox (2004) suggest a sample size for the second level of more than 50.

[13] See Section 1.3.1 below for a description of the dependent and independent variables.

variance component of the slopes is fixed to zero.[14] This model serves as a benchmark for the two variance components. Third, we set up the full model by adding the explanatory variables of the community level. Comparing this model with the model in step 3 allows us to investigate whether and to what extent the between-community variation in child mortality and child undernutrition is explained by community characteristics.

For a meaningful interpretation of the intercept, we center each explanatory variable around the grand mean by subtracting the grand mean from each variable.[15] Thus, Equation 1.4 becomes:

$$Y_{ij} = \gamma_{00} + \gamma_{10}(X_{ij} - \bar{X}) + \gamma_{01}(Z_{qj} - \bar{Z}) + \gamma_{11}(X_{ij} - \bar{X})(Z_j - \bar{Z}) + [u_{1j}(X_{ij} - \bar{X}) + u_{0j} + e_{ij}]. \quad (1.5)$$

Following the multilevel analysis, in step five, we merge all country data sets to one global data set and run the multilevel regression again testing for specific country and region fixed effects for each country in the sample to identify differences in the effects of the explanatory variables on child mortality and undernutrition between countries in South Asia and Sub-Saharan Africa. Here, the independent variables enter into the regression as the mean values per cluster to explicitly take into account regional differences within countries. In addition, we include a Sub-Saharan Africa dummy to capture regional differences and to check whether the Enigma still persists, when controlling four demographic and socio-economic characteristics. Furthermore, the region dummy is also interacted with all explanatory variables at each level. Finally, in step six, the analysis is extended by constructing a simulation of several scenarios for child mortality and undernutrition. Here, we compare changes in the outcome variables for potential changes in specific covariates to check whether the differences in the outcomes of the socio-economic characteristics between the two regions can help to explain the Enigma.

1.3 Empirical Analysis

1.3.1 Data Description

To obtain possible explanations about the regional differences in child mortality and undernutrition between South Asia and Sub-Saharan Africa, we analyze a

[14] In particular, we assume that $u_{1j} = 0$.

[15] The reason of centering the explanatory variables is the interpretation of the intercept β_0. As it is defined as the expected value of the outcome variable when all explanatory variables have a value of zero, we face the problem that this would be misleading for some dummy variables because they are coded as 1 and 0. If we center the variables around their grand mean, the intercept becomes the expected value of the outcome variable, when all variables have their mean value.

sample of five countries from these regions. We use nationally representative DHS data that provide information on anthropometric outcomes of children, information about access to the health system, and other information about the socio-economic status of children below the age of five and the mothers (aged between 15 and 49). The DHS data sets also contain information on cluster characteristics, especially on infrastructure. This information is included in the service availability recodes that are available for the South Asian countries Bangladesh (2000) and India (1999) and in Sub-Saharan Africa for Mali (2001), Uganda (1995), and Zimbabwe (1994). In total, our sample contains more than 53.000 children in South Asia and more than 29.000 children in Sub-Saharan Africa.

The underlying theoretical framework for the choice of the dependent and independent variables to study child mortality and undernutrition, i.e. the underlying determinants, closely follows the analytical framework proposed by Molsey and Chen (1984) to study child survival. The idea of this framework is the assumption that social, economic, demographic, and medical determinants, i.e. the proximate determinants, affect the survival probability of the children through a set of biological mechanism. The proximate determinants are grouped at different hierarchial levels, i.e. the individual, household, and community level. In this analysis, the Mosley and Chen (1984) framework is combined with the conceptual framework to study the causes of child undernutrition proposed by the United Nations Childrens' Fund (UNICEF, 1990), which is based on assumptions similar to the Mosley and Chen (1984) framework, and the subsequent extended model of Engle et al. (1999), which implements also the provision of health care capacities of households into the analysis of childrens' welfare.

As dependent variables, we use two dummy variables. For child mortality, the dummy is used whether the child died in the first year of life.[16] To measure child undernutrition, the DHS data sets provide information on several anthropometric outcomes of children, in particular the z-scores for weight for age, weight for height, and height for age.[17] In line with the dependent variable for child mortality, as dependent variable for child mortality, we use a dummy variable whether the child is stunted, that is, whether the stunting z-score (height for age) is below

[16]To capture the whole birth history of the children, we do not consider child mortality of children below the age of five because this throws out to many observations. We do not explicitly separate between neonatal deaths (child died in the first month) and post-neonatal death (child died between the first month and the first year of life (Adebayo et al., 2004) because this did not change the results.

[17]The z-score is defined as: $z = \frac{AI_i - MAI}{\sigma}$, where AI_i refers to the individual anthropometric indicator (height for age - stunting, weight for height - underweight, weight for age - wasting), MAI refers to the median of the reference population, and σ refers to the standard deviation of the reference population. For example, the stunting z-scores are the outcomes of the ratio of height over age minus the median of the reference population and the standard deviation of the reference population (see e.g. Klasen, 2003, 2007; Smith and Haddad, 2000).

-2 standard deviations from the median of the reference population (WHO, 1995, 2006).[18] In addition, we also use the stunting z-scores as the dependent variable to study the determinants of undernutrition.

In the empirical model, we include a set of several individual and household characteristics as well as cluster characteristics that might have an effect on the two outcome variables. For the individual characteristics, besides the household size and the number of children in the household, we include the age and sex of the child in the regression equation. The nutritional status is supposed to worsen non-linearly with increasing age of the child, and with the sex variable we control for sex differentials in mortality and undernutrition in our countries as is often to be found in the empirical literature on child mortality and undernutrition (for example, see Marcoux, 2002; Klasen, 1996). Another major determinant focussing especially on child mortality is the question whether the child was immediately breastfed after birth. Breastfeeding in the first month of life plays an important role for the development of the child because the breastmilk meets most of the childs' nutritional needs and increases the childs' resistance against diseases (Ramalingaswami et al., 1996). To avoid the problem of endogeneity when including breastfeeding and the birth order number of the child in our regression model, i.e. that these variables are affected by the age of the child, we include a dummy whether the child was breastfed immediately after birth and a dummy whether the child is the first born child in the household. In addition, we include also a variable that shows the preceding birth interval, and a variable that indicates whether the vaccination process of the child is completed, which is expected to decrease the mortality risk of the child. To avoid the problem of endogeneity, the dummy whether the vaccination process is completed is defined as follows: the first 2 month after birth are not considered as incomplete if no vaccinations were received, for the age between 3 and 6 months the dummy is one if the child has received at least 3 vaccinations, for the age between 7 and 9 months if the child has received at least 6 vaccinations and between 10 and 12 months if the child has received all 8 vaccinations.

Concerning the mother, the educational level of the mother enters the regression equation. The argument here is twofold. First, more-educated women might be able to better process information and to acquire skills in order to take care of the children, for example in the case of illness, and second, better-educated women are in a better position to earn money. In addition, the nutritional status of the mother is included, which is supposed to strongly affect the nutritional status

[18]We also consider the case of extreme stunted children where the z-score is below -3 standard deviations of the height for age reference.

of the child.[19] In particular, a bad nutritional status is expected to have a severe negative impact especially on the nutritional status of the child. Strong empirical evidence exist that show a high risk of low birth weight and birth height for children whose mother has suffered by a bad nutritional status (see e.g. Rao et al., 2001; Hasin et al., 1996; Smith and Haddad, 2000). As a proxy for the status of women within the household, we include the age of the mother at the time of the survey. To take into account the household structure, we include the household size into the model. As a strong argument can be made that the household size is endogenous, the household size enters based on an instrumental variable approach, where the mean household size in the respective cluster is used as instrument.

As we do not have information on income or expenditure in the DHS, we consider an asset-based approach in defining well-being (Sahn and Stifel, 2001). For this, we use a principal component analysis on several household assets proposed by Filmer and Pritchett (2001) to derive an index that indicates the material status of a household. In particular, as the components for the asset index, we include dummies whether the following assets exist or not: radio, TV, refrigerator, bike, motorized transport, low floor material, toilet, drinking water. Of course, one could include the assets separately into the regression, but the use of an aggregate index has two main reasons: First, it provides an income proxy of the household, which can be used to analyze distributional differences of outcomes in child mortality and undernutrition. Second, as the assets are correlated, their coefficients are likely to provide no significant effects if they are included separately, which would however lead to misleading interpretations of the estimation results. We then introduce another index into the analysis, which includes information on the access to health facilities of the household. Again, this is based on a principal component analysis using dummies whether the mother has received a tetanus vaccination before birth, whether the mother has received prenatal care, and whether the child was born at home without assistance of a doctor or a nurse. We assume that the access to health facilities is a crucial determinant both for child mortality and undernutrition. This index captures both the potential access opportunities to the health system as well as real outcomes, which means that the child or the mother have really benefited from the services. To make the coefficients of the asset index and the access to health facility index comparable across regions and countries, the calculation of both indices are based on a global data set, which includes all country samples.

[19]The recommend method to measure the nutritional status of adults is the body mass index (BMI), which is calculated by $BMI = weight(kg)/height^2(m^2)$. A mother is considered as malnourished if her BMI is less then 18.5.

Besides the individual and household characteristics, we include cluster variables.[20] In this context, the multilevel model distinguishes two different kinds of variables, namely contextual variables and global variables. Contextual variables at higher levels are variables that are simply the aggregates of the covariates at the individual level for each cluster. For example, we include the percentage of women with secondary education per cluster and the percentage of children that had recently suffered from fever per cluster. The global variables are part of the service availability recode and are not drawn from information of the individual level. In our case, these global variables provide information about the infrastructure in the cluster. We include the distance to the next health facility, which might be important for the access to heath services, and a public infrastructure index that is based on the availability of general facilities like a bank, a cinema, a post office, primary and secondary schools, a telephone, and public transportation. The weights for the index again are determined by a principal component analysis.

1.3.2 Descriptive Statistics

As can be seen in Table 1.1, the South Asia - Sub-Saharan Africa Enigma of anthropometric failure and mortality reversals is clearly discernable in our five data sets. Relatively higher undernutrition rates in both South Asian countries coincide with relatively lower infant mortality rates than in the three Sub-Saharan African countries. For example, whereas the infant mortality rate in Mali is 1.9 times higher than in India (149 compared to 79), the stunting rate in India is 15 percent higher than in Mali (43.17 compared to 37.61). This result is independent of the measure for undernutrition (i.e. stunting, wasting, underweight or the composite index of (severe) anthropometric failure (CIAF/CISAF) that indicates undernutrition by any of the preceding measures).[21] For example, whereas Bangladesh and Zimbabwe show almost equal mortality rates (80 compared to 75), the rate of severely underweight children is four times higher in Bangladesh than in Zimbabwe (13.12 and 3.26, respectively). This picture is not changed by the use of the new multi-country growth reference standard that was published by the WHO in 2006. Prevalence rates using this new reference standard are shown in parentheses. Table 1.1 shows that the anthropometric indicators that are based on the new reference standard lie all above the indicators based on the old reference standard. For example, the stunting rate in Bangladesh increases from 44.12 percent to 50.82 percent. However, this level effect does not change the picture of the Enigma, because the ratios of anthropometric indicators between South Asia and

[20]In the case of India, the service availability recode contains information on districts instead of clusters.

[21]In particular, CIAF and CISAF indicate whether a child is (severely) undernourished by either stunting, wasting, or underweight.

Sub-Saharan Africa do not change very much. For instance, the stunting ratio between India and Mali is 1.16 for the old standard and 1.17 for the new standard. This result suggests that the use of new reference standard instead of the old reference standard is not able to solve the Enigma alone.

Table 1.1: Infant Mortality and Anthropometric Indicators (percentage)

	Bangladesh 2000	India 1999	Mali 2001	Uganda 1995	Zimbabwe 1994
Infant mortality					
Infant mortality*	80	79	149	99	75
Undernutrition**					
Stunting	44.12	43.17	37.61	35.19	22.24
	(50.82)	(50.75)	(43.06)	(42.37)	(30.09)
Wasting	10.50	14.99	10.97	5.11	5.56
	(13.47)	(20.09)	(13.83)	(7.34)	(7.30)
Underweight	47.32	43.77	34.14	23.38	16.30
	(41.48)	(40.62)	(30.62)	(19.81)	(12.54)
Severe stunting	18.12	21.39	19.01	13.26	6.18
	(24.39)	(30.31)	(24.44)	(19.20)	(10.28)
Severe wasting	1.05	2.84	1.72	0.85	0.86
	(3.36)	(8.49)	(5.48)	(3.02)	(2.99)
Severe underweight	13.12	15.92	11.66	6.12	3.26
	(14.41)	(18.21)	(12.97)	(7.19)	(3.39)
CIAF***	56.63	57.21	47.86	41.21	29.82
	(61.10)	(63.58)	(52.05)	(47.01)	(36.09)
CISAF	22.16	27.33	22.85	15.39	8.05
	(29.64)	(38.37)	(29.42)	(22.37)	(13.26)

Source: Demographic and Health Surveys (DHS); own calculations.
Notes: *Child mortality shows the number of dead children per 1000 of children under one year of age who died within the last 12 month. **Children are considered as wasted, stunted, or underweight if the respective z-scores are below -2 standard deviation from the median of the reference category (WHO, 1995). If the z-scores are below -3, children are considered as severely undernourished. The numbers in parentheses refer to the new reference standard for child anthropometric failure that was published by WHO in 2006 (WHO, 2006). ***CIAF and CISAF refer to the composite index of (severe) anthropometric failure that indicates whether a child is (severely) undernourished by either stunting, wasting, or underweight.

Table 1.2 presents summary descriptive statistics of individual, household, and community characteristics four the five countries of our sample. Besides some observed similarities in the household and child characteristics, Table 1.2 shows also large differences in the covariates both between South Asia and Sub-Saharan

Table 1.2: Summary Statistics
for Individual, Household and Community Characteristics

	Bangladesh 2000	India 1999	Mali 2001	Uganda 1995	Zimbabwe 1994
Total number of children in DHS	6.944	46.569	14.328	5.799	2.438
Individual characteristics					
Age (month)	28.79	17.14	28.56	22.63	17.50
Immediate breastfeeding (%)	35.05	25.81	42.40	59.13	53.08
Household characteristics					
Household size	6.79	7.41	7.35	6.59	6.89
Total number children	3.11	2.90	4.67	4.16	3.54
Female headed household (%)	5.36	6.53	8.70	20.28	32.77
Household has					
TV (%)	17.98	38.37	16.07	5.87	12.29
Radio (%)	31.52	41.73	73.06	49.19	43.34
Flush toiled (%)	10.93	25.32	7.19	3.21	22.38
Piped drinking water (%)	6.37	40.04	27.06	12.58	31.27
Mothers' education (years)	3.19	3.90	0.91	4.13	6.38
Mother has no education (%)	45.36	50.14	83.68	26.38	12.92
Mother has primary education (%)	28.96	16.21	11.33	57.76	51.27
Mother has second. education (%)	21.18	24.45	4.62	15.67	34.58
Age at first birth	17.67	19.35	18.21	18.11	18.96
BMI of mother	19.42	19.83	22.07	21.92	23.00
BMI of mother <18.5 (%)	41.63	34.85	8.33	7.77	5.28
Community characteristics					
Number of vaccinations	5.44	4.65	3.83	5.03	5.82
Birth assistance					
Assistance at birth** (%)	14.31	44.39	22.43	44.16	67.80
Prenatal care (%)	22.51	62.88	20.88	90.46	93.55
Tetanus vaccination (%)	62.37	75.79	31.37	81.25	82.53
Born home w/o assist. (%)	85.24	55.08	60.85	22.77	31.17
Distance to health facility***	47.67****	10.05	7.87	8.69	16.19
Children had fever recently (%)	37.81	30.27	31.08	48.17	37.73

Source: Demographic and Health Surveys (DHS); own calculations.
Notes: *Child was breastfed immediately after birth. **By doctor or nurse. ***Distance to hospital and clinic in kilometers. ****As the distance to the next health facility is not included in the data set for Bangladesh the time in minutes to next health facility is used.

Africa and within these regions between countries. First, looking at regional differences in the individual, household, and community characteristics between South Asia and Sub-Saharan Africa, they provide first insights of possible explanations of the Enigma. For example, Table 1.2 shows that both the share of mothers who breastfed their children immediately after birth and the share of female headed households are considerably higher in Sub-Saharan Africa than in South Asia. If female headed households are less able to care for their children, than the high share in Sub-Saharan Africa can contribute to the existing relative high rates of child mortality. In addition, Table 1.2 shows also very large region-specific differences in the nutritional status of the mothers, which is much worse in South Asia than in Sub-Saharan Africa. In particular, whereas in Bangladesh 41.63 percent of mothers have a BMI less than 18.5, in Zimbabwe 'only' 5.28 percent are malnourished. This regional disparity is also reflected in the low mean values of the BMI of mothers in South Asia compared to countries in Sub-Saharan Africa. This regional pattern is very interesting since the nutritional status of the mother is expected to have a strong negative impact on the nutritional status of the child, which would then help to explain the Enigma. Various empirical studies exist, which analyze the reasons for the high prevalence of malnourished mothers in South Asia. Primarily, gender differences in the socio-economic status of women are identified as the most important determinants of the low BMI of mothers in Bangladesh, particularly in urban areas (see e.g. Ahmed et al., 1998). In India, women in rural areas are more likely to work full-time in farming activities than men and carry also the burden of the work in the household, which often results in chronic fatigue and undernutrition (see e.g. Barker et al., 2006). If the nutritional status of the the mother increases the risk of child undernutrition, this would then contribute to explain the higher rates of stunting in South Asia compared to Sub-Saharan Africa and contributes to explain the Enigma.

Second, country specific differences between covariates provide also interesting information regarding the explanation of the Enigma. For example, although an overall low level of mothers' education is observed for all five countries, in Mali, which was found to be the country with the highest mortality rates in our sample, the mean years of education of mothers is less than 1 year, compared to 6.38 years in Zimbabwe, where mortality rates and rates of child undernutrition were found to be rather low. Hence, given that Bangladesh, India, and Zimbabwe show relatively high levels of education and low levels of child mortality, this suggests that the educational attainment might be an important determinant for the survival probabilities of children. However, as argued in the previous section, the educational level of mothers is also expected to have an important impact on the nutritional status of the child, but Bangladesh and India show the highest rates of undernutrition. Other glaring differences between countries are found for some community characteristics, particular the access to health infrastructure. Bangladesh has the lowest rates of assistance at birth (14.31) and of prenatal care (22.51), Zimbabwe has the best access to birth assistance in the sample, with 67.8 percent of mothers who have received assistance at birth and even 93.55 percent who received prenatal care. Looking at the difference in stunting and child mortality, this result suggests a strong influence of access to health care on both outcomes of childrens' welfare.

As mentioned before, the lack of income data necessitates the use of a wealth index as a proxy for incomes or consumption. To avoid using arbitrary weights, we use a principal component analysis, which implies that the weights are equivalent to a measure of the degree of correlation between each factor and a hidden component (in our case wealth). First, the results of the principal component analysis, which are presented in Table A.1 in Appendix A, show that all weights for the factors have the assumed sign, giving positive values to durable goods like TV and radio and negative values to the lack of a toilet facility or the use of surface drinking water. Second, also when we look at the weights of our health facility index, it can be seen that the principal component analysis determines weights with the 'right' signs, which is shown in Table A.1 in Appendix A. Positive weights are generated, therefore, for the dummies for a tetanus vaccination of the mother before birth, and for prenatal care. A negative value is generated for the dummy whether a child was born at home without the assistance of a doctor or a nurse.

In addition, the results of the principal component analysis show that both factors, wealth and access to health facilities are strongly correlated with child mortality and undernutrition. First, Table 1.3 reflects the differences in the levels of child mortality and undernutrition between the two regions and between countries, and confirms the Enigma. Second, Table 1.3 show that both phenomena are a lot more prevalent in the lower quintiles of both indices meaning that the poor population is much more affected by child mortality and undernutrition than the non-poor population. As the distribution of both phenomena over the indices shows a similar pattern across regions and countries, a particularly strong connection is observable between access to health facilities and child mortality indicating that the development of the health care system is a very strong determinant for probability of the child to survive. Here, for example, the ratio of the first to the fifth quintile in Bangladesh is 9.70, and India, Uganda, and Mali even show no child mortality for their respective fifth quintile.

1.3.3 Regression Results

This section presents the regression results and discusses possible explanations of the South Asia - Sub-Saharan Africa Enigma that were asked in Section 1.1.2. First, it starts with comparing the multilevel approach to standard regression models when analyzing child mortality and undernutrition. Second, to shed more light on the South Asia - Sub-Saharan Africa Enigma, this section discusses the differences in the determinants of child mortality and undernutrition to explain the relationship between both phenomena. In particular, the results provide us with

Table 1.3: Mortality and Stunting by Asset and Access to Health Facility Index (percentage)

	Quintile 1	Quintile 2	Quintile 3	Quintile 4	Quintile 5	Ratio 1/5
			Asset index			
Infant mortality						
Bangladesh 2000	9.26	8.21	8.03	8.12	6.33	1.46
India 1999	10.32	8.43	7.64	7.20	5.69	1.81
Mali 2001	16.54	16.41	15.12	14.41	11.92	1.39
Uganda 1995	11.27	11.16	9.86	9.21	8.46	1.33
Zimbabwe 1994	8.98	7.74	6.50	6.50	8.05	1.12
Stunting						
Bangladesh 2000	54.49	49.46	43.01	32.81	16.74	3.26
India 1999	53.11	47.48	44.21	41.16	33.15	1.60
Mali 2001	46.84	40.70	40.62	37.20	23.83	1.97
Uganda 1995	41.57	37.98	31.10	21.77	16.48	2.52
Zimbabwe 1994	22.13	28.12	25.40	20.90	12.43	1.78
			Access to health facilities index			
Infant mortality						
Bangladesh 2000	21.72	7.25	7.51	0.81	2.24	9.70
India 1999	15.16	10.80	8.97	3.80	0	n.c.
Mali 2001	21.59	17.29	16.07	11.15	8.08	2.67
Uganda 1995	19.98	16.99	11.12	1.07	0	n.c.
Zimbabwe 1994	23.84	6.52	6.50	0	0	n.c.
Stunting						
Bangladesh 2000	56.62	45.90	46.73	31.90	17.51	3.23
India 1999	56.21	54.31	44.64	37.66	31.89	1.76
Mali 2001	43.06	39.85	35.21	21.27	17.16	2.51
Uganda 1995	36.96	39.54	36.32	34.36	33.94	1.09
Zimbabwe 1994	27.71	26.60	21.61	22.52	21.25	1.30

Source: Demographic and Health Surveys (DHS); own calculations.
Notes: Infant mortality shows the percentage of children under 1 year of age who died before their first birth within the last the 60 months for the respective quintile. The stunting rate shows the percentage of stunted children in the respective quintile compared to all children under 5 years of age. A child is considered as stunted if the height over age z-score is below -2 standard deviations from the reference category. The asset index is calculated based on a principal component analysis. As variables to calculate the asset index, dummies are included whether the following assets exist or not in a household: radio, TV, refrigerator, bike, motorized transport, low floor material, toilet, drinking water. Quintile 1 corresponds to the poorest and quintile 5 to the richest population sub-group.

information about socio-economic characteristics that determine child mortality and undernutrition in a similar way and characteristics that determine both phenomena in different ways, which helps to explain the Enigma. Third, regional differences between South Asia and Sub-Saharan Africa and also country-specific differences in the regression results are discussed concerning possible explanations of the Enigma.

As mentioned before, we use a multilevel model approach to examine the influence of individual, household, and community socio-economic characteristics on child mortality (Table 1.4) and child undernutrition (Tables 1.5 and 1.6). The use of a multilevel approach instead of standard regression models insures that we avoid misleading significance effects due to violations of the assumption of independent errors with a constant variance. This effect is confirmed in our regression results in which the multilevel regressions display lower levels of significance compared to the OLS regression and the logit regression with the same model specification, which are presented in Tables A.2-A.6 in Appendix A. The standard errors for the multilevel regression are higher than the standard errors for the logit and OLS regressions for mortality and for undernutrition both using a dummy whether the child is stunted and also using the stunting z-scores as dependent variable. Especially, in the case of community characteristics, a strong reduction in significance levels is observable, whereas for the individual and household characteristics the differences in significance of the coefficients are rather low. This means that the multilevel approach allows a more reliable analysis of the determinants of our household survey data through explicitly incorporating the hierarchical data structure of the data and community information.

Table 1.4: Regression Results of Infant Mortality (Multilevel Regression)

	Bangladesh 2000	India 1999	Mali 2001	Uganda 1995	Zimbabwe 1994
Constant	-3.188**	-2.591**	-2.109**	-2.234**	-2.790**
	(0.111)	(0.043)	(0.061)	(0.118)	(0.222)
Age (mother)	-0.116**	-0.224**	-0.152**	-0.094	-0.182
	(0.062)	(0.031)	(0.034)	(0.067)	(0.157)
Age^2 (mother)	0.170*	0.352**	0.241**	0.133*	0.353
	(0.106)	(0.054)	(0.053)	(0.111)	(0.260)
Sex of child (1=female)	-0.158	0.055	-0.112*	-0.070	-0.410*
	(0.106)	(0.047)	(0.061)	(0.110)	(0.231)
Immediate breastfeeding (=1)	-0.429**	-0.491**	-0.179**	-0.061	-0.501*
	(0.125)	(0.068)	(0.064)	(0.115)	(0.231)
Complete vaccination (=1)	-2.458**	-2.531**	-2.008**	-2.003**	-3.683**
	(0.227)	(0.070)	(0.130)	(0.199)	(0.393)
First born (=1)	0.295	-0.057	-0.095	0.153	0.299
	(0.187)	(0.084)	(0.116)	(0.200)	(0.403)
Preceding birth interval	-0.005	-0.006	-0.015**	-0.009*	0.013*
	(0.003)	(0.002)	(0.002)	(0.005)	(0.005)
Household size (IV)	0.200**	0.105**	0.016**	0.067	0.096
	(0.053)	(0.024)	(0.005)	(0.049)	(0.088)
Female headed household (=1)	0.055	0.100	-0.079	-0.076	-0.012
	(0.258)	(0.100)	(0.111)	(0.147)	(0.251)
Asset index	-0.167	-0.098**	-0.053	-0.145	-0.015
	(0.114)	(0.024)	(0.046)	(0.111)	(0.147)
BMI of mother	-0.042*	0.051	0.026*	-0.045	0.008
	(0.025)	(0.010)	(0.012)	(0.023)	(0.040)
$BMI^2/100$ of mother	0.484	0.040	-0.281*	0.243	-0.056
	(0.280)	(0.122)	(0.159)	(0.318)	(0.360)
Mother has sec. education (=1)	-0.174	-0.084	-0.313	-0.523**	0.057
	(0.159)	(0.064)	(0.228)	(0.207)	(0.003)
Health facility index	-0.647**	-0.326**	-0.400**	-0.287**	-0.186**
	(0.090)	(0.030)	(0.048)	(0.086)	(0.179)
Distance to health facility***	-0.003	0.001	0.002	0.009	0.003
	(0.002)	(0.004)	(0.003)	(0.005)	(0.007)
Secondary education (%)	-0.661	-0.591*	-0.394	0.173	-0.647
	(0.458)	(0.301)	(0.528)	(0.472)	(0.658)
Children had fever (%)	0.775*	-0.330	0.124	0.542*	0.545
	(0.370)	(0.357)	(0.220)	(0.301)	(0.573)
Public infrastruct. index	0.046	-0.002	0.012	0.167*	0.317*
	(0.070)	(0.036)	(0.046)	(0.079)	(0.149)
σ_u^2	0.169	0.255	0.172	0.274	0.698
	(0.086)	(0.042)	(0.041)	(0.108)	(0.375)
R^2	0.099	0.128	0.068	0.068	0.159
Obs. (level 1)	5381	28539	9852	4232	1.568
Obs. (level 2)	339	426	371	357	229

Source: Demographic and Health Surveys (DHS); own calculations.
Notes: *P-value<0.1. **P-value<0.01. For details about the variables, see Section 1.3.1. σ_u^2 refers to the variance of the residual errors of the intercepts at the household level (level 2). ***In the case of Bangladesh distance is measured in time (hours). The household size enters via an instrumental variable into the model. As instrument the mean household size per cluster is used.

Table 1.5: Regression Results of Stunting (Old Reference Standard) (Multilevel Regression)

	Bangladesh 2000	India 1999	Mali 2001	Uganda 1995	Zimbabwe 1994
Constant	-0.601**	-0.326**	-0.644**	-0.776**	-1.459**
	(0.050)	(0.030)	(0.049)	(0.075)	(0.102)
Age (mother)	0.108**	0.247**	0.156**	0.169**	0.305**
	(0.008)	(0.006)	(0.006)	(0.012)	(0.031)
Age^2 (mother)	-0.001**	-0.005**	-0.002**	-0.003**	-0.006**
	(0.000)	(0.000)	(0.000)	(0.000)	(0.001)
Sex of child (1=female)	0.027	0.008	-0.071	-0.241**	-0.049
	(0.061)	(0.025)	(0.049)	(0.069)	(0.115)
Immediate breastfeeding (=1)	-0.131*	-0.010*	-0.120*	-0.052	-0.072
	(0.065)	(0.031)	(0.052)	(0.071)	(0.118)
Complete vaccination (=1)	-0.051	-0.091	-0.111	-0.568	-0.189
	(0.139)	(0.434)	(0.104)	(0.134)	(0.297)
First born (=1)	-0.241*	-0.291**	-0.335**	-0.213*	-0.254
	(0.100)	(0.041)	(0.088)	(0.118)	(0.196)
Preceding birth interval	-0.008**	-0.005**	-0.010**	-0.007**	-0.004
	(0.002)	(0.001)	(0.002)	(0.002)	(0.003)
Household size (IV)	0.034	0.058**	-0.003	-0.047*	0.055
	(0.029)	(0.016)	(0.005)	(0.027)	(0.039)
Female headed household (=1)	-0.161	-0.140**	-0.049	0.057	-0.126
	(0.137)	(0.052)	(0.089)	(0.089)	(0.126)
Asset index	-0.430**	-0.178**	-0.090*	-0.203**	-0.127*
	(0.064)	(0.013)	(0.039)	(0.069)	(0.070)
BMI of mother	-0.090**	-0.065**	-0.075**	-0.073**	-0.060**
	(0.015)	(0.005)	(0.010)	(0.015)	(0.020)
$BMI^2/100$ of mother	0.309	-0.084*	-0.130	-0.092	0.294
	(0.217)	(0.082)	(0.145)	(0.258)	(0.253)
Mother has sec. education (=1)	-0.354**	-0.251**	-0.561**	-0.291*	-0.346*
	(0.086)	(0.031)	(0.163)	(0.116)	(0.156)
Health facility index	-0.246**	-0.243**	-0.023	-0.061	-0.248**
	(0.047)	(0.017)	(0.036)	(0.059)	(0.086)
Community characteristics					
Distance to health facility***	0.001	-0.004	0.005*	0.006*	0.001
	(0.001)	(0.003)	(0.003)	(0.003)	(0.003)
Secondary education (%)	-0.162	-1.520**	-2.403**	-1.280**	-0.290
	(0.260)	(0.203)	(0.484)	(0.297)	(0.345)
Children had fever (%)	0.215	-0.582*	0.160*	-0.421*	-0.206
	(0.218)	(0.268)	(0.227)	(0.186)	(0.288)
Public infrastruct. index	0.054	-0.021	-0.094	-0.074	-0.025
	(0.042)	(0.024)	(0.046)	(0.054)	(0.081)
σ_u^2	0.097	0.252	0.326	0.134	0.082
	(0.033)	(0.025)	(0.045)	(0.042)	(0.080)
R^2	0.109	0.140	0.118	0.106	0.121
Obs. (level 1)	5284	34797	9258	4518	2057
Obs. (level 2)	339	424	368	354	227

Source: Demographic and Health Surveys (DHS); own calculations.
Notes: *P-value<0.1. **P-value<0.01. For details about the variables, see Section 1.3.1. σ_u^2 refers to the variance of the residual errors of the intercepts at the household level (level 2). ***In the case of Bangladesh distance is measured in time (hours). The household size enters via an instrumental variable into the model. As instrument the mean household size per cluster is used.

Table 1.6: Regression Results of Stunting (New Reference Standard) (Multilevel Regression)

	Bangladesh 2000	India 1999	Mali 2001	Uganda 1995	Zimbabwe 1994
Constant	-0.243**	0.089**	-0.340**	-0.356**	-0.925**
	(0.046)	(0.030)	(0.046)	(0.069)	(0.091)
Age (child)	0.107**	0.152**	0.135**	0.127**	0.171**
	(0.007)	(0.005)	(0.005)	(0.010)	(0.023)
Age^2 (child)	-0.001**	-0.002**	-0.002**	-0.002**	-0.003**
	(0.000)	(0.000)	(0.000)	(0.000)	(0.001)
Sex of child (1=female)	-0.060	-0.132**	-0.162**	-0.344**	-0.209
	(0.059)	(0.023)	(0.046)	(0.065)	(0.105)
Immediate breastfeeding (=1)	-0.130*	-0.039*	-0.132*	-0.093*	-0.011*
	(0.063)	(0.029)	(0.049)	(0.067)	(0.107)
Complete vaccination (=1)	0.090	0.047	0.204	-0.012	0.177
	(0.130)	(0.038)	(0.092)	(0.198)	(0.244)
First born (=1)	-0.173*	-0.222**	-0.204*	-0.187*	-0.309*
	(0.096)	(0.038)	(0.082)	(0.111)	(0.175)
Preceding birth interval	-0.007**	-0.004**	-0.008**	-0.008**	-0.005
	(0.001)	(0.001)	(0.001)	(0.002)	(0.003)
Household size (IV)	0.012	0.044**	-0.008	-0.043*	0.022
	(0.029)	(0.016)	(0.005)	(0.026)	(0.038)
Female headed household (=1)	-0.112	-0.084	-0.127*	-0.066	-0.126
	(0.132)	(0.048)	(0.084)	(0.084)	(0.114)
Asset index	-0.387**	-0.160**	-0.109**	-0.202**	-0.157**
	(0.061)	(0.012)	(0.036)	(0.065)	(0.068)
BMI of mother	-0.072**	-0.056**	-0.059**	-0.064**	-0.049**
	(0.014)	(0.005)	(0.009)	(0.014)	(0.018)
$BMI^2/100$ of mother	0.362*	0.000	-0.126	-0.404*	0.157
	(0.155)	(0.001)	(0.129)	(0.244)	(0.216)
Mother has sec. education (=1)	-0.290**	-0.223**	-0.466**	-0.175	-0.260*
	(0.081)	(0.029)	(0.143)	(0.107)	(0.138)
Health facility index	-0.219**	-0.222**	-0.040	-0.085	-0.184*
	(0.046)	(0.016)	(0.034)	(0.055)	(0.080)
Community characteristics					
Distance to health facility***	0.001	-0.006*	0.004	0.010**	0.002
	(0.001)	(0.003)	(0.003)	(0.003)	(0.003)
Secondary education (%)	-0.253	-1.278**	-1.740**	-1.042**	-0.271
	(0.258)	(0.205)	(0.437)	(0.277)	(0.325)
Children with fever (%)	0.276	-0.586*	0.194	-0.470**	-0.124
	(0.217)	(0.273)	(0.218)	(0.178)	(0.276)
Public infrastruct. index	-0.005	-0.020	-0.060	-0.121*	-0.042
	(0.041)	(0.024)	(0.043)	(0.051)	(0.078)
σ_u^2	0.113	0.284	0.312	0.137	0.167
	(0.034)	(0.027)	(0.042)	(0.040)	(0.079)
R^2	0.100	0.114	0.100	0.094	0.097
Obs. (level 1)	5503	37880	9750	4771	2114
Obs. (level 2)	339	424	368	355	227

Source: Demographic and Health Surveys (DHS); own calculations.
Notes: *P-value<0.1. **P-value<0.01. For details about the variables, see Section 1.3.1. σ_u^2 refers to the variance of the residual errors of the intercepts at the household level (level 2). ***In the case of Bangladesh distance is measured in time (hours). The household size enters via an instrumental variable into the model. As instrument the mean household size per cluster is used.

Figure 1.1: Mean Stunting Z-Scores By Age

(a)
(old reference standard)

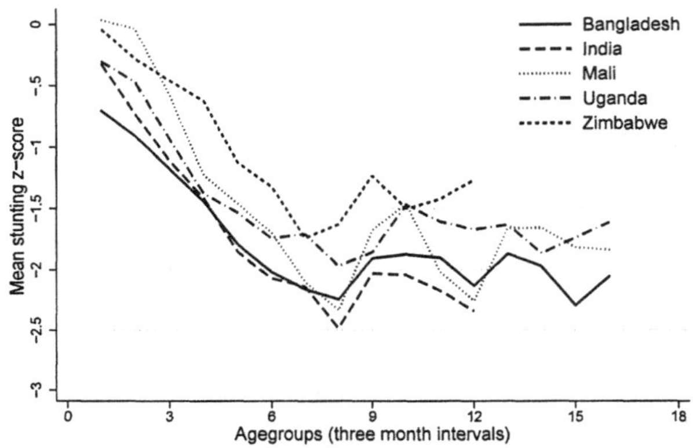

(b)
(new reference standard)

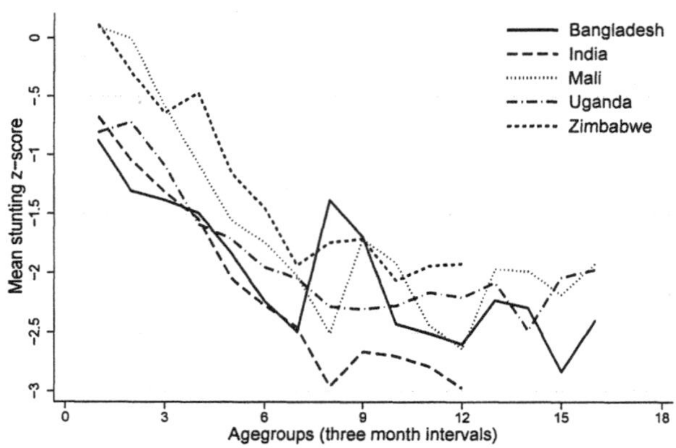

Source: Demographic and Health Surveys (DHS); own calculations.

Turning to the estimation results and possible explanations of the South Asia - Sub-Saharan Africa Enigma, Tables 1.4-1.6 show the regression results for infant mortality and stunting both for the old and the new reference standard. As expected, the age of the mother has a significant non-linear negative influence on child mortality in all cases, meaning that the number of child deaths decreases non-linearly with age, which reflects the increasing experience of mothers to take care of their children when they got older compared to very young mothers. At the same time, the age of the child influences undernutrition positively in a well known non-linear way in all countries as is also shown in Figure 1.1, which presents the stunting z-score by age for the respective country and reference standard.[22] Figure 1.1 shows that the stunting z-scores strongly decrease within the first two years of live and then remain constant or starts to raise slowly. This pattern of decreasing z-scores in early childhood can be explained by the critical phase for the child when the mother replaces breast milk to complementary food or liquids. If the mother stops breastfeeding, the child is exposed to malnutrition and diseases, particularly if the complementary food is nutritionally inadequate or not hygienic (see e.g. UNICEF, 1998; Klasen, 2007). Again, as described in Section 1.3.2, Figure 1.1 demonstrates the differences in the levels of the z-scores between the old and the new reference standard to calculate the z-scores.

Concerning the relationship between child mortality and undernutrition and their respective determinants, Tables 1.4 through 1.6 show that mortality and undernutrition have both very similar determinants across countries and also determinants that affect both phenomena in different way. The results are confirmed when using the stunting z-scores as dependent variable. Very similar effects across countries are found when looking at individual characteristics like immediate breastfeeding. As expected, a positive breastfeeding practice like the immediate initiation of breastfeeding after birth has a negative and, in most cases, a significant effect on mortality. This complies with the general observation of the importance of the colostrum, which contains a large number of antibodies and basically works as a first immunization or vaccination. Furthermore, a strong and significant decreasing effect on the mortality risk is found if the vaccination process of the child is complete. In addition, also the preceding birth interval has a positive effect the survival probability and the nutritional status of the child. Analogous to this findings, we also find a consistent pattern of the effect of the household structure, measured by the household size, which enters based on a instrumental variable approach. The household size increases both the mortality risk and the risk of undernutrition.

[22]For India and Zimbabwe, the DHS provide information on anthropometric indicators for children only until the age of 3 years.

Tables 1.4, 1.5, and 1.6 also show determinants that affect mortality and undernutrition in different directions and at different significance levels. For example, being the first born significantly decreases the risk of being malnourished in all countries except of Zimbabwe. In contrast, a positive but insignificant effect was found for the risk of dying within the first year of life. Interesting to note is that we find no clear gender bias in a way that girls have higher mortality risks than boys. Being female even has a significant negative effect on the mortality risk in Mali. This might be due to the higher susceptibility of boys to diseases in early years, which also results in a worse nutritional status of boys. Particularly, when using the new reference standard, we find significantly lower undernutrition rates for girls. In addition, being a girl significantly increases the risk of being stunted in South Asia, whereas it decreases the risk of undernutrition in Sub-Saharan Africa.

Differences in the determinants are not only found in different directions of the coefficients but also in different magnitudes of the impacts and different significance levels. For example, whereas the asset index strongly influences the nutritional status of children in all five countries, no such overall significant effect was found for the mortality risk. Here, only India shows a significant reducing effect of the asset index on mortality. The effect of the asset index on undernutrition reflects that material welfare strongly increases the capacities to care for children, resulting in higher investments in children and higher outcomes of their status of well-being, but also that it seems to be more important for the nutritional status of the child rather for the probability of the child to survive. In addition, whereas a strong impact on the child mortality risk was found if the vaccination process of the child is complete, no such clear effect is found for undernutrition. Another difference concerning the determinants of child mortality and undernutrition is found for the nutritional status of the mother, measured by the BMI. As already discussed in Section 1.3.2, the nutritional status of the mother has a very strong effect on the nutritional status of the child. What is interesting to note here is that when looking at the results of undernutrition based on the new reference standard, Table A.8 shows that the BMI of the mother affects the childs' nutritional status non-linearity way in Bangladesh, which is reflected in the BMI squared, in the sense that the positive effect decreases with high values of BMI (see also Kandala et al., 2001). This reflects the possibility that the high BMI is simply due to the intake of many calories that are, however, nutritionally inadequate. In contrast, the nutritional status of the mother seems to play no significant role for the probability of the child to survive.

In addition, also the mothers' educational attainment affects both phenomena in different ways. We found a clear negative and significant effect if the mother has achieved secondary schooling level on undernutrition both at the individual level and also at the community level, measured as the percent of secondary education in the cluster.[23] In contrast, and quite surprisingly, the educational attainment of the mothers exhibits a much lower influence on child mortality than originally expected. Here, we find only a significant negative impact on mortality for Uganda. One explanation of this result might be that the mothers' education level seems to have no clear direct significant influence on child mortality and only influences it indirectly via other determinants like better feeding practices and lower fertility, instead. Thus, as was also found for the asset index and the nutritional status of mother, the mothers' educational attainment is more important for undernutrition than for mortality.

When also taking into account regional and country-specific differences between the determinants of mortality and undernutrition, Tables 1.4-1.6 provide interesting results that also can help to explain the Enigma. On the one hand, the largest and most significant effect on mortality is exerted by the access to health facilities, which is measured by our health facility index and which strongly decreases the mortality risk of children. This index includes information on whether the mother received prenatal care as well as a tetanus injection before birth, whether the child was born at home without the assistance of a doctor or a nurse and on the mean number of vaccinations per child in a household. On the other hand, the health index has no such clear effect on child undernutrition. Whereas the health index strongly decreases the risk of being malnourished in South Asia, Zimbabwe is the only country in Sub-Saharan Africa where the index shows a significant negative effect. First, this results suggest that the access to health facilities is more important for mortality than for undernutrition and, second that in South Asia, the access to health facilities is also more important to reduce undernutrition than in Sub-Saharan Africa.[24] Another regional difference between South Asia and Sub-Saharan Africa is found for the preceding birth interval in the case of infant mortality. Here, we found a significant reducing effect only for the Sub-Saharan African countries, whereas the effect is smaller and not significant in South Asia. Therefore, an overall short time period between two births would contribute to the relatively higher mortality rates in Sub-Saharan Africa compared to South Asia.

Looking at the effects of the community characteristics, except for the percentage of secondary education per cluster, we find only very small effects on child mortality and undernutrition for other variables at the community level when using the multilevel approach. This is the case despite the variation of the intercept of the community level σ_u^2 being significant and, therefore, showing that informa-

[23]The same result was find if the variable was included whether the mother has primary education.

[24]However, looking at the regression results of the logit regression model, Table A.3 shows also an overall high and significant effect of the health index on undernutrition.

tion of this level plays a role in explaining child mortality.[25] However, especially the results of the higher level covariates show large country-specific differences. For example, only for Uganda and Zimbabwe, we find a significant mortality increasing effect of the public infrastructure index and no significant reducing effect on undernutrition at all. The percentage of children with fever in a cluster significantly increases the mortality risk only in Bangladesh and Uganda, but it has a clear negative effect on undernutrition in India, Mali, and Uganda. Other country-specific differences are found for the sex of the child. If the sex of the child is female strongly reduces the risk of being malnourished only in Uganda, whereas it reduces the mortality risk only in Mali. These examples of differences in the determinants and their significance levels between countries reflect that the Enigma cannot only be solved by identifying region-specific determinants of child molality and undernutrition but that also country-specific variations play an important role.

After concentrating on the country-specific regression results and the differences and similarities of infant mortality and undernutrition, we now turn again directly to differences and similarities between the two regions of South Asia and Sub-Saharan Africa. Table 1.7 shows the additional regressions that were implemented using a combined data set of all children in the five countries, which confirm the results of the country regressions. In addition to the covariates of the country-specific regression models, Table 1.7 includes also a region dummy for Sub-Saharan Africa that captures the unexplained part of the Enigma and also some interactions between Sub-Saharan Africa and individual and community characteristics. The region dummy for Sub-Saharan Africa in Table 1.7 shows that the Enigma still remains and underlines that significant differences between the two regions still exist, even when we control for the large set of explanatory variables. Whereas the dummy variable for Sub-Saharan Africa has a strong significant positive effect on mortality, it has a strong negative effect on undernutrition. In particular, the first row in Table 1.7 shows that mortality is significantly larger in Sub-Saharan Africa than in South Asia and the second and third row show that it is the other way round when we look at stunting, both for the old and the new reference standard. Besides the significant region dummy, the inclusion of region interaction effects shows that the coefficients for almost all variables differ significantly between regions. For example, the effect of the interaction of female headed households and Sub-Saharan Africa shows a strong negative impact on mortality. The same holds for the effect of immediate breastfeeding and for the effect of a complete vaccination process on child mortality. In addition, also the effect of the access to health facility on child mortality and the asset in-

[25] Again, higher significance for the variables at the community level are found for the logit and OLS regression (see Tables A.2-A.6 in Appendix A).

dex on undernutrition are significantly higher in Sub-Saharan Africa than in South Asia. In contrast, the effect of the percentage of children with fever on undernutrition is lower in Sub-Saharan Africa than in South Asia. What is also interesting to note is that if the nutritional status of mother is interacted with the Sub-Saharan Africa dummy, this shows no clear significant decreasing effect, whereas it does for South Asia.

To summarize the estimation results, we have found that, first, the multilevel approach allows to correct for too high significance levels compared to standard regression models. Second, the estimation results provide new insights for solving the South Asia - Sub-Saharan Africa Enigma. Concerning the relationship between mortality and undernutrition, we have identified determinants that affect both phenomena in a similar way like breastfeeding. However, we have also found differences in the determinants between child mortality and undernutrition. In particular, the material welfare, the nutritional status of the mother, and her educational attainment are relatively more important to reduce undernutrition risk, whereas a complete vaccination process and the access to health facility are relatively more important to reduce the mortality risk of children. Thus, although similar determinants of both phenomena are identified, both phenomena are not perfectly correlated, which would then also allow to explain some of the differences in the outcomes in the two regions. In particular, the low levels of the mothers' BMI in South Asia can partly explain the high levels of child undernutrition in Bangladesh and India. Moreover, we have also found large regional and country-specifics differences in the determinants of mortality and undernutrition concerning their magnitude and significance levels, which can also help to explain the Enigma. For example, the access to health facilities is relatively more important in Sub-Saharan Africa. This seems to be very important to explain the relatively high mortality rates in this region, since countries in Sub-Saharan Africa face higher risks of infectious diseases induced by the tropical climate like Malaria and also face much higher risks of HIV infections, which is supposed to be a strong determinant of mortality and which cannot be observed by our data set.[26] In addition, we also found that country-specific factors are important that show no regional trend and that countries in Sub-Saharan Africa differ among each other as well as countries in South Asia. However, even if we have identified some factors that can help to explain part of the Enigma, the global regression has shown that still much behind the Enigma persists, which can not be solved by our regression results.

[26]The empirical analysis of Section 2.4 in Essay 2 shows that the HIV infection of mothers strongly increases the mortality risk of children, mainly via mother-to-child-transmission of the epidemic. In addition, also Klasen (2007) using macro-data shows that the HIV prevalence rate is a strong determinant of child mortality and can partly explain the Enigma.

Table 1.7: Global Regression of Infant Mortality and Stunting (Multilevel Regression)

	Infant mortality		Stunting (old ref. standard)		Stunting (new ref. standard)	
Constant	-2.694**	(0.054)	-0.445**	(0.029)	-0.036**	(0.028)
Age	-0.158**	(0.019)	0.147**	(0.003)	0.126**	(0.002)
Age^2	0.245**	(0.031)	-0.002**	(0.000)	-0.002**	(0.000)
Sex of child (1=female)	-0.033	(0.033)	-0.023	(0.019)	-0.141**	(0.018)
Immediate breastfeeding (=1)	-0.472**	(0.057)	-0.089**	(0.025)	-0.104**	(0.024)
Complete vaccination (=1)	-2.438**	(0.063)	-0.102**	(0.038)	-0.020	(0.035)
First born (=1)	0.025	(0.072)	-0.297**	(0.036)	-0.235**	(0.033)
Preceding birth interval	-0.005**	(0.001)	-0.005**	(0.001)	-0.004**	(0.001)
Household size (IV)	0.082**	(0.014)	0.066**	(0.008)	0.058**	(0.007)
Female headed household (=1)	0.036	(0.091)	-0.143**	(0.047)	-0.096*	(0.043)
Asset index	-0.070**	(0.022)	-0.167**	(0.011)	-0.156**	(0.011)
BMI of mother	-0.038**	(0.008)	-0.076**	(0.004)	-0.062**	(0.004)
$BMI^2/100$ of mother	0.008	(0.082)	0.020	(0.061)	0.028	(0.052)
Mother has sec. education (=1)	-0.224**	(0.055)	-0.272**	(0.026)	-0.233**	(0.025)
Health facility index (global)	-0.353**	(0.022)	-0.221**	(0.013)	-0.202**	(0.012)
Sec. education in cluster (%)	-0.463*	(0.182)	-1.136**	(0.089)	-1.076**	(0.084)
Child. w. fever in cluster (%)	0.083	(0.190)	-0.364**	(0.100)	-0.380**	(0.095)
Public infras. index	-0.007	(0.023)	-0.008	(0.011)	-0.004	(0.011)
Region fixed effects						
Sub-Saharan Africa (=1)	0.664**	(0.080)	-0.363**	(0.126)	-0.411**	(0.074)
Region interaction effects						
SSA * household size	-0.070**	(0.015)	-0.070**	(0.008)	-0.065**	(0.008)
SSA * female headed hh	-0.140	(0.121)	0.097	(0.070)	-0.034	(0.066)
SSA * vaccination	0.409**	(0.116)	0.329**	(0.077)	0.176*	(0.069)
SSA * first born	-0.109*	(0.111)	0.054	(0.072)	0.091	(0.067)
SSA * preceding birth int.	-0.004	(0.002)	-0.002	(0.001)	-0.001	(0.001)
SSA * breastfeeding	-0.342**	(0.077)	-0.013	(0.045)	-0.003	(0.042)
SSA * asset index (global)	0.002	(0.066)	-0.094*	(0.046)	-0.152**	(0.042)
SSA * mothers' BMI	-0.036**	(0.032)	0.008	(0.008)	0.004	(0.007)
SSA * health facility index	-0.127**	(0.062)	-0.055	(0.043)	0.001	(0.040)
SSA * sec. education (%)	0.008	(0.306)	0.335*	(0.192)	0.510**	(0.174)
SSA * children w. fever (%)	0.140	(0.232)	0.081	(0.139)	0.110	(0.130)
SSA * infras. index (global)	0.044	(0.040)	-0.030	(0.027)	-0.037	(0.025)
R^2	0.110		0.125		0.110	
Obs.	49572		55914		60018	

Source: Demographic and Health Surveys (DHS); own calculations.
Notes: *P-value<0.1. **P-value<0.01. The variables 'age' and 'age^2' denote the age of the mother in the child mortality regression and the age of the child in the two undernutrition regressions. For more details on the variables, see Section 1.3.1.

1.3.4 Simulations

To shed more light on the South Asia - Sub-Saharan Africa Enigma, in this section, we take explicitly into account the regional and country-specific differences between the outcomes of individual, household, and community characteristics and their respective effects on mortality and undernutrition. We compare the effects of covariates on undernutrition and child mortality by simulating the effects for cases, in where one country would have the outcome and the distribution of covariates of another country. In particular, we create rank preserving transformations of selected covariates between countries. This means, for example that we assign the value of the best educated mother in Uganda to the best educated mother in India. Thus, we ask what would be the outcome of child mortality or undernutrition if the mothers in India had the same level and distribution of education as mothers in Uganda.

We simulate the effects on child mortality and undernutrition based on this rank preserving transformation for a large set of several covariates and countries in South Asia and Sub-Saharan Africa. For example, based on the result that the nutritional status of mothers has a greater impact on child undernutrition in South Asia, we assign the outcome and the distribution of the BMI of mothers from Mali to mothers in India and Bangladesh and estimate the difference in the effect on undernutrition. However, we found an overall small effect. If mothers in India and Bangladesh had the nutritional status of mothers from Mali, this would change the rate of undernutrition of 0.2 percent and 0.3 percent, respectively. In addition, since also the educational attainment of mothers has a greater effect on undernutrition in South Asia, we assign the education of the mothers from Uganda to the mothers in Bangladesh and India. But also here, the effect is only very small.

Furthermore, based on the result that the access to health facilities has a larger impact on child mortality in Sub-Saharan Africa, we assign the values and the distribution of the access to health facilities index from India to Mali. Here, we found that mortality would decrease in Mali by 2 percent if Mali had the access to health facilities as India. However, for the case, where we assign the asset index of Bangladesh to Uganda and Zimbabwe, we only find a very small effect on mortality in both countries. In addition to the rank preserving transformation of selected covariates, we also simulate the effect of mean improvements in these variables. This means, for example that we simulate the effect of an overall increase of the BMI of the mothers by 30 percent. However, also these simulation can only account for small changes in rates of mortality and undernutrition.

Concerning the explanations of the South Asia - Sub-Saharan Africa Enigma, non of these simulations had the potential to fully explain it. But using these simulations, we were able to test the economic significance of the different explanatory variables, meaning that we were able to see what effects certain improvements in the different determinants have on both phenomena. One clear result was that changes in the explanatory variables would result in very different changes in the two forms of deprivation. Again, the strongest influence on child mortality is exerted by the access to health facilities. Although the influence on stunting was also very significant, the magnitude was by far not as large. At the same time, we confirmed the preceding results that increases in material wealth will result in significant reductions of undernutrition and mortality. Even stronger improvements in the incidence of undernutrition could be generated by increases in the level of education of mothers, which has only a limited positive effect on changes in mortality rates by it own.

1.4 Conclusion

In this paper, we analyzed the regional puzzle of child mortality and undernutrition between South Asia and Sub-Sahara Africa. We investigated the effects of individual, household and community socio-economic characteristics on child mortality and undernutrition using a multilevel approach for a set of five developing countries in South Asia and Sub-Saharan Africa. We find strong evidence supporting the existence of the South Asia Sub-Saharan Africa Enigma using micro-data.

The results show large differences in the determinants and their significance levels between mortality and undernutrition, across the two regions, and also between countries. While finding very similar patterns across countries indicating a close relationship between child mortality and undernutrition, we also find that the determinants of mortality and undernutrition differ significantly from each other, which helps to explain the Enigma. And although very similar patterns in the determinants of each phenomenon are discernable, there are large differences in the magnitude of the coefficients. Accounting for the high rates of child mortality in Sub-Saharan Africa, strong evidence is found that the access to health infrastructure is more important for mortality than for undernutrition and the impact is of greater magnitude in Sub-Saharan Africa than in South Asia, whereas the individual and household characteristics like wealth and educational attainment and nutritional characteristics of mothers play a larger role for anthropometric shortfalls. Especially, the nutritional status of mothers has a greater effect in South Asia accounting partly for the high rates of undernutrition, since the overall nutritional status of the mother is even worse in South Asia than in Sub-Saharan Africa. As our study has also shown, there are determinants at the community level that have a significant influence on mortality as well as on undernutrition like the percentage of children with fever or public infrastructure. Besides, regressions using a combined data set of all five countries show that there are still significant unexplained differences between the two regions although taking account of a large set of covariates. Therefore, our results are only partly be able to solve the Enigma.

One hypothetical explanation for the regional differences remains the quality of the data. There might be biases and errors especially in the African data sets. However, these biases cannot account for the differences in the determinants of both phenomena, since the same data sets and explanatory variables are used for the explanation of child mortality and undernutrition in all countries.

Explaining the high rates of child mortality in Sub-Saharan Africa, clearly unobserved socio-economic characteristics play an important role. For example Klasen (2003) emphasizes the importance of the mortality decreasing effect of lower fertility. Another possible explanation for the Enigma might lie in the different prevalence of diseases like HIV/AIDS and Malaria, which heavily affects countries in Sub-Saharan Africa. Therefore, given the data constraints on infectious diseases and their consequences at the individual level, further studies should try to estimate the impact of HIV/AIDS and other diseases on mortality rates.[27] Future research should also try to capture differences in the quality of health facilities and in the composition of nourishments.

Accounting for the high rates of undernutrition in South Asia, one possible explanation might still be how undernutrition is measured. Klasen (2007) suggests that measurement issues play a significant role for the high rates of undernutrition in South Asia. He identifies both the arbitrary cut-off of a z-score of -2 and the reference standard by the WHO (old and new) to calculate the z-scores as two important issues that might lead to an overestimation of undernutrition in South Asia. In particular, he emphasizes that already small genetic differences in the growth potential of children in South Asia considerably overestimate undernutrition in South Asia. Therefore, a closer investigation of the role of the genetic differences as a possible explanation for the high rates of undernutrition in South Asia is of high priority. Another reason for the high rates of undernutrition in South Asia could also be the effects of past undernutrition of the mothers during their childhood, which might has an impact on the status of their children, even if they grow up an a healthy and wealthy environment (Klasen, 2007).

To investigate further explanations of the Enigma, high research priority should also be given on other factors like interactions and non-linearities between risk factors and that they might effect child mortality and undernutrition in a rather multiplicative than additive way (see e.g. Pelletier, 1994).

Finally, one part of the explanation of the South Asia Sub-Saharan Africa Enigma could be the insight that child mortality and undernutrition are not as closely correlated as generally assumed. Our study finds considerable evidence for large differences in the determinants of both phenomena. These differences make

[27] See also Essay 2.

it highly unlikely that child mortality and undernutrition are as closely correlated as found by the studies of Pelletier et al. (1995, 2002) and cited by numerous other publications. And in order to achieve both Millennium Development Goals concerning child mortality and undernutrition it is, therefore, important that both phenomena are taken into account as separate goals, which are to be achieved by different policy measures.

Essay 2

The Impact of HIV on Childrens' Welfare

Abstract: Children living in HIV/AIDS-affected households bear the heaviest burden of the epidemic. Besides direct vertical transmission, HIV/AIDS potentially worsens childrens' welfare indirectly through its socio-economic impact on affected households. This paper uses household survey data including information about individual HIV infection status to analyze the direct and indirect effects of HIV-infected household members on child mortality, undernutrition, and school enrollment for Burkina Faso, Cameroon, Ghana, and Kenya. The results indicate that the main channel through which HIV affects the child mortality risk is mother-to-child-transmission. Whereas no effect of HIV is found on undernutrition, a negative effect of the HIV status of the mother on school enrollment is found for Burkina Faso and Ghana.

2.1 Introduction

As is well known, the HIV/AIDS epidemic dramatically increases mortality rates among young adults in many developing countries, which may also have severe negative consequences for the surviving household members. The region most strongly affected by the epidemic is Sub-Saharan Africa, exhibiting also relatively poor socio-economic indicators. In Sub-Saharan Africa, the demographic impact of HIV/AIDS is much higher than in other affected regions of the developing world. On average, life expectancy at birth has decreased from 50 years in 1990 to 46 years in 2004 (World Bank, 2005). In 2002, about 22 million persons died from AIDS and more than 40 million were living with HIV/AIDS, which accounts for 70 percent of all infected persons worldwide. About 100 million additional deaths are expected until 2025, as a result of the epidemic (UN, 2004).

HIV/AIDS may have similar negative welfare impacts, from the national to the individual level. At the national level, the decline of human capital might hamper economic development. At the household and individual level, the impact of the epidemic might be not only due to loss of lives, but it also might impose a heavy burden on surviving family members, particularly on children. Childrens' welfare potentially worsens via two channels. First, directly through mother-to-child-transmission of the epidemic and, second, indirectly via the socio-economic impact of the epidemic. The latter means that HIV/AIDS might negatively influences the childrens' health, nutritional status, and educational attainment, which goes beyond the effects of direct vertical transmission. Children living in a household in which the mother or another household member is HIV positive may have higher mortality risk and lower nutritional status and educational attainment than children in unaffected households, even if they are not directly infected. In particular, children might suffer indirectly from the epidemic as a result of the diminishing capacities of their main caregivers in the household to provide certain key inputs for the children, as a result of a loss of household income due to HIV/AIDS.

During the last 15 years, many researchers have addressed the demographic, social, and socio-economic impacts of HIV/AIDS. To study the effects of the epidemic on childrens' welfare, clearly it would be ideal to have large-scale panel data including HIV infection rates and information who already suffers from AIDS, to follow the evolution of the epidemic and the resulting consequences for the household. However, such data virtually do not exist for developing countries. In addition, reliable cross-sectional data on HIV/AIDS at the individual level is also still very limited, especially in Sub-Saharan African countries, which hampers the micro-analysis of the determinants and the effects of the epidemic. Therefore, only very limited empirical evidence exists regarding the impact of HIV on childrens' welfare through channels that go beyond the mother-to-child-transmission. For example, Taha et al. (1995) find a considerable higher child mortality risk of HIV-infected mothers in Mali, whereas Ryder et al. (1994) find only very little differences in social indicators among orphans whose mother was HIV positive, compared to orphans whose mother was non-infected in Zaire. However, these studies suffer from the lack of data on HIV/AIDS at the individual level and are based on small-scale surveys with few observation and lacking of socio-economic information.

This paper tries to close the gap and contributes to the literature by analyzing the effects of HIV on different outcomes of childrens' welfare at the micro-level using large-scale Demographic and Health Surveys (DHS). In particular, the paper analyzes the impact of HIV-infected household members that were alive at the time of the survey on child mortality, child undernutrition and school enrollment. So far, no such analysis exists, using large scale household survey data including information about individual HIV infection status of currently living individuals to investigate the impact of HIV on child mortality, undernutrition, and education. Unfortunately, the DHS data provide no information whether the HIV-infected individuals already suffer from AIDS, which might weaken the result with respect to the impact on childrens' welfare. First, there might be exist big differences between the impact of those who are HIV positive and those who already suffer from AIDS with respect to their physical status (i.e. their ability to work and to take care for the children), which might influence the results in a sense that the impact on children is likely to be lower for HIV-infected individuals than for AIDS-affected individuals. Second, the DHS data provide only information about household member currently alive. Therefore, the effect on children of those who already had died as a result of AIDS is not captured, which might lead to an underestimation of the socio-economic impact of the epidemic. However, since the information about the HIV status is very likely to be highly correlated with those who suffer from AIDS and as long as no information about AIDS is available at the individual level, analyzing of the effect of HIV infection is a useful approach to investigate the direct and indirect impact of HIV/AIDS. If a negative impact of the HIV status of the mother or a male partner on the outcome of the childrens' welfare can be identified, this would not only show the diminishing capacities to care of affected households but would also underline the thesis that the effects of those who suffer from AIDS are expected to be even higher.

The aim of the paper is to shed more light on the effects of the HIV/AIDS epidemic on the welfare of children that are caused both by direct vertical transmission and by worsening socio-economic conditions. For the econometric modelling, first a survival model framework is used to estimate the impact of the HIV status of household members on child mortality, which allows for accounting for unobserved heterogeneity. Second, an ordinary least squares (OLS) regression model and a logistic regression model are used to estimate the impact on child undernutrition and education. The model is estimated for four African countries:

Burkina Faso, Cameroon, Ghana, and Kenya using Demographic and Health Surveys (DHS).

The paper is organized as follows. Section 2.2 describes the channels through which HIV/AIDS affects economic development and childrens' welfare, and provides a review of the empirical literature on the impact of HIV/AIDS. Section 2.3 describes the methodology of the empirical approach to estimate the the impact of HIV/AIDS on childrens' welfare. Section 2.4 presents the empirical analysis. Starting with the description of the data sources and the description of the history of HIV/AIDS in the four countries, this section presents the descriptive statistics and the estimation results of the analysis. Section 2.5 concludes.

2.2 Literature Review on the Impact of HIV/AIDS

2.2.1 Development of the HIV/AIDS Epidemic

The main transmission channel of HIV/AIDS is sexual intercourse, which accounts for around 80 percent of all HIV transmissions. Due to biological, socio-economic, and socio-cultural factors, women have a considerably higher infection risk than men (World Bank, 1997). The second important transmission channel is mother to child transmission, which accounts for around 5 percent of all transmissions.

Morgan et al. (2002) estimated based on longitudinal data from rural Uganda that the median time from seroconversion to AIDS is about nine years and from AIDS to death about nine months.[1] Piwoz and Preble (2002) show that the time period between HIV infection and AIDS related death is considerably shorter in developing countries than in industrialized countries because of the higher exposure to other diseases, poor health care (especially missing antiretroviral (ARV) treatment of AIDS), sanitation, and malnutrition.

The national history of HIV/AIDS is assumed to follow a similar pattern in most developing countries. In the early stages of the epidemic, it is generally the wealthier and better educated population in urban regions that is affected. Several studies using data for African countries from the beginning of the 1990s show a higher infection risk among the better educated population group (see e.g. Grosskurth et al., 1995; Hargreaves et al., 2001; Smith et al., 1999; Cogneau and Grimm, 2006). Once the epidemic reaches the poor population, i.e. those with very limited knowledge about HIV transmission and prevention, the epidemic

[1] Two forms of the HIV virus are classified: HIV type-1 and HIV type-2. HIV type-1 is the worldwide most diffused infection type, whereas HIV type-2 is still most prevalent in Sub-Saharan Africa. Mother to child transmission of HIV type-2 is less frequently than mother to child transmission of HIV type-1.

begins to spread across the society as a whole, which is reflected in increasing prevalence of the epidemic. In the next stage, the literature shows that the better educated, i.e. those who are more able to acquire knowledge about HIV/AIDS and its infection risk, change their sexual behavior (see e.g. Kremer, 1996; Glynn et al., 2004). This, accompanied by policy instruments to promote knowledge about the epidemic and the use of condoms, then leads to a slow down in the spread of the epidemic and countries experience a decline of HIV/AIDS cases. The poor are often bypassed by this decline, however, because they still have limited knowledge about HIV/AIDS. Especially the very poor population do not change sexual behavior. Since the very poor have to fight to satisfy their daily basic needs (see e.g. UN, 2005a; Haddad and Gillespie, 2001), their focuss is on short term risks and they cannot afford to deal with HIV as a long term risk.[2]

2.2.2 The Macro-Economic Impact of HIV/AIDS

HIV/AIDS has various channels through which it affects welfare, from the national to the individual level. At the macro-level, economic researchers indicate two main channels through which the HIV/AIDS epidemic has negative macroeconomic effects. First, it kills people, which directly reduces welfare. From an perspective of the 'surviving' economy, the cost of HIV/AIDS, therefore, are mainly through the impact of HIV/AIDS on human capital. In the short run, HIV/AIDS directly decreases human capital because it primarily affects the working age population, and higher mortality rates shrink the labor supply. Indirectly, and especially in the long run, HIV/AIDS can hamper the accumulation of future human capital through higher child mortality and orphaned children (see e.g. Bell et al., 2003). Both effects can hamper economic development, especially if the relatively scarce skilled worker are more affected than unskilled worker. Second, the epidemic makes people ill. Longer and more frequent times absent from work as a result of the epidemic may lower labor productivity of infected workers. In addition, the epidemic leads to the rise of public health care expenditures both through the rise of people needing medical services and higher the cost of the antiretroviral (ARV) treatment of AIDS as compared to the treatment of other diseases (see e.g. Hellinger, 1993). Both impacts have negative effects on savings and investments leading to an overall decline in growth.

---

[2]This has important policy implications. The usual argument of political instruments to reduce HIV/AIDS is to improve the knowledge about the epidemic and its transmission channels and to spread the use of condoms. While this is a very important instrument, it might not be enough, especially when the very poor are the target group of such initiatives and if they are not willing to change their behavior. Recent data show that the very poor are relatively less likely to use condoms (UN, 2005a). Therefore, instruments to reduce HIV/AIDS through, for example, the use of condoms have to be accompanied by measures to reduce poverty and inequality.

During the last two decades, a growing body of literature on the macro-economic impact of HIV/AIDS has developed. For example, Over (1992) estimates a decline in GDP of one third of a percentage point due to the effect of HIV/AIDS on savings and on skilled labor supply. Cuddington (1993) developed a Solow-type growth model and estimates a loss in GDP in 2010 by 15 to 20 percent for Tanzania. Arndt and Lewis (2000) find substantial divergencies in growth of GDP between two scenarios of AIDS and non-AIDS for South Africa. They estimate that the level of GDP is about 17 percent lower by the year 2010 compared to the non-AIDS scenario, mainly as a result of higher public expenditures for health services and lower labor productivity, which results in lower growth of investments. Bonnel (2000) estimates an annual decline in GDP growth of 0.7 percentage points using cross-country regression for Africa between 1990 and 1997.[3] More recently, Bell et al. (2003) emphasizes the importance of human capital and transmission mechanism across generation and argue that the long run impact of HIV/AIDS on GDP growth is even stronger and may even lead to a collapse of the economy of South Africa.

However, researchers also indicate some channels through which the epidemic has a compensating or even positive effect on economic growth, suggesting that the effect of HIV/AIDS on GDP per capita is generally overstated for several reasons (see e.g. Bloom and Mahal, 1997). First, the often existing labor surplus of unskilled worker could moderate the effect of lower labor productivity due to rising mortality and morbidity among the working age population as a result of AIDS. Second, social and economic adjustments could mitigate the rising public expenditures for health care services due to HIV/AIDS. Third, changes in behavior over time are usually not considered when forecasting the number of infected persons. Finally, higher infection rates among the poor could diminish the overall impact on average per capita terms of well-being. If the decline in GDP is absorbed by higher infection rates and resulting higher number of deaths among the poor, i.e. when the denominator of GDP per capita shrinks more than the nominator, this might lead to misleading welfare implications of only small shrinking or even rising GPD per capita.[4]

---

[3]Similar negative effects on GDP growth due to the epidemic are found, for instance, by Jamison, Sachs, and Wang (2001) and MacFarlan and Sgherri (2001).

[4]This problem of not taking into account premature mortality into analysis of per capita well-being is not only of particularly relevance in the case of the HIV/AIDS epidemic. In the context of the worldwide demographic change, the incorporation of variations in life expectancies, changes in population size, and mortality when performing aggregate welfare comparison over time and space is recently discussed in a growing literature. For theoretical implications see, for example, Kanbur and Mukherjee (2003), Becker, Philipson and Soares (2005), Blackorby, Bossert, and Donaldson (2005), and for empirical illustrations Ravallion (2005) and Grimm and Harttgen (2007).

Bloom and Mahal (1997) found only an insignificant impact of HIV/AIDS on GDP per capita, based on a cross-country analysis for 51 developing and developed countries. Young (2005) identifies decreasing fertility rates and higher per capita investments in human capital as another channel through which AIDS may affect the economy in a positive manner and which stands against the negative long term growth effect of a loss in human capital due to higher mortality rates.[5] Other studies find only a small or insignificant effect of the epidemic on the macro-economic performance of African countries. Botswana, where almost one in three persons is HIV positive, experiences a strong growth of GDP per capita (World Bank, 2005).

2.2.3 The Micro-Economic Impact of HIV/AIDS

At the micro-level, the empirical evidence also shows the severe negative economic and social impact of HIV/AIDS on household and individuals. Limited labor productivity of sick household members causes income and substitution effects. HIV/AIDS-affected households experience a temporary loss of income if an income earner is not able to work. Finally, the death of an income earner leads to a permanent loss of income. Often, affected households have to sell assets to compensate the loss of income (Mutangadura, 2000; Béchu, 1998). Particularly poor households, which are more vulnerable to shocks, are most strongly affected. Poor households can cope, if at all, only to a limited extent with losses in income as they own no assets to sell, or cannot afford medical care for affected household members. In general, poverty increases both the infection risk and the impact of HIV/AIDS. For example, Booysen (2003) shows that in South Africa poor households that experienced an AIDS-related death were more than twice as likely to fall into long term poverty than non-affected households. In addition, high expenditures for medical care and the loss of income of sick or dead income earners leads to a reallocation of resources within HIV/AIDS-affected households. For example, affected households often experience a decline in consumption including a reduction in food consumption resulting in higher rates of undernutrition (Topouzis, 1994).[6]

[5] In particular, he compares a negative welfare effect of the decreasing accumulation of human capital through orphaned children with a positive welfare effect of a lower fertility. He states that when countries are affected by high infections rates, the fertility rate decreases directly via less unprotected sexual activities because of higher risks and indirectly via shrinking labor supply, which increases the value of the time of women. Using a Beckerian household model, he finds that the fertility effects dominated the effect of a shrinking human capital accumulation of orphaned children in South Africa resulting in a potentially higher future per capita income.

[6] In many countries, the death of the income earner leads in addition to high expenditure through high funeral costs (Menon et al., 1998).

Children living in HIV/AIDS-affected households might face the heaviest burden resulting from the direct loss in income and intra-household resource reallocations. This paper focusses on three socio-economic channels of which HIV/AIDS might affect childrens' welfare: the impact on child mortality, on undernutrition and on school enrollment. The empirical literature shows that HIV/AIDS is one of the leading causes of child mortality in Africa (see e.g. Hill et al., 2001). Under-five mortality risk for children whose mother is HIV-infected is estimated to be two to five times higher than for those whose mother is HIV negative (see e.g. Adetunji, 2000; Taha et al., 1995). The epidemic affects the mortality risk of children directly through mother-to-child-transmission during pregnancy, delivery and breastfeeding.[7] Without any interventions about 20 to 40 percent of HIV-infected mothers transmit the infection to their children (De Cock et al, 2000; World Bank, 1997) and the median age of death of such an HIV-infected child in Africa is about two years (see e.g. Spira et al., 1999). However, besides the direct effects of HIV/AIDS on child mortality, the epidemic may also have indirect effects on the mortality risk of children through the socio-economic consequences of HIV/AIDS-affected households that stem from reduced capacities of the infected parents to care for their children and from higher risk of illness, which is analyzed in this paper by estimating separately the effect of the HIV status of the mother and her partner on the mortality risk of children controlling for a set of socio-economic individual and household characteristics and environmental factors.

HIV/AIDS may have also direct and indirect effects on the nutritional status of HIV-affected children. Empirical evidence exists that HIV-infected mothers often directly affect the nutritional status of the children, since HIV infection increases the risk a low birth weight, which again leads directly to an increased risk of morbidity, mortality as well as chronic undernutrition (see e.g. Dreyfuss et al., 2001). In addition, undernutrition directly accelerates the progression of the disease towards AIDS-related death through effects on the immune system and its impact on nutrients intake, absorption and utilization (Piwoz and Preble, 2000).[8] Indirectly, HIV/AIDS might affect the precondition of a secure nutritional status of a child and increases the risk of chronic undernutrition because the quantity and quality of food decreases as a result of reduced capacities to care, which plays an important role for the current and future development of the children, a channel, which has rarely been analyzed yet. Therefore, in this analysis, the focuss is

[7] Similarly, breastfeeding of HIV-infected mothers bears also considerable risk for the mother. The high energy demand of breastfeeding weakens the mother, which leads also to an acceleration of the progress of the disease. Mortality rates among HIV-infected mothers who gave breast milk is three times higher than for infected mothers who did not (Nduati et al., 2001).

[8] In contrast, a good nutritional status, particularly of vitamin A reduces the infection risk (Haddad and Gillespie, 2001).

on the impact of HIV on chronic undernutrition of the children living an affected households.

There is also empirical evidence indicating severe negative effects of the epidemic on the educational attainment of children living in HIV/AIDS-affected households. Because of resource reallocations within households as the result of sick or deceased income provider, children often have to be taken out of school to reduce costs resulting in lower potential for future earnings. For instance, Mutangadura (2002) finds for Zimbabwe that the share of children visiting school decreases by 20 percent after an AIDS-related death because of lack of money, or because the children have to go to work to compensate the loss in household income. Topouzis (1994) finds that only every fifth child remains in school after the death of a household member. The impact of HIV/AIDS on education is even worse for children who become orphans, because it decreases strongly their future welfare perspective (see e.g. Bicego et al., 2003; Case et al., 2004). If orphans live with other adults, these adults might not invest in the children because they are not expected to care for them in retirement age (Ainsworth and Semali, 2000). However, since these studies are based on small-scale data sets with only few observations, and since these studies analyze the effect of AIDS-related deaths on children, no information is provided whether HIV-infected household members who are still alive already have an impact on the enrollment status of children living in those households. Only very limited empirical evidence exists on these possible indirect effects of HIV-infected household members on the enrollment status of children. For example, Graff Zivin et al. (2006) estimate the impact of antiretroviral treatment on childrens' schooling and nutritional status in Kenya and finds that the treatment of adult household members raises weekly schooling hours by 20 percent and also improves the nutritional outcome of children. However, also this study is based on a small-scale population survey and much scope for further research is left. This paper tries to fill this gap in the literature by using large scale DHS data for four Sub-Saharan African countries: Burkina Faso, Cameroon, Ghana, and Kenya.

2.3 Methodology

2.3.1 Survival Model Framework

To analyze the impact of HIV on child mortality, this paper applies a survival model framework. The idea of survival or hazard models is to analyze the time to the occurrence of an event, which is in this case the death of the child.[9] In partic-

[9]In general, survival analysis can be defined as the analysis of rates of the occurrence of the failure during a specific risk period (Yamaguchi, 1991). Survival analysis has become a common

ular, this paper employs a semi-parametric Cox proportional-hazard-continuous-time model (Cox, 1972), which is the most popular form of survival model when analyzing patterns of child mortality. Besides, taking the time to the event (i.e. the time to the death of a child) explicitly into account, an advantage of hazard rate models for the analysis of survival data as compared to standard cross-section regression models, is their capacity to deal with several kinds of censored observations. The most typical form of censoring when analyzing child mortality rates is right censoring, which means that the subject (child) has not had the event (death) when the observation time ends, e.g. the child is three years old when the observation time ends and one does not have information whether the child is going to die before she reaches the age of five. Standard regression models (in this case, for example, a logistic regression model) are then restricted to the events that occur within the observed follow-up period. But simply omitting the right-censored cases from the sample reduces the sample size a lot resulting in a loss of information and can generate serious biases in the parameter estimation. In survival analysis, one can include the information about the right-censored subjects up to the time of censoring without making any assumption about the date the event occurs in the future.[10]

Based on Cox (1972), to illustrate the model, let T be the non-negative survival time, which is the time period between non-occurrence and occurrence of failure, i.e. the age between zero and five years. The immediate risk of failure of an individual i, which is alive at time t, is defined as the hazard rate or the or age-specific failure rate and expressed through the hazard function.[11] Let $h(t)$ denote the hazard function of survival time T and $x_i = (x_{1i}, x_{2i}, \dots, x_{pi})$ be a vector of p independently observed covariates for individual i. The hazard function for individual i given the vector x can then be written as

$$h_i(t|x) = h_0(t)g(x_i), \tag{2.1}$$

where $g(x_i)$ is a function of the covariates and the term $h_0(t)$ is defined as the baseline hazard function, which is the hazard for the respective individual when all independent covariates are equal to zero. Assuming continuously distributed survival times and no ties, the hazard function can be written as

$$h_i(t|x) = h_0(t)exp(\beta_1 x_{1i} + \beta_2 x_{2i} + \dots + \beta_p x_{pi})$$

econometric instrument to analyze the determinants of child mortality (see e.g. Ridder and Tunali, 1999; Van der Klaauw and Wang, 2004).

[10]For a detailed description of survival models, see e.g. Lee (1992).

[11]In the context of child mortality, the hazard rate can also be termed as the age-specific mortality rate (Ridder and Tunali, 1999). The mortality rate at time (age) t refers to the magnitude of the child mortality at this age, given that the child has survived to age t.

$$= h_0(t)exp\left(\sum_{j=0}^{p}\beta_j x_{ji}\right). \quad (2.2)$$

Equation 2.2 shows that the underlying hazard rate is a function of a set of independent covariates.[12] To simplify the model, Equation 2.2 can be linearized by dividing both sides by $h_0(t)$ and then taking the logarithm of both sides:

$$log_e\frac{h_i(t)}{h_0(t)} = \beta_1 x_{1i} + \beta_2 x_{2i} + \ldots + \beta_p x_{pi}$$

$$= \left(\sum_{j=0}^{p}\beta_j x_{ji}\right). \quad (2.3)$$

The left-hand side of Equation 2.3 shows the hazard, i.e. the relative risk of individual i and the right-hand side is a linear function of the covariates x_{ji} with their respective coefficients β_j.[13] To estimate Equation 2.3, a maximum likelihood approach is used. In contrast to parametric models, the semi-parametric Cox proportional hazard model does not require the specification of a parametric form of the hazard function $h_0(t)$.[14]

One of the problems that arise is the possible existence of unobserved heterogeneity. The child mortality risk may also depend on unobserved individual and household characteristics and on unobserved biological frailties. It is important to account for this unobserved heterogeneity to avoid inefficient and inconsistent parameter estimation (Van der Klaauw and Wang, 2004).[15] Therefore, the model is

---

[12]Given that there exist no left-censored observation, the likelihood function to estimate the hazard rate for a set of independent observations of duration $i = 1,...,I$ can be expressed as $\prod_{i=1}^{I} h_i(t_i)^{\delta_i} S_i(t_i)$, where t_i is the duration of risk for individual i, $S_i(t_i)$ is the survival function, defined as the probability that an individual survives longer than t ($S(t) = P(T > t)$), and δ_i is a dummy whether the event occurred for i at time t_i ($\delta_i = 1$) or the observation was right censored at time t_i ($\delta_i = 0$). Both $h(t)$ and $S(t)$ depend on the values of the covariates of subject i. For a right-censored observation the contribution to the likelihood function remains $S_i(t_i)$, i.e. the probability of not having the event between 0 and t_i. Therefore, also the information of right-censored observation can be included into the model (Yamaguchi, 1991).

[13]The function $exp()$ is simply chosen to avoid that the hazard function ever turn negative. Semi-parametric means that the analysis makes no assumption about the distribution of the hazard function, whereas the effects of covariates are still parameterized to affect the baseline hazard function in a specific way.

[14]Therefore, the semi-parametric Cox proportional hazard model is more robust than parametric models, because it is not vulnerable to miss-specification of the baseline hazard. The disadvantage of this approach, however, is a loss in efficiency. If one would know the true functional form of $h_0(t)$ one would obtain more efficient estimation results of the β_j.

[15]When unobserved heterogeneity exists and if it is not considered in the model, one either overestimates a negative duration effect or underestimates a positive duration effect (Yamaguchi, 1991).

extended to incorporate also unobserved heterogeneity. Thus the hazard function 2.3 becomes to

$$log_e \frac{h_i(t)}{h_0(t)} = \sum_{j=0}^{p} \beta_j x_{ji} + \alpha_i, \tag{2.4}$$

where α_i is the group i level frailty, which is assumed to be gamma distributed.

The impact of HIV is separately estimated both through the HIV status of the mother or the male partner. As the dependent variables for the analysis of the impact of HIV on child mortality, the hazard rate of children under five years of age is used.[16]

2.3.2 Ordinary Least Squares and Logistic Model

To analyze the impact of HIV on undernutrition and school enrollment, controlling for individual and household socio-economic and demographic characteristics and environmental factors, a standard ordinary least squares (OLS) and a logistic regression model are applied. For each country, the following equation is estimated:

$$\begin{aligned} y_i &= \beta_1 x_{1i} + \beta_2 x_{2i} + ... + \beta_p x_{pi} + u_i \\ &= \sum_{j=0}^{p} \beta_j x_{ji} + u_i, \end{aligned} \tag{2.5}$$

where y_i represents either the dependent variable to analyze child undernutrition or the dependent variable to analyze school enrollment for child i. As dependent variable to analyze the impact of HIV infected mothers or partners on child undernutrition the stunting z-score of children under five years of age is used.[17] To analyze the impact on school enrollment, a dummy variable is used that shows whether all children aged between five and fifteen per household are enrolled in school.[18]

[16]This paper does not separate between neonatal deaths, i.e the child dies within the first month of life and post-neonatal death, i.e. the child died between the second month and the first year of life, as for example proposed by Adebayo et al. (2004) because this did not change the estimation results.

[17]The z-score is defined as $z = \frac{AI_i - MAI}{\sigma}$, where AI_i refers to the individual anthropometric indicator (height for age - stunting, weight for height - underweight, weight for age - wasting), MAI refers to the median of the reference population, and σ refers to the standard deviation of the reference population (see e.g. Klasen, 2003, 2007; Smith and Haddad, 2000). A child is considered as stunted if the stunting z-score (height for age) is below -2 standard deviations from the median of the reference category (WHO, 2006).

[18]For the logistic regression model, the dependent variable y_i enters the regression as $log \frac{p_i}{p_i - 1}$, where $p_i = pr(y_i = 1|X)$, which is the probability that all children aged between 5 and 15 living in the same household are enrolled in school, conditional on a vector of covariates X.

2.4 Empirical Analysis

2.4.1 Data Description

Fortunately, DHS conducted in recent years include HIV test results at the individual level for selected Sub-Saharan African countries. These DHS surveys are the first large-scale households survey data sets providing HIV testing results.[19] Thus, the data sets provide interesting scope for the analysis of the impact of HIV on the households' welfare and may give new insights into the causes and impact of the epidemic. Besides the information on HIV testing results, the DHS surveys provide also information on anthropometric outcomes of children, child mortality and socio-economic individual and household characteristics.

The Sub-Saharan African countries analyzed in this paper are Burkina Faso (2003), Cameroon (2004), Ghana (2003), and Kenya (2003). Concerning human development, Ghana is the only country of the sample that is classified as a 'Medium Human Development' country by the United Nations with a Human Development Index (HDI) rank of 138. The other three countries are classified as 'Low Human Development' countries with HDI ranks of 148 (Cameroon), 154 (Kenya) and 177 (Burkina Faso, which is only higher ranked than Sierra Leone and Niger) (UN, 2005b). In all countries, poverty rates[20] are around 50 percent and GDP per capita is low. In 2003, Cameroon, Kenya, and Burkina Faso had a life expectancy between 46 and 48 years, whereas the situation in Ghana was better with a life expectancy of about 60 years (World Bank, 2005). In addition, all countries suffer from high incidence of child mortality of more than 100 per 1000 children and of child undernutrition of around 40 percent, compared to African average rates of 17.1 percent for child mortality and 29.4 percent for malnutrition (weight for age) (World Bank, 2005). At present, it is not very likely that the four countries will reach the Millennium Development Goals (MDG) in 2015.[21]

The underlying theoretical framework to study the impact of HIV on childrens' welfare, controlling for socio-economic individual and households characteristics, the paper follows the theoretical framework for the study of child mor-

[19]In particular, the DHS data sets provide a sub-sample including HIV infection testing results for males and females. As the DHS data sets are representative at the national level, the HIV sub-sample is compared to the full sample regarding the question if also the sub-sample is national representative. Table B.1 compares the two data sets by estimating the probability of being in the full sample on a the set of variables that are used in the analysis of this paper. Almost all variables are not significant indicating that the results of the analysis using the HIV sub-sample can be interpreted as representative at the national level. However, the urban dummy is significant in Burkina Faso, Cameroon, and Kenya indicating the results are only to a limited extent interpretable as national representative.

[20]Considering the poverty line of below 1 USD PPP per day.

[21]However, among these countries, Ghana has the best chance to reach the goals.

tality proposed by Mosley and Chen (1984), and for undernutrition by UNICEF (1990) and Engle et al. (1999).[22] In total, the data sets contain information on 13734 children living in 5629 households.[23] As independent variables, a set of household socio-economic and child characteristics are included into the regression models. In addition, to control for urban areas, the household size,[24] the number of children, and a dummy whether the household is female headed are included.[25] As the DHS surveys provide no information on income or consumption, an asset-based approach is applied to obtain information about the material well-being of the households (Sahn and Stifel, 2001). For this, an index based on a principal component analysis, proposed by Filmer and Pritchett (2001), is derived. Assets to calculate the index are dummy variables whether household possesses a radio, TV, refrigerator, bike, motorized transport, low floor material, toilet, and drinking water.[26]

The sex of the child is included to control for a possible gender bias, which is often found in the literature (see e.g. Marcoux, 2002; Klasen, 1996). Other important determinants of child mortality and undernutrition are whether the child is the first born child, the preceding birth interval, and if the child was immediately breastfed after birth by the mother.[27] In addition, the regression models capture also the access to health services, by including a dummy whether the child received all possible vaccinations,[28] whether the child received vitamin A, and

[22]See also the data description of Section 1.3.1 in Essay 1.

[23]See Section 2.4.2 for descriptive statistics.

[24]As the household size is arguably endogenous, i.e. households in which many children die tend to be larger to compensate the loss of the dead children, the variable is not included directly into the regression. Instead in instrumental variable approach is applied, where as instrument variable the mean household size per cluster is used (see also Section 1.3.1 in Essay 1).

[25]HIV/AIDS contributes to a rising share of female headed households, which potentially worsens the situation of food security for the children.

[26]As already discussed in Section 1.3.1 in Essay 1, the reasons why one includes the asset index instead of separate dummies for each assets are, first that the index provides an income proxy of the household which can be used to analyze distributional differences of the impact of HIV or the distribution of HIV itself. Second, as the assets are correlated, their coefficients are likely to provide no significant effects if they are included separately, which would however lead to misleading interpretation of the estimation results.

[27]Breastfeeding in the first month of life plays an important role for the development of the child, because the breast milk meets most of the childs' nutritional needs and makes the child more resistent against diseases (see e.g. Ramalingaswami et al., 1996). However, breastfeeding is also a channel of mother to child transmission, which means that it might have a negative effect when the mother is HIV positive.

[28]As described in Section 1.3.1 in Essay 1, to avoid the problem of endogeneity, i.e. that the number of vaccinations is an increasing function of the age of the child, the dummy whether the vaccinations process is completed is defined as follows: the first 2 month after birth are not considered as incomplete if no vaccinations were received, for the age between 3 and 6 months the dummy is one if the child has received at least 3 vaccinations, for the age between 7 and 9

whether the mother received prenatal care. Furthermore, concerning the status of the mother, the education of the mother is included to take into account the direct ability to acquire skills to take care of the children and indirectly the earning potential of the mother, which is expected to positively affect childrens' welfare outcomes. In addition, the nutritional status of the mother is included since a malnourished mother is expected to have a negative impact on the nutritional status of the child.[29]

For the estimation of the impact of HIV on child education, the described household socio-economic characteristics enter the regression model as well. Apart from the educational level of the household head, the information on the educational status of the mother is included. Information whether the mother works for cash is also included, because it might have a positive effect on the probability that children are sent to school. This argument holds especially for female children. For example, in South Asian countries, the gender bias in education of children is found to be lower if the mother works and, therefore, strengthens her bargaining power position in the household (Alderman et al., 1996).

2.4.2 Descriptive Statistics

The countries have experienced different histories regarding the development of the epidemic over the past 20 years. In Kenya, the first official AIDS case was reported in 1984, followed by Cameroon in 1985. In Burkina Faso and Ghana, the first cases were reported in 1986. Figure 2.1 shows the number of reported AIDS cases by year and country and describes the history and different stages of the epidemic for the countries over time.[30]

months if the child has received at least 6 vaccinations and between 10 and 12 months if the child has received all 8 vaccinations.

[29] As the measure of the nutritional status of the mother the body mass index (BMI) is used. A mother is considered as malnourished if the BMI is below 18.5 (see also Section 1.3.1). The BMI enters also as the BMI squared into the regression to capture the possibility that the BMI of the mother affects the childs' nutritional status non-linearly. In particular, this captures the possibility that a very high BMI might effect the nutritional status of the child in a negative way, because the high value of the BMI might be simply due to the intake of many calories that are, however, nutritionally inadequate.

[30] However, one should be careful when comparing the reported AIDS cases across countries. The number of reported AIDS cases is only a very crude indicator of the actual HIV/AIDS prevalence and depends heavily on the existing and spatial distribution of reporting systems within countries. For example, if the share of people living in urban areas strongly differs between countries, than comparing the numbers of AIDS cases across countries can be misleading if, first, the prevalence of AIDS is higher in urban areas than in rural areas and, second, because reporting institutions are usually located in urban areas resulting in higher reporting in urban than rural areas. One should also be careful when interpreting the evolution of AIDS over time within a country,

All countries exhibit the initial growth in AIDS prevalence as described in Section 2.2.1. During the first years of the epidemic, Kenya experienced the highest increase in AIDS cases in the sample. Already at the beginning of the 1990s, the number of new infections began to decline rapidly. Compared to Kenyas' development, Ghana, Cameroon and Burkina Faso are in an earlier stage of the epidemic but show a similar history of the epidemic. After a continuous rise, AIDS cases started to decline around the year 2000 in Ghana and Burkina Faso.

Table 2.1 shows the HIV infection rates by sub-groups for the four countries. Overall, the HIV prevalence in the DHS data sets is consistent with the prevalence published by UNAIDS (UNAIDS, 2006). In addition, in a recent paper, Oster (2006) provides a new methodology to estimate the HIV prevalence based on mortality data on siblings. By providing consistent estimates of HIV prevalence over time and across countries, she found that the HIV prevalence of the DHS surveys are not underestimated. Cameroon and Kenya are affected considerably stronger by the epidemic than Burkina Faso and Ghana. In Kenya and in Cameroon 7 and 6 percent, respectively, of all households have at least one HIV-infected person, compared to about 2 and 3 percent in Burkina Faso and Ghana, respectively. Whereas the age group between 25 and 59 years is more affected in Burkina Faso, Cameroon and Ghana, the opposite is found for Kenya. The distribution of HIV over age is also shown in Figure 2.2, which illustrate the results from Table 2.1.

The spatial distribution of the epidemic follows the usual pattern. HIV infection rates are considerably higher in urban than in rural areas in Burkina Faso, Cameroon, and Kenya, which might indicate more frequent changes in partnerships in urban areas. In Burkina Faso, HIV infection rates are more than 3 times higher in urban areas than in rural areas (4.01 compared to 1.22 percent). Only in Kenya is the HIV infection rate only slightly higher in rural than in urban areas, which might indicate that the rural population has less knowledge about the epidemic and the risk factors of HIV transmission. Looking at the infection rates of mothers, Table 2.1 shows a similar picture as for the total household. The highest rates are found in Kenya at 8.88 percent and the lowest infection rates are found in Burkina Faso, at 1.50 percent.

To get a picture of how HIV infections are distributed across welfare groups in the countries, Table 2.2 shows the HIV infection rates for the asset index quintiles. In Burkina Faso, Cameroon, and Ghana the poorest quintile has the lowest infection rate, whereas the richest quintile has the highest rate. This indicates that especially the wealthier population group is affected by the epidemic. For example, the ratio of infections of the first to the fifth quintile is 0.10 in Burkina

because the number and distribution of reporting institutions as well as the reporting behavior can change a lot over time.

Figure 2.1: Number of Reported AIDS Cases
by Years

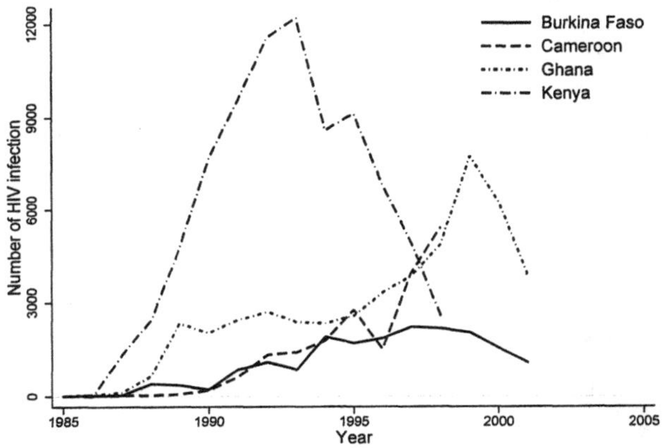

Source: WHO (2006a), own calculations.

Table 2.1: HIV Infection Rates

HIV infection* (percentage)	Burkina Faso 2003	Cameroon 2004	Ghana 2003	Kenya 2003
Adults				
Total	1.88	5.50	2.71	6.84
Agegroup 15-24	1.34	3.38	1.18	4.13
Agegroup 25-59	2.26	7.05	3.65	8.64
Urban	4.01	6.66	2.90	5.82
Rural	1.22	3.40	2.59	7.42
Mother				
Total	1.50	5.78	2.21	8.88
Agegroup 15-24	1.16	4.88	1.82	8.88
Agegroup 25-59	1.63	6.25	2.31	8.92
Urban	4.46	8.03	1.85	13.39
Rural	1.04	4.04	2.38	7.85

Source: Demographic and Health Surveys (DHS); own calculations.
Note: *Positive tested for HIV type-1 or HIV type-2.

Figure 2.2: HIV Infection by Age

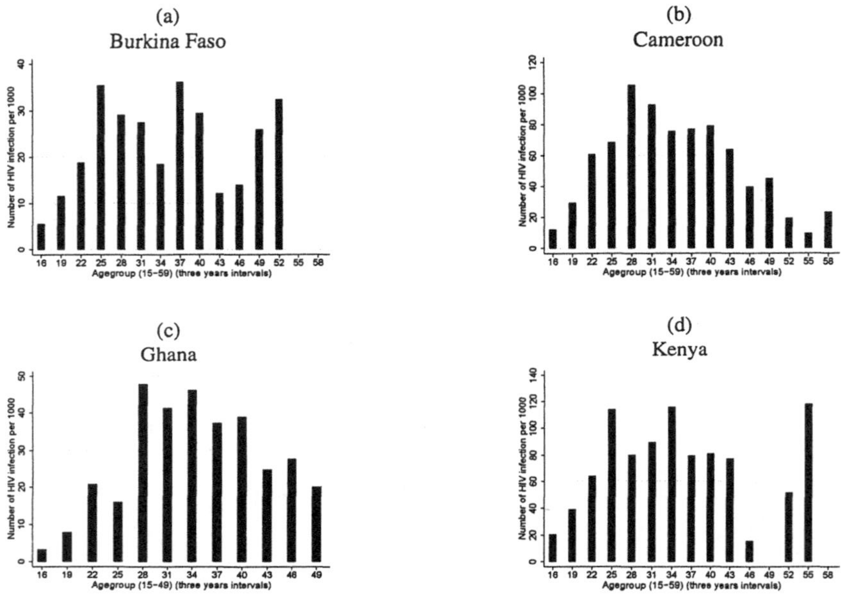

Source: Demographic and Health Surveys (DHS); own calculations.

Faso. Interesting to note is, as Cogneau and Grimm (2006) already pointed out for Côte d'Ivoire, high infection rates are also observed for the second quintile, i.e. whom they call 'the rich of the poor'. For example, looking at the second and fourth quintile in Burkina Faso, the poorer quintile has considerably higher infection rates than the richer quintile (1.33 compared to 2.27). In contrast, Kenya shows the opposite picture. Here, Table 2.2 shows that the poorest quintile has the highest infection rates, which is reflected in a ratio of the first to the fifth quintile of 1.16. The distribution of HIV over asset index quintiles is also shown in Figure 2.3, which also indicates the slightly higher infection rates among the wealthier population groups.

Figure 2.3: HIV Infection by Asset Index

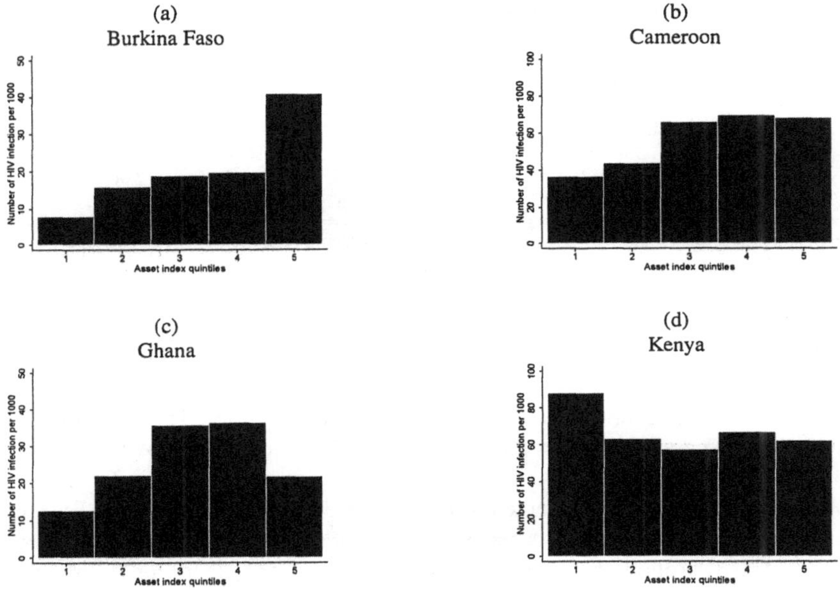

Source: Demographic and Health Surveys (DHS); own calculations.

This again indicates that Kenya has reached a different stage of the epidemic than the other countries. Comparing these findings about the socio-economic distribution of HIV infections to the findings of the empirical literature described in Section 2.2.1, only Kenya has yet reached the stage in the history of the epidemic where infection rates spread away from the wealthier to the poorer population.[31] The other countries show, in spite of decreasing overall infection rates that still higher rates persist among the richer population group among the lower middle class.[32]

Table 2.3 presents some descriptive statistics for child mortality, undernutrition, and education for the total data set and by asset index quintiles. The absolute values for child mortality are high in all four countries. In contrast to HIV infections, Burkina Faso has the highest rates of child mortality at 164, as compared

[31] As also found, for example, by Glynn et al. (2004).

[32] This was also found, for example, by Hargreaves et al. (2001) and Cogneau and Grimm (2006).

Table 2.2: HIV Infection by Asset Index

	Quintile 1	Quintile 2	Quintile 3	Quintile 4	Quintile 5	Ratio 1/5
HIV infection						
Burkina Faso 2003	0.87	1.33	3.90	2.27	8.99	0.10
Cameroon 2004	5.66	8.05	17.69	18.48	20.73	0.27
Ghana 2003	1.91	2.53	4.10	4.15	2.90	0.66
Kenya 2003	12.21	9.60	7.13	7.56	10.51	1.16

Source: Demographic and Health Surveys (DHS); own calculations.
Notes: The asset index is calculated based on a principal component analysis. As variables to calculate the asset index, dummies are included whether the following assets exist or not in a household: radio, TV, refrigerator, bike, motorized transport, low floor material, toilet, drinking water. Quintile one corresponds to the poorest and quintile five to the richest population sub-group.

to Ghana with the overall lowest child mortality rate of 106.[33] The percentage of stunted children are also considerably high in all four countries. Whereas more than one third of all children under five years of age are stunted in Cameroon, Ghana, and Kenya, even 44 percent suffer from chronic undernutrition in Burkina Faso. In addition, also the percentage of households in which all children between 5 and 15 are enrolled in school is worse in Burkina Faso. Here, only 7 percent households show complete school enrollment, which is more 7 times less than in Cameroon and Kenya, where 49 and 48 percent of households show complete school enrollment, respectively.

The distribution of child mortality, undernutrition, and complete school enrollment over the asset index shows a clear bias against the poor. On average, child mortality rates are about two times higher for the poorest quintile than for the richest quintile. Inequality is even worse in the case of undernutrition. In Ghana, half of all children in the first quintile are stunted (47 percent) compared to 'only' 15 percent in the fifth quintile. Cameroon, Ghana, and Kenya have quite similar total undernutrition rates of about 35 percent. Again, in Burkina Faso the situation is worse with a stunting rate of even 44 percent. The situation of school enrollment is also alarming. Concerning the distribution of educational opportunities for different welfare groups, Table 2.3 shows substantial inequalities between the quintiles in Burkina Faso, Cameroon, and Ghana. For example, the ratio of

[33]The level and evolution of the survival rates is also shown in Figure B.1 in Appendix B. Figure B.1 illustrates the differences in the levels of survival rates over age between the four countries. During the first year of live, the survival rates do not differ very much between countries. But then, the survival rates begin to spread and Burkina Faso shows the lowest level of survival rates. In contrast, the highest survival rates are found for Ghana and Kenya.

Table 2.3: Child Mortality, Undernutrition, and Education by Asset Index

	Quintile 1	Quintile 2	Quintile 3	Quintile 4	Quintile 5	Total	Ratio 1/5
Child mortality							
Burkina Faso 2003	170	196	180	156	106	164	1.60
Cameroon 2004	156	146	132	159	89	143	1.76
Ghana 2003	107	104	108	109	75	106	1.43
Kenya 2003	119	141	88	104	84	113	1.42
Stunting (%)							
Burkina Faso 2003	0.52	0.47	0.47	0.38	0.29	0.44	1.80
Cameroon 2004	0.44	0.42	0.41	0.27	0.17	0.36	2.59
Ghana 2003	0.47	0.37	0.36	0.27	0.19	0.36	2.47
Kenya 2003	0.45	0.37	0.37	0.24	0.19	0.35	2.37
School enrollment (%)							
Burkina Faso 2003	0.03	0.04	0.04	0.10	0.24	0.07	0.13
Cameroon 2004	0.40	0.41	0.49	0.58	0.73	0.49	0.55
Ghana 2003	0.14	0.21	0.27	0.30	0.35	0.23	0.40
Kenya 2003	0.43	0.45	0.50	0.50	0.51	0.48	0.84

Source: Demographic and Health Surveys (DHS); own calculations.
Notes: Child mortality shows the number of children per 1000 of under five years of age who died within the last 60 months, compared to all children under five years of age living in the respective quintile. The stunting rate shows the percentage of stunted children in the respective quintile compared to all children under five years of age. A child is considered as stunted if the height over age z-score is below -2 standard deviations from the new reference category (WHO, 2006). School enrollment refers the percentage of households where all children between five and fifteen are enrolled in school. The asset index is calculated based on a principal component analysis. As variables to calculate the asset index, dummies are included whether the following assets exist or not in a household: radio, TV, refrigerator, bike, motorized transport, low floor material, toilet, drinking water. Quintile one corresponds to the poorest and quintile five to the richest population sub-group.

the first to the firth quintile shows that in Cameroon and Ghana complete school enrollment is twice as high for the richest quintile than for the poorest quintile. Only in Kenya, the inequality in education is found to be lower.

To provide more specific insights into the situation in the countries, Table 2.4 provides descriptive statistics on specific household demographic, and socio-economic characteristics, on sexual behavior, and on knowledge about HIV/AIDS. For example, Burkina Faso has the highest rates of malnourished mothers at 18.11 percent and the mean value of the BMI is almost 13 percent lower than in Cameroon (22.69 compared to 23.35). Cameroon has the highest school enrollment rates as well as has the highest rates of primary education of the household head (48.09 percent). The overall bad situation of access to piped drinking water is also worth noting. In Burkina Faso, only 3.54 percent of households have piped drinking water and Ghana and Cameroon also show rates below 10 percent. Only in Kenya the situation is slightly better where almost 14 percent of households have piped drinking water. Looking at the situation of knowledge about HIV/AIDS, Table 2.4 shows that nearly all respondents have heard of AIDS in all countries. For example, in Cameroon 46 percent know someone with AIDS and 62 spoke about AIDS with the spouse. However, the knowledge about specific transmission risk factors is still very limited. In Kenya, where 95.25 percent know about mother-to-child-transmission, only 12.47 percent know about other risk factors like prostitution or sharing razor blades with intra-venous drug users. The knowledge about risk factors of HIV-transmission is even worse in rural areas compared to urban areas in all four countries.

Table 2.4: Summary Statistics
for Individual and Household Characteristics and AIDS Knowledge

	Burkina Faso 2003	Cameroon 2004	Ghana 2003	Kenya 2003
Urban (%)	14.71	37.35	26.85	22.93
Female headed household (%)	5.97	18.42	23.00	24.64
Household size	8.05	7.98	6.19	5.89
Age of head	45.31	41.54	41.31	38.17
Head has primary education (%)	7.16	42.26	37.25	30.55
Head has secondary education (%)	1.10	4.79	7.69	21.29
Mothers' BMI<18.5 (%)	18.11	5.56	8.60	13.49
Mothers' BMI	20.69	23.35	22.60	22.14
Age of first birth	18.81	18.24	19.93	19.04
Age of first marriage	17.23	17.16	18.69	18.51
Married (%)	86.64	71.41	83.29	78.01
Number of children	4.34	4.00	3.93	3.89
Sex of child is female (%)	49.41	49.95	49.21	49.45
Immediate breastfeeding (%)	40.44	34.00	53.51	54.80
Immediate breastfeeding (HIV-positive) (%)	40.00	34.85	45.45	53.50
Stunting z-score	-1.65	-1.39	-1.44	-1.37
Complete vaccination (%)	57.88	64.40	74.41	70.28
Prenatal care (%)	50.81	52.12	65.95	58.07
Child received vitamin A (%)	27.95	34.84	49.16	14.75
Child had recently fever (%)	85.43	48.89	32.50	69.43
Piped water (%)	3.54	7.43	8.19	13.92
AIDS knowledge and sexual behavior				
Ever heard from AIDS (%)	96.74	97.99	97.30	97.81
Knows someone with AIDS (%)	47.45	45.43	37.72	71.98
Spoke with spouse about AIDS (%)	35.84	60.29	56.13	61.17
Knowing about MTCT* (%)	64.46	70.37	75.72	95.65
Knowing risk factors** (%)	9.09	24.10	35.47	12.47
Knowing risk factors** (%) (rural)	6.85	15.59	33.34	13.06
Knowing risk factors** (%) (urban)	16.54	27.87	47.12	11.53
Obs.	3578	3952	3627	2447

Source: Demographic and Health Surveys (DHS); own calculations.
Note: *Dummy variable whether knowing about mother to child transmission of HIV/AIDS. **Dummy variable whether knowing at least about one of the following risk factors: Prostitution, partner with many partners, sex with intra-venous drug users, sharing razor blades with AIDS patients.

2.4.3 Estimation Results

Table 2.5 shows the regression results for child mortality. Overall, Table 2.5 shows the familiar pattern, which was also found in Section 1.3.3 in Essay 1 for countries in South Asia and other Sub-Saharan countries. Regarding the socio-economic characteristics of the child, very similar effects are found across countries. Three main determinants of child mortality can be identified: breastfeeding, prenatal care and a complete vaccination process. As expected, breastfeeding immediately after birth significantly reduces the mortality risk of children, which is in line with the general knowledge about the importance of the colostrum, which contains a large number of antibodies and basically works as a first immunization. In addition, a strong negative effect on child mortality is also observed if the vaccination process of the child is completed and if the mother has received prenatal care, which reflects the access to the medical care system. Differences between determinants are found across countries for the effect of female-headed households. Whereas in Ghana living in a female-headed household significantly increases the mortality risk, it significantly decreases the risk in Burkina Faso, and has no significant effect in the other two countries. Interestingly, no significant gender bias in the sense that girls have a higher mortality risk than boys could be identified in any of the four countries. In Kenya, an even negative and significant effect on child mortality is found if the sex of child is female.[34]

Quite surprisingly, some characteristics of the mother have a much lower effect on child mortality than expected. For example, the mothers' educational level, measured by the mother having secondary education, has only a significant mortality decreasing impact in Ghana.[35] The same holds for the nutritional status of the mother, measured by the BMI. Even more surprising is the low influence of wealth, measured by the asset index, on the reduction of the child mortality risk. Whereas no significant effect was found for Burkina Faso, Cameroon, and Kenya, the asset index even has a positive and significant effect in Ghana.[36] In, addition, the percentage of children who recently suffered from fever only has a significant positive effect on mortality in Ghana. Although the percentage of access to piped drinking water show the right sign, it is insignificant in all countries.

Turning to the impact of HIV on child mortality, Table 2.5 shows a strong and significant effect of the HIV status of the mother in all four Sub-Saharan African countries. The mother being HIV positive considerably increases the mortality risk. For example, simulating for all HIV-infected mothers in the sample being HIV negative yields a reduction in the hazard rate by about 8 percent in Cameroon

[34]This can partly be explained because girls are less vulnerable to diseases than boys in the first months of live.

[35]However, the educational level of the mother influences other determinants of child mortality, which directly affects child mortality like fertility or feeding practices, which are separately considered in the regression model.

[36]One possible explanation of this questionable result is the problem of underreporting. Especially the very poor and bad educated population sub-group is very likely to conceal the death of a child, which then might lead to distorted estimation results.

and Kenya and by around 3 percent in Ghana and Burkina Faso. The question is, how can this result be interpreted in the light of the question through which channel HIV affects the welfare of the children? Does this result shows only the mother-to-child-transmission of the epidemic, or can we also draw conclusions about the indirect effect of lower capacity to care of HIV-infected mothers? The main effect of this variable seems to be due to mother-to-child-transmission. This can be verified by including the variable whether the male partner is HIV-infected, instead of considering the status of the mother. If the HIV status of a male household member has a significant impact on child mortality, this would suggest that the socio-economic consequences of HIV are also captured and would also play an important role for the mortality risk.[37]

[37] In addition, interesting to note is that if the variable whether the child was breastfed immediately after birth is excluded from the model, the negative effect of the HIV status increases, which reflects the higher risk of mother-to-child-transmission due to breastfeeding.

Table 2.5: Regression Results of Child Mortality (HIV Status of Mother) (Cox Proportional Hazard Model)

	Burkina Faso 2003	Cameroon 2004	Ghana 2003	Kenya 2003
Age (mother)	-0.145*	-0.150*	-0.053	-0.165*
	(0.060)	(0.063)	(0.076)	(0.092)
$Age^2/100$ (mother)	0.235**	0.238*	0.086	2.854*
	(0.091)	(0.100)	(0.113)	(1.437)
Sex of child (1=female)	0.047	-0.111	-0.095	-0.352*
	(0.099)	(0.102)	(0.122)	(0.151)
Urban (=1)	0.304	0.043	-0.098	-0.258
	(0.213)	(0.148)	(0.183)	(0.258)
Asset index	0.014	-0.170	0.187*	0.213
	(0.113)	(0.105)	(0.124)	(0.176)
Household size (adults) (IV)	0.009	0.019	0.010	0.083
	(0.023)	(0.031)	(0.051)	(0.076)
Female headed household (=1)	-0.498*	-0.253	0.297*	0.013
	(0.287)	(0.154)	(0.154)	(0.191)
First born (=1)	-0.445*	-0.333*	0.043	-0.557*
	(0.210)	(0.184)	(0.222)	(0.272)
Preceding birth interval	-0.015**	-0.007*	-0.002	-0.006
	(0.004)	(0.003)	(0.003)	(0.004)
Prenatal care (=1)	-0.493**	-0.618**	-0.706**	-0.621**
	(0.119)	(0.118)	(0.131)	(0.165)
Immediate breastfeeding (=1)	-0.228**	-0.346**	-0.754**	-0.820**
	(0.107)	(0.121)	(0.130)	(0.164)
Mother has sec. education (=1)	-0.395	-0.113	-0.330*	0.015
	(0.474)	(0.147)	(0.161)	(0.238)
BMI of mother	-0.014	0.043	0.025	0.038
	(0.024)	(0.017)	(0.022)	(0.026)
$BMI^2/100$ of mother	-0.072	-0.002	-0.057	0.253
	(0.352)	(0.198)	(0.183)	(0.248)
Complete vaccination (=1)	-0.900**	-0.975**	-0.630**	-0.758**
	(0.117)	(0.116)	(0.130)	(0.163)
Vitamin A (=1)	0.178*	0.031	-0.138	-0.042
	(0.092)	(0.109)	(0.125)	(0.223)
Recently had fever (% in cluster)	0.274	0.351	0.899*	-0.138
	(0.273)	(0.322)	(0.375)	(0.377)
Piped drinking water (% in cluster)	-0.627	-0.475	-0.508	-0.478
	(0.629)	(0.423)	(0.434)	(0.467)
HIV positive (mother) (=1)	0.860**	0.867**	1.015**	0.586**
	(0.305)	(0.179)	(0.274)	(0.245)
Obs.	3344	3671	3406	2267

Source: Demographic and Health Surveys (DHS); own calculations.
Notes: *P-value<0.1. **P-value<0.01. The household size enters via an instrumental variable into the model. As instrument the mean household size per cluster is used.

Table 2.6: Regression Results of Child Mortality (HIV Status of Partner) (Cox Proportional Hazard Model)

	Burkina Faso 2003	Cameroon 2004	Ghana 2003	Kenya 2003
Age (mother)	-0.143**	-0.131*	-0.041	-0.165*
	(0.056)	(0.062)	(0.076)	(0.091)
Age^2/100 (mother)	0.231**	0.209*	0.073	2.810*
	(0.084)	(0.100)	(0.113)	(1.432)
Sex of child (1=female)	0.053	-0.118	-0.081	-0.332*
	(0.097)	(0.102)	(0.122)	(0.150)
Urban (=1)	0.346*	0.050	-0.146	-0.224
	(0.207)	(0.148)	(0.185)	(0.257)
Asset index	0.024	-0.153	0.216*	0.214
	(0.111)	(0.106)	(0.122)	(0.176)
Household size (adults) (IV)	0.009	0.014	0.005	0.089
	(0.022)	(0.031)	(0.051)	(0.076)
Female headed household (=1)	-0.445*	-0.158	0.335*	0.044
	(0.273)	(0.151)	(0.154)	(0.190)
First born (=1)	-0.457*	-0.304	0.066*	-0.555
	(0.225)	(0.184)	(0.221)	(0.270)
Preceding birth interval	-0.015**	-0.006*	-0.001	-0.006
	(0.005)	(0.003)	(0.003)	(0.004)
Prenatal care (=1)	-0.479**	-0.596**	-0.703**	-0.604**
	(0.112)	(0.117)	(0.131)	(0.165)
Immediate breastfeeding (=1)	-0.122**	-0.367**	-0.766**	-0.829**
	(0.104)	(0.121)	(0.131)	(0.164)
Mother has sec. education (=1)	-0.380	-0.077	-0.329*	0.018
	(0.453)	(0.147)	(0.161)	(0.238)
BMI of mother	-0.016	0.040	0.023*	0.038
	(0.024)	(0.017)	(0.022)	(0.026)
BMI^2/100 of mother	-0.071	-0.002	-0.056	0.218
	(0.352)	(0.199)	(0.184)	(0.249)
Complete vaccination (=1)	-0.896**	-1.021**	-0.635**	-0.772**
	(0.128)	(0.116)	(0.130)	(0.163)
Vitamin A (=1)	0.154	0.038	-0.140	-0.033
	(0.083)	(0.109)	(0.125)	(0.222)
Recently had fever (% in cluster)	0.286	0.371	0.835*	-0.094
	(0.253)	(0.328)	(0.373)	(0.374)
Piped drinking water (% in cluster)	-0.723	-0.452	-0.475	-0.420
	(0.594)	(0.428)	(0.438)	(0.470)
HIV positive (partner) (=1)	0.525	0.194	-0.129	-0.421
	(0.390)	(0.276)	(0.713)	(0.479)
Obs.	3344	3671	3406	2667

Source: Demographic and Health Surveys (DHS); own calculations.
Notes: *P-value<0.1. **P-value<0.01. The household size enters via an instrumental variable into the model. As instrument the mean household size per cluster is used.

As shown in Table 2.6, the HIV status of a male household member (where the mother is not infected) has no significant effect on child mortality in all countries. This result seems to indicate that the main effect of HIV is then through mother-to-child-transmission rather due to the socio-economic impact of HIV. In other words, if a child lives in a HIV-affected household, and if the infected person is not the mother, this does not seem to automatically increase the mortality risk of the child. The effect of the HIV status of the partner might be mitigated by the asset index because HIV worsens the material well-being as a consequence of less ability to work and, therefore, reduce the capacity to care and might increase the child mortality risk. Indeed, if the asset index is excluded from the regression, the coefficient becomes also positive in Ghana Faso and Kenya, but still remains insignificant. However, the effect of the HIV status of the mother could also include the effect of less care capacity and not only the effect of mother-to-child-transmission, even if the HIV status of the male partner shows no significant result. In general, the mother is the main care provider of the child. Therefore, if a HIV-infected mother suffers from the epidemic, resulting in reduced care for the children, this is expected to have a much higher impact on the survival probability than less care capacities of an HIV-infected male household member.

In addition, being HIV positive is clearly not the same as the household member already having started to suffer from AIDS, which is expected to have a clearer and significant negative impact on the household and on the welfare of the child. One possible way to statistically separate HIV-infected mothers among those who already suffer from AIDS is to compare them by their nutritional status. However, including only those mothers with a BMI less then 18.5 instead of HIV positive mothers did not change the results significantly.

It is most likely that the effect of HIV on child mortality is underestimated. As the information one child mortality rates are based on retrospective data collected from mothers that were alive at the time of the survey, the analysis leaves out the mortality among children whose mother had already died from AIDS. The higher risk of dying for children whose mother died from AIDS is not evaluated, resulting in a possible underestimation of the impact on HIV on child mortality.[38]

An additional regression is implemented based on a combined data set of all children in the four countries. The results of this global regression are shown in Table B.2 in Appendix B and confirm the results from Table 2.5 and Table 2.6. Again, the HIV status of the mother has a strong impact on the mortality risk of the child, whereas a positive test result of a male household member has no significant effect.

[38]However, this problem may be weakened by the fact that fertility rates are much lower among HIV-infected women (see e.g. Gray et al., 1998; UN, 2005a).

Table 2.7 shows the regression results for stunting. The coefficients of the stunting z-score follow the usual pattern across the four countries.[39] Besides the age of the child, which effects the nutritional status of the child in the well known non-linearity way, again, three main determinants are identified that strongly reduce the risk of children to be stunted. First, in contrast to the impact on child mortality, the material welfare, proxied by the asset index shows a strong and significant decreasing effect on child undernutrition in all four countries. Second, the educational attainment of the mother also has a significant positive impact on the nutritional status of the child in all four countries. Third, the same holds for the nutritional status of the mother. A higher BMI of the mother significantly increases the z-score of her children. Interesting to note is that the impact of the nutritional status has a significant non-linear impact on the child in Ghana. As was already found in the regression results for child mortality, no gender bias in the sense that girls have a worse nutritional status than boys could be identified. In Burkina Faso, Cameroon, and Kenya being a female child significantly increases the z-scores. In contrast to that, the preceding birth interval significantly decreases the stunting z-scores of children. In addition, being the first born child in the household significantly increases the risk of being stunted in Cameroon and Ghana. Quite surprisingly, a significant positive effect of breastfeeding is found only for Ghana.

Considering the impact of HIV on undernutrition, no significant effect is found in all four countries.[40] Whether the mother is HIV positive or not seems to be of low importance for the nutritional status of the child when controlling for other socio-economic characteristics. These finding holds even if the nutritional status of the mother is excluded, which might capture the effect of HIV on the the mother. Also in this case, the HIV status has no significant impact on the nutritional status of the child. In addition, also excluding the asset index from the regression does not change this results. These results seem to indicate again that being HIV positive does not automatically decrease the nutritional status of the child.[41] Furthermore, no significant effect is found on the stunting z-scores if the male partner is HIV positive, which is shown in Table B.3 in Appendix B.

Table 2.8 shows the results for school enrollment. Again, the coefficients show the expected directions. For example, urban households are more likely to show complete school enrollment than rural areas. In contrast to the results for child mortality and stunting, Table 2.8 shows a significant gender bias in education. In Cameroon and Kenya, girls are less likely to be enrolled than boys, whereas the no

[39] Overall, the results of the regression reflect the results that are found in Section 1.3.3 in Essay 1 for Uganda, Mali, and Zambia.

[40] This results is also confirmed by the results of the global regression of the HIV status of the mother or male partner on undernutrition, which are shown in Table B.4 in Appendix B.

[41] However, an underestimation of the impact of HIV is again very likely.

significant effect is found for Burkina Faso and Ghana. The asset index has also a significant increasing effect on the probability of complete school enrollment reflecting that richer households have better access to the educational system and invest more resources into the education of their children. Quite surprisingly, the educational level of the household head plays no significant role for the probability of complete school enrollment, whereas the educational level of the mother has a significant positive impact of the school enrollment of the children. The same result is found for female headed households, which strongly increases the probability of complete school enrollment. The socio-economic status of the mother is not only captured in her educational level but also in the variable whether the mother works for cash, which has a significant positive influence on the enrollment status of the children in Ghana and Kenya.

Turning to the effect of the HIV status of the mother on school enrollment, two different results are found. For Cameroon and Kenya, no significant effect of HIV on school enrollment is found, which tends to confirm the previous results. However, for Burkina Faso and Ghana, a significant negative impact of HIV on school enrollment is found.[42] Concerning the question of the impact of HIV on the welfare of children this negative effect is a very interesting result. Whereas HIV seems to have no impact on undernutrition, and whereas the impact on mortality was identified as mainly due to mother-to-child-transmission, this result seems to indicate that already being HIV-infected, without any information whether the individual already suffers from AIDS, has also a negative impact on childrens' education. A significant effect on school enrollment is also found if a male household member is HIV positive (where the mother is not infected), which is shown in Table B.5 in Appendix B.

[42]The results of the global regression of the impact of the HIV status on school enrollment is shown in Table B.6 in Appendix B.

Table 2.7: Regression Results of Stunting
(OLS Regression)

	Burkina Faso 2003	Cameroon 2004	Ghana 2003	Kenya 2003
Age (child)	-0.131**	-0.094**	-0.102**	-0.096**
	(0.007)	(0.007)	(0.006)	(0.008)
$Age^2/100$ (child)	0.175**	0.131**	0.142**	0.137**
	(0.012)	(0.011)	(0.010)	(0.013)
Sex of child (1=female)	0.139*	0.028	0.213**	0.242**
	(0.062)	(0.056)	(0.049)	(0.066)
Urban (=1)	0.248*	0.083	0.058	0.135
	(0.118)	(0.070)	(0.069)	(0.097)
Asset index	0.178**	0.335**	0.291**	0.253**
	(0.057)	(0.044)	(0.041)	(0.057)
Household size (adults)(IV)	0.006	-0.023	-0.025	0.053*
	(0.011)	(0.015)	(0.021)	(0.030)
Female headed household (=1)	0.260*	0.089	-0.129	0.123
	(0.139)	(0.077)	(0.064)	(0.079)
First born (=1)	0.143	0.264**	0.264**	0.124
	(0.116)	(0.089)	(0.081)	(0.102)
Preceding birth interval	0.007**	0.007**	0.004**	0.002
	(0.002)	(0.001)	(0.001)	(0.002)
Prenatal care (=1)	0.047	-0.028	0.204**	-0.121
	(0.074)	(0.065)	(0.061)	(0.080)
Immediate breastfeeding (=1)	0.053	0.066	0.179**	0.005
	(0.064)	(0.070)	(0.058)	(0.092)
Mother has sec. education (=1)	0.335**	0.186**	0.125**	0.185**
	(0.192)	(0.069)	(0.058)	(0.091)
BMI of mother	0.128**	0.125**	0.148**	0.107*
	(0.071)	(0.057)	(0.041)	(0.065)
BMI of $mother^2/100$	0.011	-0.004	-0.234**	0.067
	(0.150)	(0.110)	(0.077)	(0.132)
Age of first birth	0.014	0.007	-0.007	0.024*
	(0.011)	(0.009)	(0.007)	(0.011)
Complete vaccination (=1)	0.014	0.007	-0.007	0.024
	(0.011)	(0.009)	(0.007)	(0.011)
Vitamin A (=1)	0.087	0.005	0.080	0.005
	(0.069)	(0.066)	(0.062)	(0.080)
HIV positive (mother) (=1)	-0.023	-0.054	0.033	0.021
	(0.279)	(0.131)	(0.180)	(0.127)
Constant	-1.124	-0.926	-2.302**	-1.320
	(0.864)	(0.740)	(0.576)	(0.845)
R^2	0.195	0.145	0.193	0.138
Obs.	2538	2844	2828	1856

Source: Demographic and Health Surveys (DHS); own calculations.
Notes: *P-value<0.1. **P-value<0.01. The household size enters via an instrumental variable into the model. As instrument the mean household size per cluster is used.

Table 2.8: Regression Results of School Enrollment (Logistic Regression)

	Burkina Faso 2003	Cameroon 2004	Ghana 2003	Kenya 2003
Age (child)	0.013	0.000	-0.019*	0.004
	(0.016)	(0.008)	(0.009)	(0.010)
$Age^2/100$ (child)	-0.009	0.008**	0.047	0.004
	(0.027)	(0.014)	(0.015)	(0.017)
Age (mother)	0.003	0.017*	0.034**	0.054**
	(0.008)	(0.004)	(0.007)	(0.010)
Urban (=1)	1.080**	0.172*	0.067	-0.423**
	(0.206)	(0.090)	(0.114)	(0.137)
Household size (adults) (IV)	-0.108**	0.056**	0.051	0.277**
	(0.031)	(0.021)	(0.039)	(0.050)
Female children in household (%)	-0.360	-0.442**	-0.012	-0.696**
	(0.268)	(0.131)	(0.148)	(0.175)
Asset index	0.501**	0.289**	0.228**	0.197**
	(0.104)	(0.062)	(0.066)	(0.081)
Head has no education (=1)	0.411	-1.044**	-0.624**	-0.629**
	(0.427)	(0.196)	(0.179)	(0.148)
Head has prim. education (=1)	0.535	-0.172	-0.144	-0.150
	(0.429)	(0.187)	(0.159)	(0.146)
Mother has sec. education (=1)	0.367*	0.598**	0.269**	1.080**
	(0.194)	(0.074)	(0.100)	(0.103)
Complete vaccination (=1)	0.784**	0.219**	0.314**	0.444**
	(0.174)	(0.079)	(0.107)	(0.108)
Female headed household (=1)	0.693**	0.473**	0.394**	0.558**
	(0.241)	(0.098)	(0.109)	(0.117)
Mother works for cash (=1)	-0.231	0.164*	-0.017	0.344**
	(0.205)	(0.082)	(0.136)	(0.097)
HIV positive (mother) (=1)	-0.764*	0.063	-0.448*	0.223
	(0.450)	(0.157)	(0.260)	(0.180)
Constant	-3.339**	-0.995**	-2.388**	-3.280**
	(0.569)	(0.246)	(0.296)	(0.323)
Pseudo R^2	0.171	0.094	0.049	0.146
Obs.	3323	3575	3421	2261

Source: Demographic and Health Surveys (DHS); own calculations.
Notes: *P-value<0.1. **P-value<0.01. The household size enters via an instrumental variable into the model. As instrument the mean household size per cluster is used.

2.5 Conclusion

This paper analyzed the effects of HIV-infected household members on child mortality, undernutrition, and educational attainment for Burkina Faso, Cameroon, Ghana, and Kenya. All four Sub-Saharan African countries are strongly affected by the HIV/AIDS epidemic and suffer from high rates of child mortality, undernutrition, and from an overall low rate of school enrollment. The aim of the paper was to shed more light on the effects of the HIV/AIDS epidemic on the welfare of children caused by direct vertical transmission and by worsening socio-economic conditions as a result of the epidemic.

The results show strong evidence for a severe direct negative impact of HIV on child mortality through mother-to-child-transmission in all four countries. When controlling for other individual and household characteristics, no indirect negative socio-economic effect of HIV was found for child mortality and undernutrition. One possible explanation for the limited socio-economic effects of HIV found is that the data cannot sperate between those mothers who are HIV positive and those who already suffer from AIDS. This could lead to underestimation of the indirect impact of the HIV status of the mother or the male partner on children. In addition, another reason for the overall low indirect impact might be that the analysis captures only those household members that were alive at the time of the survey and, therefore, omits the effect on children whose mother or other infected household member had already died from AIDS. A negative relationship between HIV and school enrollment is found in Burkina Faso and Ghana, however. This seems to confirm that negative socio-economic impact of HIV on the welfare of children do exist that go beyond the direct transmission of the epidemic.

One should be very careful when drawing any policy implications from the result of an overall low indirect impact of HIV on childrens' welfare outcomes. Again, the analysis cannot distinguish who already suffers from AIDS, which clearly lead to reduced capacities to care and, therefore, to indirect negative effects on children. However, the negative impact of HIV on child mortality and education, which was also recently found by Graff Zivin et al. (2006), strongly argues for better treatment opportunities for HIV-infected persons. Better treatment opportunities would not only reduce the impact of the epidemic on the infected person, the results show that this also would have a positive impact on the situation of other household member, especially on the children. The future development of the HIV/AIDS epidemic and its impact depends heavily on improved education regarding the infection risks in order to reduce further spreading. The socio-economic impact depends heavily on appropriate policy instrument that mitigate the reduced care capacities of households affected by the epidemic. Therefore, future research on the impact of HIV/AIDS on households and children should further focus on the indirect impact of the epidemic, but will also depend heavily on data availability regarding AIDS at the individual level.

Essay 3

Measuring Pro Poor Growth in Non-Income Dimensions

Abstract: In order to track progress on MDG1 and explicitly link growth, inequality, and poverty reduction, several measures of pro-poor growth have been proposed in the literature. However, current concepts and measurements of pro-poor growth are entirely focused on the income dimension of well-being, which neglects the multidimensionality of poverty and well-being. There are no corresponding measures for tracking progress on non-income dimensions of poverty. In this paper, we propose to extend the approach of pro-poor growth measurement to non-income dimensions of poverty by applying the growth incidence curve to non-income indicators. The approach allows a much more detailed assessment of progress towards MDGs 2-6 by focusing on the distribution of progress, rather than simply focusing on mean progress. Moreover, this extension allows the assessment of the linkage between progress in income and non-income dimensions of poverty. We illustrate this empirically for Bolivia between 1989 and 1998. We find that growth was pro-poor both in the income and in the non-income dimension, but results for the non-income dimensions are less clear when the poor are ranked by income.

---

based on joint work with Melanie Grosse and Stephan Klasen.

3.1 Introduction

Pro-poor growth has recently become a central issue for researchers and policy makers, especially in the context of reaching the Millennium Development Goals (MDG). The various proposals to measure pro-poor growth have also allowed a much more detailed assessment of progress on reducing poverty as they explicitly examine growth along the entire income distribution.

However, one existing shortcoming of current pro-poor growth concepts and measurements is that they are completely focused on income, thus focused only on MDG1 with the aim to halve the incidence of poverty until 2015.[1] The shortcoming of the one-dimensional focus on income is that a reduction in income poverty does not guarantee a reduction in non-income dimensions of poverty, such as education or health. This means that finding pro-poor growth in income does not automatically mean that non-income poverty has been also reduced (see e.g. Klasen, 2000; Grimm et al. 2002). In this context, Kakwani and Pernia (2000) note that it would be 'futile' if one operationalizes poverty reduction via pro-poor growth using just one single indicator because poverty is a multidimensional phenomena, and thus pro-poor growth is also multidimensional. For this reasons, multidimensionality of poverty and pro-poor growth as two main research areas have to be combined. While non-income indicators have recently received more and more attention in the concept and measurement of poverty they have not in the concept of pro-poor growth and no attempts have been made to measure pro-poor growth on the basis of non-income indicators.[2]. Also international organizations point to the importance of the direct outcomes of poverty reduction such as health and education (see e.g. World Bank, 2000; UN 2000; UN 2000a).

The aim of this paper is to introduce the multidimensionality of poverty into the pro-poor growth measurement. The basic idea of implementing the multidimensionality of poverty into the pro-poor growth concept goes back to Sen's capability approach (Sen, 1987, 1988). Defining human well-being in terms of functionings and capabilities[3], Sen (1987, 1988) considers poverty as a multidimensional phenomenon and focusses on direct outcomes of human well-being. Since money-metric indicators of poverty reflect only the ability to achieve functionings, it serves only as an indirect measure of the standard of living, whereas direct measures are, for example, the status and access to health and education.

[1]In this paper, we only consider income as the money-metric measure of living standard and do not distinguish between income and consumption.

[2]Examples for recent studies examining the multidimensional casual relationship between economic growth and poverty reduction are Bourguignon and Chakravarty (2003), Mukherjee (2001), and Summer (2003)

[3]Where functionings are the achievements of human well-being and capabilities reflect the ability to achieve these functionings.

Based on this approach, many poverty assessments including social indicators have been done using aggregate data or household-level data (see e.g. UN, 1996; Klasen, 2000; Grimm et al., 2002). However, non-income indicators have not been considered in the pro-poor growth measurement so far.

We introduce the multidimensionality of poverty into to the pro-poor growth measurement by applying the growth incidence curve (GIC) by Ravallion and Chen (2003) to non-income indicators and call our resulting graphs non-income growth incidence curves (NIGIC). We illustrate this approach using micro-data for Bolivia for 1989 and 1998. We distinguish between ranking the sample by each non-income indicator and ranking the sample by income and investigate based on this income ranking the changes of the non-income indicator, with respect to the position in the income distribution. In addition to investigating growth rates, we investigate absolute changes of the non-income indicators. We find that growth was pro-poor both in the income and in the non-income dimension, but results for the non-income dimensions are less clear for the non-income development when the poor are ranked by income.

The paper is organized as follows. Section 3.2 briefly gives an overview of the concept of pro-poor growth and the need to investigate it in a multidimensional perspective. Section 3.3 explains our methodology to apply the GIC to non-income indicators and discuss some limitations. Section 3.4 presents the results of the GIC and the NIGIC for selected variables and for a composite welfare index. Section 3.5 summarizes and gives an outlook for future research.

3.2 The Concept of Pro-Poor Growth

3.2.1 Definition of Pro-Poor Growth

According to some, pro-poor growth is simply economic growth that benefits the poor (e.g. UN, 2000; OECD, 2001, 2006). This definition, however, provides little information how to measure or how to implement it. What remains to be specified is, first, if economic growth benefits the poor and, second, if yes to what extent. For example, Klasen (2004) provides more explicit requirements that a definition of pro-poor growth needs to satisfy. The first requirement is that the measure differentiates between growth that benefits the poor and other forms of economic growth, and it has to answer the question by how much the poor benefited. The second requirement is that the poor have benefited disproportionately more than the non-poor. The third requirement is that the assessment is sensitive to the distribution of incomes among the poor. The fourth requirement is that the measure allows an overall judgement of economic growth and not focuses only on the gains of the poor. Besides this approach there exist several other attempts conceptualizing pro-poor growth.[4]

Categorizing the different and conflicting definitions, we speak of three definitions of pro-poor growth in our paper: weak absolute pro-poor growth, relative pro-poor growth, and strong absolute pro-poor growth (see also Klasen, 2005). Pro-poor growth in the weak absolute sense means that the income growth rates are, on average, above 0 for the poor. Pro-poor growth in the relative sense means that the income growth rates of the poor are higher than the average growth rates, thus that relative inequality falls (i.e. in which some indicator considering the relative gap between the rich and the poor falls). Pro-poor growth in the strong absolute sense requires that absolute income increases of the poor are stronger than the average, thus, that absolute inequality falls (i.e. some measure considering the absolute gap between the rich and the poor falls, e.g. Klasen, 2004).[5]

The different definitions of pro-poor growth are illustrated in Table 3.1, which is taken from Klasen (2005). Table 3.1 shows a country in which the poor earn \$100 per capita and the non-poor \$500 per capita in the initial period. In year 1, the income of the poor grow by 3 percent and the income of the non-poor grow by 2 percent. In terms of the pro-poor growth definitions, this is pro-poor in the weak absolute sense (i.e. growth rates are above 0) and in the relative sense (i.e. growth rate for the poor is higher than for the non-poor). In year 2, the income of the poor grow by 1 percent and the income of the non-poor also by 1 percent. This is pro-poor only in the weak absolute sense, since the the poor have benefited from growth, which illustrates the importance of the the relative and absolute definition of pro-poor growth in order to reduce inequality. In year 3, the income of the poor grow by 6 percent and the income of the non-poor by 9 percent. This illustrates the advantage of the weak absolute definition of pro-poor growth. Even if the benefit is not pro-poor in the relative sense, only the weak absolute definition captures that the poor also have been made improvements (even if inequality rises). In year 4, the income of the poor grow more than the income of the non-poor showing pro-poor growth in the weak absolute and relative sense. Moreover, the growth is

[4]For a detailed review on the different definitions and measures of pro-poor growth, see, for example, Son (2003). Other approaches to define pro-poor growth are provided, for example, by White and Anderson (2000), Ravallion and Datt (2002), Klasen (2004), Hanmer and Booth (2001). The most common measures that have evolved in pro-poor growth measurement are the 'poverty bias of growth' of McCulloch and Baulch (2000), the 'pro-poor growth index' of Kakwani and Pernia (2000), the 'poverty equivalent growth rate' of Kakwani and Son (2002), the 'poverty growth curve' of Son (2003), and the 'growth incidence curve' of Ravallion and Chen (2003).

[5]Most inequality measures, including the Gini, Theil, and Atkinson measures as well as decile or quintile ratios are relative inequality measures, but these measures can also be turned into absolute measures of inequality, e.g. absolute Gini coefficients (Ravallion, 2005a). For a discussion of the merits of also considering absolute inequality measures, see Atkinson and Brandolini (2004).

also pro-poor in the strong absolute sense since the absolute increase in income for the poor ($20) is higher than for the non-poor ($15).

Table 3.1: Illustration of Pro-Poor Growth Definitions

Year	Poor	Growth (%)	Non-Poor	Growth (%)	Pro-Poor?
0	100	-	500	-	-
1	103	3	510	2	relative, weak absolute
2	104	1	560	1	weak absolute
3	110	6	610	9	weak absolute
4	130	18	625	10	relative, weak and strong absolute

Source: Klasen, 2005.

Table 3.1 illustrates that the definition of strong absolute pro-poor growth is obviously the strictest definition of pro-poor growth and the hardest to achieve, which is also shown empirically by White and Anderson (2000). This is why most researchers concentrate, in general, on the weak absolute and relative definition. But this ignores that decreases in relative inequality might be - and often are - accompanied by increases in absolute inequality, which is seen as undesirable by many and can be an important source of social tension (e.g. Atkinson and Brandolini, 2004; Duclos and Wodon, 2004; Klasen, 2004). Conversely, growth that is associated with falling absolute inequality would be particularly pro-poor and, therefore, it is useful to consider this strong absolute concept as well. This is particularly important when examining pro-poor growth in the non-income dimension of poverty where even pro-poor growth in the relative definition might not be seen as sufficiently pro-poor. Consider the case where the poorly educated increased their education level from 1 to 2 years, an increase of 100 percent while the rich increased their education levels from 10 to 12 years, an increase of 20 percent. This would be pro-poor growth in the relative definition as relative inequality falls, but most observers would also note the rise in absolute inequality and might, therefore, not consider this type of educational expansion 'pro-poor' since no degree is achieved. Besides, concentrating only on percentage changes in education misses that the poor should catch up to the non-poor regearing specific degrees in education. Concentrating also on absolute changes allows one to examine, for example, whether a poor individual achieved the level of primary or secondary education.[6]

[6]See also the discussion below in Section 3.3.4.

3.2.2 Multidimensionality of Pro-Poor Growth

The most glaring shortcoming of all attempts to define and measure pro-poor growth is that they rely exclusively on one single indicator, which is income. This means that they are only focussed on MDG1 but leave out the multidimensionality of poverty, which is taken into account in the other MDGs.

Income enables households and/or individuals to obtain functionings. This means, income serves to expand peoples' choice sets (capabilities) (Sen, 1987, 1988) and is, therefore, an indirect measure of poverty. In contrast, certain non-income indicators measure the functionings of households and individuals directly. Measuring poverty only with income assumes that income growth is accompanied by non-income growth. However, the problem of focussing only on MDG1 is that an improving income situation of households need not automatically imply an improving non-income situation, thus, reaching the other MDGs is not automatically guaranteed (for example, as shown in Klasen (2000) or Grimm et al. (2002)). While non-income indicators have recently received more and more attention in the concept and measurement of poverty[7] they have not in the concept of pro-poor growth and no attempts have been made so far to measure pro-poor growth on the basis of non-income indicators.

Following Sen (1987, 1988), our conceptual approach to introduce non-income indicators in the pro-poor growth measurement starts with the selection of non-income indicators determining the most important functionings of human welfare. In line with the MDGs (UN, 2000) we select education, health, nutrition, and mortality as non-income indicators of poverty and, therefore, follow the spirit of the most prominent multidimensional poverty indices such as the Human Development Index, the Human Poverty Index, and the Physical Quality of Life Index by UN (1991) and UNDP (2000). After having selected the indicators and defined related variables we investigate whether non-income growth was pro-poor between two periods. We do this exemplarily in applying the methodology of the growth incidence curve (GIC) to non-income indicators, but non-income pro-poor growth can also be applied to other pro-poor growth measures. We also compare the results based on non-income indicators with those based on income.

[7]Examples for recent studies examining the multidimensional casual relationship between economic growth and poverty reduction are Bourguignon and Chakravarty (2003), Mukherjee (2001) and Summer (2003). Also international organizations point to the importance of the direct outcomes of poverty reduction such as health and education (see e.g. World Bank, 2000; UN, 2000; UN, 2000a).

3.3 Methodology

3.3.1 The Growth Incidence Curve

To answer the question if and to what extent growth was pro-poor one can investigate the growth rates of the poor, i.e. those who were below the poverty line in the initial period. A useful tool for this purpose is the GIC (Ravallion and Chen, 2003), which shows the mean growth rate g_t in income y at each percentile p of the distribution between two points in time, t–1 and t. The GIC links the growth rates of different percentiles and is given by

$$GIC : g_t(p) = \frac{y_t(p)}{y_{t-1}(p)} - 1. \tag{3.1}$$

By comparing the two periods, the GIC plots the population percentiles (from 1–100 ranked by income) on the horizontal axis against the annual per capita growth rate in income of the respective centile. If the GIC is above 0 for all percentiles ($g_t(p) > 0$ for all p), then it indicates weak absolute pro-poor growth. If the GIC is negatively sloped it indicates relative pro-poor growth. It is important to note that we assume anonymity throughout, i.e. we consider the growth rates of percentiles, even though they contain different households in the two periods.[8] For a discussion of this and results when the anonymity axiom is lifted, see Grimm (2007).

Starting from the GIC, Ravallion and Chen (2003) define the pro-poor growth rate (PPGR) as the area under the GIC up to the poverty headcount ratio H. The PPGR is formally expressed by

$$PPGR = g_t^p = \frac{1}{H_t} \int_0^{H_t} g_t(p)dp, \tag{3.2}$$

which is equivalent to the mean of the growth rates of the poor up to the headcount. What is normally done in poverty assessments is to compare the PPGR with the growth rate in mean (GRIM). The GRIM is defined by

$$GRIM = \gamma_t = \frac{\mu_t}{\mu_{t-1}} - 1, \tag{3.3}$$

where μ is mean income. If the PPGR exceeds the GRIM, growth is declared to be pro-poor in the relative sense.

[8]One should be cautious when deducing policy implications from the GIC when assuming anonymity. In particular, the GIC allows not to show if, for example, specific policy measures were beneficial to those who where poor in the initial period, but can show if the poor in both periods have benefited more from the measures than the non-poor.

Examining pro-poor growth in the strong absolute sense, one has to concentrate on the absolute changes in income of the population percentiles between the two periods. We define the absolute GIC or by

$$GIC_{absolute} : c_t(p) = y_t(p) - y_{t-1}(p), \tag{3.4}$$

which shows the absolute changes for each percentile. By comparing the two periods, the absolute GIC plots the population percentiles on the horizontal axis against the annual per capita change in income of the respective percentile on the vertical axis. If the absolute GIC is negatively sloped it indicates strong absolute pro-poor growth.

Starting from the absolute GIC, we define 'pro-poor change' (PPCH) as the area under the absolute GIC up to the headcount H. The PPCH is formally expressed by

$$PPCH = c_t^p = \frac{1}{H_t} \sum_{1}^{H_t} c_t(p), \tag{3.5}$$

which is equivalent to the mean of the changes of the poor up to the headcount. We compare the PPCH with the change in mean (CHIM), which is defined by

$$CHIM = \delta_t = \mu_t - \mu_{t-1}. \tag{3.6}$$

If the PPCH exceeds the CHIM, growth is declared to be pro-poor in the strong absolute sense.

3.3.2 The Non-Income Growth Incidence Curve

The calculation of the non-income growth incidence curves (NIGIC) broadly follows the concept of the GIC. Instead of income (y), we apply Equations (3.1) through (3.6) to selected non-income indicators to measure pro-poor growth directly via outcome-based welfare indicators. Thus, the NIGIC measures pro-poor growth not in an income sense but in a non-income sense, e.g. the improvement of the health status or the educational level between two periods for each percentile of the distribution.

We calculate the NIGIC in two different ways. The first way we call the unconditional NIGIC in which we rank the individuals by each respective non-income variable and generate the population percentiles based on this ranking. For example, using average years of schooling of adult household members, the 'poorest' percentile is now not the income-poorest percentile but the one with the lowest average household educational attainment.

The second way, we call conditional NIGIC in which we rank the individuals by income and calculate based on this income ranking the population percentiles of the non-income variable. With the conditional NIGIC, we capture the problem that the assignment of the households to income percentiles on the one hand (GIC) and to non-income percentiles on the other hand (unconditional NIGIC) might not be the same. For example, the income-poorest group might not be the education-poorest group at the same time. This means that, in the conditional NIGIC, the percentiles are income percentiles, thus that the 'poorest' percentile is the one with lowest income, but that the growth rates are non-income growth rates, thus, are calculated for, e.g. years of schooling of the income percentiles. With the conditional NIGIC, we measure how the development of the non-income indicators is distributed across income groups.

Both ways of calculating the NIGIC are of particular relevance for policy making. The unconditional NIGIC mirrors the development of the social indicators that are relevant for human welfare. Thus, it can monitor how the non-income MDGs (especially MDGs 2-6) have developed over time for different points of the non-income distribution. In order to reach the MDGs, improvements will be particularly important for those at the lower end of the non-income achievements and the NIGIC allows such an assessment. The conditional NIGIC give an additional tool to investigate how the progress in non-income dimensions of poverty was distributed over the income distribution. This is also of relevance when evaluating distributional impacts of aid and public spending. Standard benefit incidence studies, for example, analyze the impact of public spending by calculating shares of the total spending to each percentile and comparing the shares of the income poorest with the income richest centile (see e.g. Van de Walle, 1998; Van de Walle, 1995; Lanjouw and Ravallion, 1998; Roberts, 2003). But the share of public spending for the poor serves only as a proxy for a real welfare impact in terms of non-income achievements. With the conditional NIGIC, it is than possible to analyze the actual improvements in the particular social indicator over the income distribution. For example, it provides an instrument to assess if public social spending programs has reached the targeted income-poorest population groups and if the public resources are effective allocated and used. For example, Berthélemy (2005) shows that education policies in Sub-Saharan Africa are biased against the poor. On average, policies favor the non-poor because they are concentrated on improvements in secondary and tertiary education and only little attention is paid to improvements in primary eduction, i.e. to the poor population. In this respect, the conditional NIGIC might be a useful tool in the pro-poor spending analysis to understand who benefits from public spending and to what extent.

When interpreting the NIGIC, three issue need to be discussed. First, in comparing the GIC and the NIGIC, one cannot deduce any causality between income and non-income indicators. For example, from the curves, we can neither say that an improvement in income causes an improvement in the health status nor that an improvement in the health status causes an improvement in income. They simply show how improvements in income and non-income indicators are related to each other, which might be due to causal or spurious correlations. Second, one cannot compare the absolute values of the growth rates of income and non-income variables because the variables are measured in different dimensions such as monthly income and years of schooling. One can only compare if the growth rates are positive or negative and by how much the PPGR exceeds the GRIM. Lastly, due to the different dimensions of the income and non-income indicators, and the fact that many of the non-income indicators are bounded above (i.e. there is an upper limit to survival prospects or to educational achievements)[9], it may well be plausible that different definitions of 'pro-poor growth' would be appropriate for different indicators. While one may be satisfied that income growth was pro-poor if it met the relative definition (i.e. the poor had higher income growth rates than the rich), one may only call growth in educational achievements pro-poor if the poor had higher absolute increments than the non-poor.[10]

3.3.3 Specification of the Non-Income Indicators

We calculate the unconditional and conditional NIGIC for education, health, nutrition, and for a composite welfare index (CWI) as described below. We are working with DHS data for Bolivia from the years 1989 and 1998 that do not contain information on income or consumption due to its focus on demographics, health, and fertility. However, in our DHS data set, we use simulated incomes based on a dynamic cross-survey micro-simulation methodology introduced by Grosse et al. (2004).[11] The basic idea of this simulation methodology is the following. The authors use two kinds of surveys: first, the DHS (of 1989 and 1998)

[9]See discussion in Section 3.3.4 below.

[10]A different way to deal with this problem would be to re-scale the non-income variables by, for example, transforming the education indicator into a percentage shortfall from a maximum level, say 16 years of education, and then define growth as the percentage reduction in that shortfall, which was also discussed by Sen (1981) and Kakwani (1993). With such an indicator, one may well decide to choose the relative definition as sufficient to define pro-poor growth. As discussed below, this issue will also arise when comparing the Gini coefficients of incomes with Gini coefficients in non-income indicators. We do not apply this approach in this paper, because we do not want to give achievements at higher levels more weight than achievements at the lower levels in education since we are interested into the question whether the poor can catch-up to the non-poor. See Section 3.3.4 for a more detailed discussion on this particular issue.

[11]For the calculation of the PPGR in the next chapter, we use the headcount of 77 percent as found in Klasen et al. (2004) for the moderate poverty line. We use the same headcount for the calculation of the PPGR of all non-income indicators.

and, second, the Bolivian household surveys (the 2nd EIH of 1989 and the ECH of 1999). Then they estimate an income correlation in the household survey, apply the coefficients to the DHS and predict, i.e. simulate, incomes in the DHS.[12]

For each non-income indicator, we identify alternative variables to capture particular aspects of the non-income dimension in question. For education, we specify eight different variables. We calculate average years of schooling for all adult household members and for males and females separately.[13] Age plays an important role when analyzing changes in non-income indicators, especially for education. In particular, not much improvements in education can be expected among the adult population (the education of 30-40 year olds in 1989 should not be be very different from the education of the 40-50 year olds in 1999). To avoid misleading conclusion from potential low improvements, we, therefore, restrict the sample to women aged between 20 and 30 as only this age group is likely to have experienced a change in their educational achievement (the 20-30 year olds in 1999 represent a new cohort of women who were educated later than the other cohorts). In addition, we calculate the maximal education per household instead of the average for all adults, males, females, and females aged between 20 and 30. The idea behind using these variables as an indicator is that it might be sufficient that one household member is well educated to generate income for the whole household and to invest in education of other household members (i.e. intra-household externalities) (Basu and Foster, 1998).[14] To take into account possible intra-household inequalities in education, we also calculate gender gaps

[12]To provide some more detail, the authors estimate an income/consumption expenditure model in the 1999 Living Standard Measurement Survey (LSMS) data restricting the set of covariates to those which are also available in the 1998 DHS data and interacting all variables with a rural dummy. They then use the regression to predict incomes in the DHS and add a randomly distributed error term. They then repeat the procedure for the EIH of 1989, which is only available in urban areas. When imputing incomes in rural areas, they use the model for urban areas in 1989 and add the results of the rural interaction terms from 1999, thus assuming that the difference in the impact of income correlates between 1989 and 1999 did not change over time. While the results work well in a validation test for 1999, there is a tendency that the simulated income growth is higher than the observed one. This overprediction should not bias the results in this paper, but it might be useful to test the results generated here with a survey that contains detailed information both on income and on non-income variables.

[13]The DHS only includes households with at least one woman in reproductive age, i.e. aged between 15 and 49 who serve as respondents in the DHS. The education for the male household members has to be taken from the memory of the respondents concerning the education of their husband or partner (with the age of the men being unknown). Households without women in reproductive age are excluded as well as unmarried men.

[14]An important issue is to be noted here: An overall problem of years of schooling as a variable for educational attainment is that years of schooling do not say anything about educational quality and, therefore, the indicator should be treated with some caution. This problem might be solved by using other data such as education test scores (like Pisa scores). However, these data are not always available and certainly not in the same data sets.

in eduction within households. In particular, we calculate the female minus male education in the households (in years of education).

For health, we specify three different variables. We calculate infant survival rates of children aged under 1 years and also for children aged under 5 year.[15] Furthermore, we take the average vaccinations of children aged between 1 and 5 per household, with a maximum of 8 possible vaccinations for each child.[16] The vaccination rate is a variable that represents access to health care and preventive medicines. A similar variable has, for example, been used in the monitoring of the health sector reform project in Bolivia in 1999 Montes (2003).

For nutrition, we use stunting z-scores as the variable that measures chronical undernutrition for children aged between 1 and 5 years. The stunting z-scores are defined as the difference of height at a certain age and the median of the reference population for height at that age divided by the standard deviation of the reference population.[17] It takes values between approximately -6 and 6, where values below -2 are considered as being moderately undernourished and below -3 as being severely undernourished (see e.g. Klasen, 2003, 2007). Problematic might be that the z-score contains a lot of 'genetic noise' in the sense that, for example, a low z-score interpreted as being undernourished might simply appear because the parents are genetically short but the child is small but well nourished and vice versa.

An alternative possibility to address the issue of the multidimensionality is to aggregate several indicators to a composite welfare index (CWI).[18] Here, we follow the methodology of the Human Development Index (HDI) to address the problem of difference scales of the variables (UN, 2000). Each variable that enters the index is normalized to be between 0 and 1 in subtracting the individual value from the minimum value observed in the data set divided by the range

$$CWI = \frac{1}{n}\sum_{i=1}^{n} \frac{individual_n - minimum}{maximum - minimum}. \tag{3.7}$$

The CWI is constructed by simply averaging the sum of the selected variable scores n. It includes four of the above explained variables: average education

[15]In our calculation, we use household child survival rates instead of child mortality rates. An improvement in child mortality comes out as a lower value but this lower value is mathematically interpreted as a deterioration. The linear transformation used is: survival rate = (mortality rate − 1) $*$ (−1). This means, for example that a reduction of child mortality from 80 percent to 60 percent is transformed into an increase in child survival from 20 percent to 40 percent.

[16]The possible vaccinations are 3 against polio, 3 against DPT, 1 against measles, and 1 BCG.

[17]See also Section 1.3.1 and 2.4.1 in Essay 1 and Essay 2.

[18]For a detailed overview about several composite welfare indices and how they are calculated, see e.g. UN (2006).

of all adult household members, stunting z-scores, under 1 survival, and average vaccinations.[19]

As not all variables are given for all households (e.g. health and nutrition variables are only available for households who have children), we calculate the CWI for two different samples. The first sample, called small sample, is the one for which all variables are available for all households. This reduces the sample size enormously (in 1989, e.g. from 6,053 to 1,306 households) and, more importantly, in a non-random fashion.[20] The second sample, called big sample, includes all households, but the index is averaged over fewer variables for those households, which do not have data for nutrition and/or health variables. The advantage of creating the CWI based on the big sample is the higher number of observations but the disadvantage is that the results for some percentiles are driven by very few, or even only one variable. The smaller sample has fewer observations but contains for all households the same number of variables. For both, the small and the big sample, we also augment the indices by also including simulated income as a fourth indicator.

3.3.4 Limitations of the Indicators

While we show below that these indicators yield important information, there arise also a number of problems when analyzing non-income indicators of welfare, which also are important to note for the use of the NIGIC, but can also be seen as general inherent limitations of non-income indicators of human well-being to be aware of and which we want to highlight. The first limitation is the informational value of the calculated growth rates of the NIGIC, where we interpret an ordinal relation in a cardinal fashion. Examining an ordinally scaled variable one can say that 6 years of schooling is better than 3 years but one cannot be sure to that the household is twice as well educated.[21] This ordinal scaling leads to two different kinds of interpretation problems.

First, averaging an ordinally scaled variable leads to a ranking problem when assuming that education is one of the most important determinants to generate income and reduce poverty (Osberg, 2000). For example, comparing two households, A and B, with two adults in each household where the household members of A have 0 and 12 years of schooling and of B have 6 and 7 years of schooling,

[19]The latter two variables do not enter separately but form a health sub-index as the simple average of the two scores. In contrast to the HDI, we use the maximum and minimum values defined by the data sets and do not use fixed maximum and minimum values.

[20]This reduction in observations translates into the calculation of the percentiles resulting in higher standard errors than for the large sample.

[21]The same problem exists when interpreting income in a cardinal fashion, despite the lacking foundation for such an interpretation, but this issue is normally neglected in applied discussions.

household B has a higher average education than A. Now, when B is ranked higher than A, one ignores any kind of educational degrees and the resulting differentials in returns to education. This means that the person with 12 years of schooling might earn disproportionally more income than both members of household B together, thus, household A should be ranked higher than B. We address this problem in also using maximal education per household.

In addition, averaging the years of schooling over the household ignores also possible intra-household inequalities in education. Taking into account the distribution of education within the household and, therefore, taking into account possible intra-household inequalities in education, we additionally focus on the individual educational attainment (instead of only on the average of the household) and on the potential gender gap in education of households.

Second, concerning the usual problem of absolute versus relative changes, increases in years of schooling, just comparing growth rates might be misleading and might not reflect their true achievements. For example, Table 3.2 shows for average education an increase of 80 percent for the 2nd decile compared to 6 percent of the 9th decile, which might be overstating the improvement for the poor because the years of schooling of the poor increase from 1.31 to 2.37 years of schooling and those of the non-poor from 11.73 to 12.43. In addition, improvements in tertiary education mighty be harder to achieve than improvements in primary education, which should also be taken into account. This problem is related to the fact that many of the non-income indicators are bounded above, i.e. there are firm or likely upper limits on such achievements. 100 percent survival in the first year is the upper limit for health, more than 18 or 19 years of education is very rare, more than 8 vaccinations is not recommended, done, or measured, etc. One may assume 'declining marginal returns' to improvements in non-income indicators, which would suggest that a marginal year of schooling or another vaccination is less valuable when the level of schooling is already high.

This problem is also discussed by Kakwani (1993). He derives an achievement function for non-income indicators based on the assumption that the value of the achievement increases non-linearly with the achievement level, i.e., an increase in 1 year of tertiary education reflects greater achievement than 1 year of primary education.[22] However, the value of this increase is based on the effort made to achieve but does not consider the value of the outcomes of this achievement. Since we are interested in the question whether the poor can catch-up to the non-poor and, therefore, rather interested in investigating improvements in direct outcomes of social indicators than in the effort of these achievements, we do not

[22] In particular, based on the achievements function Kakwani (1993) derives an improvements index, which takes into account both the asymptotic limit of non-income indicators of standard of living and the non-linearity of the values of achievements.

weight the improvements in relative achievements.[23] Besides, in addition to the relative changes, we calculate the absolute NIGIC and pro-poor changes examining directly the absolute improvements in years of education. However, even when we use absolute changes, which equal approximately 1, a further question remains open. An increase of 1.06 years of schooling of the 2th decile might be less beneficial because perhaps the persons are still more or less illiterate, compared to the increase of 0.70 years of schooling in the 9th decile, which might mean completing secondary schooling and getting a degree.

An another issue that arise due to the bounded above problem of social indicators is that it may be the case (and indeed is the case in Bolivia) that some households have reached the upper limit and further growth is not possible. However, our main focus is on the bottom of the distribution. Even if we observe improvements in, for example, education only for the lower deciles, we still can interpret these findings regarding the pro poorness of improvements in the educational system, particularly whether the poor have benefited from these improvements.

The third type of problem in comparing relative changes relates to the stunting z-score. In our data sets, it ranges roughly from -6 to 6. Relative changes in the stunting z-score cannot be calculated because of the coexistence of negative, positive and 0 values in the variable range. For example, how to compare the relative improvement from -2 to -1 with an improvement from 1 to 2 from the year 1989 to 1998? We reduce this problem by transforming the z-score in such a way that all values are positive, which means by adding the minimum value of both data sets (in our case -5.89) to each z-score to get a range of only positive numbers.

Another limitation is the problem of weighting, which we illustrate with the example of child mortality. For example, comparing two households, A and B, where A has 1 child and B has 10 children the households should be weighted differently when in each of the two households 1 child dies. Household A has a child mortality rate of 100 percent whereas B of 'only' 10 percent. From an intrinsic point of view, it is obvious that both deaths are equally lamentable. In this case, one could think of just counting the death per household independently of the total number of children. However, it is less obvious from an economic point of view where children can be partly considered as investment goods. Here, a higher mortality rate mirrors the more heavy loss of one child in the one-child household A compared to the 10-children household B. The investment-good character comes from absence or lack of social security systems in which case the children care for the parents in the cases of unemployment, sickness, and old age (see e.g. Ehrlich

[23]Another way to address this would be a logarithmic transformation of non-income achievements as is done for the income component of the HDI.

and Lui, 1997).[24] Following these two extreme points of view, one might think of weighting the death of children in households taking both arguments somehow into account. But any weighting would, however, be quite arbitrary and induce difficulties in justifying it with economic or welfare-theoretical judgments. Keeping this critical issue in mind we use unweighted child survival rates.

Weighting problems are also difficult with the nutrition indicator. A negative stunting z-score indicates malnourishment. But the z-score should not be interpreted as a linear variable in the sense that an increasing z-score is always equivalent to an improvement in the nutritional status. From a certain threshold onward, increasing z-scores might no longer reflect improvements of the nutritional status but indeed quite the opposite. For example, a child with a very high z-score of 3 might not be better off as one with 0 because she might be too tall for her age. This problematic holds even stronger if one would consider wasting z-scores (weight over age). Here, increasing z-scores strongly above 0 reflect obesity that negatively affects the health status (see e.g. De Onis and Blössner, 2000).[25]

Another limitation when calculating the NIGIC is that some variables of the non-income indicators do not vary much between households. This holds especially for under 5 and under 1 survival, which is very low in Bolivia at the household level. For both years, Table 1 shows that from the 2nd decile upwards, the maximum value of 100 percent survival is already reached in both years, so that no improvement is possible any more. This translates into growth rates of 0, so that the unconditional NIGIC becomes flat and takes the value of 0 from the 2nddecile onward. The problem of flat curves always arises when the variable values are bounded above (as for example a maximum of 19 years of schooling or 8 vaccinations).

Dealing with this limitation in a more general way, the discussed variables have a more discrete character (in the sense that one either has survived or not, which makes it difficult to observe relative differences among individuals, households, and over time. This is why these indicators (such as mortality rates) are mostly generated and interpreted at an aggregate level. The only, but small, variation evolves from taking household averages instead of individual data. This is why these variables – and all kinds of dummy variables – show little variation for the pro-poor growth analysis using the NIGIC.

[24]One complicating aspect arises when taking gender preferences for the children into account. The loss of one child when considered as an investment good might depend on the cultural habits (e.g. labor market opportunities for females and males, marriage agreements, and the question who takes care of the parents in old age).

[25]In particular, several studies show that obesity in childhood negatively affects the development of the child and which is an increasing concern in developing countries (see e.g. Dietz, 1998; Martorell, 1998).

More interesting to examine in these cases is the conditional NIGIC, in which we link the non-income variables to income. Here, low variation is less problematic than for the unconditional NIGIC because the variables are ranked by income. As Table 3.3 and all figures show, there is no flat part any more. Now we generate interesting information regarding the changes on the non-income indicators when ranked according to their income situation and how improvements are distributed.

3.4 Empirical Analysis

3.4.1 Inequality

Bolivia is one of the countries with a very unequal income distribution in Latin America. Table 3.2 shows the distribution of income and the non-income indicators (unconditional) and Table 3.3 shows the distribution of the non-income indicators for the conditional case, i.e. when the non-income indicators are ranked by income.

We find high and persisting income inequality as measured with the Gini coefficient that falls from 0.56 in 1989 to 0.54 in 1998. This high inequality is also reflected in the high and only slightly falling 100:10 ratio. Turning from inequality to growth, we find that all deciles increased their incomes. Especially in the 1990s, Bolivia experienced relatively high growth rates (which also were pro-poor in urban and rural areas). However, Bolivia was and is one of the poorest countries of the region, and the positive economic trend has reversed since 1999 combined with some episodes of social and political turmoil. Bolivia used to show much worse outcomes in social indicators than other countries in the region. However, there have been notable and sustained improvements in many social indicators since the late 1980s, which continued to improve during the recent economic slowdown (see e.g. Klasen et al., 2004).

Locking at the unconditional case (Table 3.2), the Ginis for education variables are all in the range of 0.40 to 0.50.[26] As stated above, due to the boundeness of the variable, one cannot infer directly from this that educational inequality is

[26] It is important to note that the values for the Gini coefficients can not be compared between income and non-income indicators and not among non-income indicators, because the values of the indicators have different ranges. For example, whereas the values for income can take values in a nearly infinite range, all non-income indicators are bounded above resulting in generally lower Gini coefficients. As Klasen (2007) notes, this is only the case for countries (like Bolivia), where the education richest groups are already close to the upper bound. This is, for example, not the case for many African countries as shown by Thomas et al. (2000) who calculate Gini coefficients for education.

in some sense substantively smaller than income inequality.[27] For all educational variables, the Ginis fall between 1989 and 1998, which is likely due to the fact that the rich have already reached high levels of education and the poor are catching up. Interesting to note is that the highest Ginis exist for the group of all respondents both for average and maximal education indicating a gender bias in educational achievements. These findings are also reflected in the 100:10 ratio. The conditional deciles, which are shown in Table 3.3 also show that the level of schooling increases with increasing income for all educational variables, but the 100:10 ratio is much lower than in the unconditional case. We find that an improvement has been made for all educational variables in all deciles for both the unconditional and the conditional case (Tables 3.2 and 3.3). However, as already both tables shows, improvements where much higher in the unconditional than in the conditional case indicating that the improvements in non-income indicators of poor, when they are ranked by income, are less clear than if the improvements are linked to the initial level in the respective non-income indicator.

The extremely low Ginis for the under 1 and under 5 survival rates (both for the unconditional and conditional ranking) can be explained by the overall low incidence of child mortality in Bolivia at the household level. For both age groups, child mortality is below 10 percent. The conditional deciles indicate that mortality seems to be more or less randomly distributed over the income distribution (Table 3.3).[28] For vaccination, the Gini falls strongly from 1989 to 1998, and we find clear improvements, especially for the lower deciles (except the lowest decile), which is also due to the fact that the best vaccinated deciles had only limited room for improvements. The inequality of the stunting z-score is relatively low and falls slightly. Malnutrition decreases with an increasing position in the income distribution, but the differences for the income deciles are quite low.

Table 3.4 shows the distribution of the composite welfare index. The CWI reflects the findings from above where the Gini coefficients decrease for the selected variables. For the CWI (both excluding and including income), the Gini coefficient is higher for the big sample than for the small sample indicating between-group inequality.[29] Table 3.4 also illustrates the difference in the values of the indices if income is included and excluded. If income is included into the index,

[27]One should also be aware of the fact that the calculation of the Ginis of the social indicators are based on discrete variables. Although income also is strictly discrete, it has a much more continuous character then social indicators like years of education. Thus, it is much more difficult to calculate a Lorenz curve for years of schooling given the lower boundary (0) and upper boundary (18), and the Ginis should be interpreted with caution. An attempt to face this problem as addressed by Thomas et al. (2000).

[28]As explained below, reasons for this might be the overall low mortality risk in Bolivia and the tendency for underreporting among poorer population groups.

[29]This between-group inequality is driven by the higher degree of homogeneity in the small sample.

the level of values decreases, both in the unconditional and the conditional case, which is driven by the high and persisting income inequality in Bolivia.

Table 3.2: Income and Non-Income Indicators (Unconditional) (Bolivia, 1989 and 1998)

	1	2	3	4	5	6	7	8	9	10	Mean	100:10	Gini
	Mean of the Deciles (unconditional), 1989												
Income	21.88	40.27	57.50	77.33	100.61	132.39	177.08	246.12	368.36	863.39	213.39	39.46	0.56
Education													
Ave. educ.	0.22	1.31	2.26	3.20	4.28	5.61	7.32	9.38	11.73	15.20	6.03	69.09	0.43
Ave. educ. all respondents	0.00	0.00	1.29	2.27	3.34	4.72	6.24	8.58	11.56	15.13	5.31	n.d.	0.51
Ave. educ. respondents (20-30)	0.13	1.72	2.95	4.10	5.18	7.01	8.92	11.25	12.00	14.48	6.69	111.38	0.39
Ave. educ. partners	0.00	1.35	2.83	4.13	5.30	6.52	8.57	11.35	12.70	16.77	6.95	n.d.	0.42
Max. educ. household	0.48	2.52	3.52	4.82	5.88	7.50	9.78	11.99	13.87	16.98	7.64	35.36	0.38
Max. educ. household (respondents)	0.00	0.00	1.29	2.27	3.34	4.72	6.24	8.58	11.56	15.13	5.40	n.d.	0.51
Max. educ. household (20-30)	0.11	1.67	2.90	3.86	5.00	6.64	8.65	11.11	12.00	14.70	6.58	133.63	0.40
Max. educ. of partners	0.00	1.37	2.85	4.25	5.40	6.75	8.88	11.64	12.84	16.89	7.09	n.d.	0.42
Health													
Under 5 child survival rate (%)	38.43	64.06	75.81	94.64	100.00	100.00	100.00	100.00	100.00	100.00	87.04	2.60	0.11
Under 1 child survival rate (%)	41.51	88.31	100.00	100.00	100.00	100.00	100.00	100.00	100.00	100.00	92.55	2.41	0.07
Ave. vacc. per child (age>=1)	0.08	1.88	3.49	4.67	5.67	6.46	7.10	7.98	8.00	8.00	5.30	100.00	0.28
Nutrition													
Stunting z-score	-4.17	-3.01	-2.50	-2.11	-1.70	-1.33	-0.90	-0.25	-0.00	0.88	-1.54	n.d.	0.19

Table continues on next page.

(Unconditional, Bolivia, 1989 and 1998)

	1	2	3	4	5	6	7	8	9	10	Mean	100:10	Gini
	Mean of the Deciles (unconditional), 1998												
Income	36.37	63.60	89.26	119.22	155.89	203.15	269.64	369.20	555.27	1242.66	312.10	34.17	0.54
Education													
Ave. educ.	0.87	2.37	3.51	4.78	6.06	7.34	8.70	9.81	12.43	16.04	7.21	18.44	0.35
Ave. educ. respondents	0.00	1.36	2.72	3.95	5.16	6.68	8.34	9.42	10.75	16.39	6.48	n.d.	0.41
Ave. educ. respondents (20-30)	0.99	3.45	5.00	6.45	7.98	8.99	9.99	9.99	13.71	16.59	8.05	16.76	0.31
Ave. educ. partners	0.54	2.23	3.85	5.13	7.51	8.58	9.50	10.00	14.23	17.04	7.86	11.59	0.36
Max. educ. household	1.47	3.48	4.87	6.44	8.23	9.01	10.00	10.71	15.76	17.04	8.74	11.60	0.31
Max. educ. household (respondents)	0.00	1.36	2.72	3.95	5.16	6.68	8.34	9.42	10.75	16.39	6.58	n.d.	0.41
Max. educ. household (20-30)	0.89	3.00	4.45	5.35	7.08	8.40	9.28	10.00	12.70	16.46	7.82	18.49	0.32
Max. educ. partners	0.54	2.25	3.89	5.19	7.64	8.73	9.66	10.00	14.69	17.04	7.96	31.56	0.36
Health													
Under 5 child survival rate (%)	46.03	70.36	90.70	100.00	100.00	100.00	100.00	100.00	100.00	100.00	90.62	2.16	0.08
Under 1 child survival rate (%)	43.67	93.29	100.00	100.00	100.00	100.00	100.00	100.00	100.00	100.00	93.63	2.29	0.06
Ave. vacc. per child (age>=1)	0.09	2.13	3.74	4.92	5.88	6.74	7.14	8.00	8.00	8.00	5.48	88.89	0.26
Nutrition													
Stunting z-score	-3.61	-2.43	-1.92	-1.55	-1.19	-0.79	-0.30	-0.00	0.05	1.11	-1.06	n.d.	0.16

Notes: The explanation for the variables is the following. Income: Real household income per capita in Bolivianos per month (CPI of 1995=100). Education: All variables for education are measured in average single years per household. Respondents and partners are only couples, for which the respondent knows the education of her partner. Health: Under 5 (1) survival rates are estimated with life table estimations taking the sample of children born 10 (5) years prior to the sample. Survival rates are averaged over the household. Vaccinations: Average vaccinations of the children in the household older than 1, where the possible vaccinations are 3 against polio, 3 against DPT, 1 against measles, and 1 BCG. Nutrition: Stunting z-score of the last born child of each respondent (averaged over the household). A a child is defined as stunted if her z-score is below -2.
Source: Demographic and Health Survey (DHS); own calculations.

Table 3.3: Income and Non-Income Indicators (Conditional)
(Bolivia, 1989 and 1998)

	1	2	3	4	5	6	7	8	9	10	Mean	100:10
	Mean of the Deciles (conditional), 1989											
Income	21.88	40.27	57.50	77.33	100.61	132.39	177.08	246.12	368.36	863.39	213.39	39.46
Education												
Ave. educ.	3.04	3.48	4.11	4.47	5.54	6.07	6.99	7.94	9.37	11.47	6.03	3.77
Ave. educ. respondents	2.20	2.93	3.25	3.75	4.69	5.41	6.34	7.19	8.70	10.68	5.51	4.85
Ave. educ. respondents (20-30)	3.30	4.62	5.20	5.91	6.78	8.06	8.32	8.84	9.24	10.47	6.69	3.17
Ave. educ. partners	3.88	4.03	4.96	5.20	6.40	6.73	7.65	8.68	10.04	12.26	6.98	3.16
Max. educ. household	4.41	4.77	5.52	5.91	7.08	7.75	8.70	9.73	11.23	13.29	7.64	3.00
Max. educ. household (respondents)	2.20	2.93	3.25	3.75	4.69	5.41	6.34	7.19	8.70	10.68	5.63	4.85
Max. educ. household (20-30)	3.19	4.50	4.83	5.72	6.55	7.52	8.48	8.16	9.53	10.82	6.58	3.39
Max. educ. partners	4.00	4.10	5.02	5.31	6.52	6.91	7.84	8.85	10.18	12.40	7.11	3.10
Health												
Under 5 child survival rate (%)	84.54	86.94	86.83	85.02	85.82	87.44	88.16	88.41	91.06	91.00	87.04	1.08
Under 1 child survival rate (%)	91.46	91.03	91.96	92.74	92.34	93.85	93.45	94.35	93.39	92.43	92.55	1.02
Ave. vacc. per child (age>=1)	5.19	4.79	5.07	5.35	5.09	5.47	5.77	6.82	6.16	6.39	5.30	1.23
Nutrition												
Stunting z-score	-1.75	-1.73	-1.89	-1.71	-1.52	-1.57	-1.27	-1.26	-1.18	-0.82	-1.54	n.d.

Table continues on next page.

(Conditional, Bolivia, 1989 and 1998)

	1	2	3	4	5	6	7	8	9	10	Mean	100:10
	Mean of the Deciles (conditional), 1998											
Income	36.37	63.60	89.26	119.22	155.89	203.15	269.64	369.20	555.27	1242.66	312.10	34.17
Education												
Ave. educ.	3.92	4.47	5.20	6.45	6.45	7.10	8.09	8.82	9.85	12.35	7.21	3.15
Ave. educ. respondents	3.10	3.72	4.48	4.84	5.83	6.51	7.62	8.20	9.29	11.74	6.53	3.79
Ave. educ. respondents (20-30)	4.59	5.35	6.22	7.35	7.91	8.71	9.28	9.88	10.43	11.84	8.05	2.58
Ave. educ. partners	4.74	5.22	5.92	6.26	7.06	7.69	8.56	9.44	10.40	12.96	7.82	2.73
Max. educ. household	5.34	5.86	6.63	6.97	7.99	8.78	9.72	10.46	11.44	13.79	8.74	2.58
Max. educ. household (respondents)	3.10	3.72	4.48	4.84	5.83	6.51	7.62	8.20	9.29	11.74	6.63	3.79
Max. educ. household (20-30)	4.34	5.05	5.77	7.07	7.53	8.47	8.54	9.71	10.37	12.12	7.82	3.03
Max. educ. partners	4.79	5.29	5.99	6.32	7.18	7.78	8.68	9.56	10.55	13.06	7.92	2.73
Health												
Under 5 child survival rate (%)	86.98	90.13	89.29	88.94	90.82	89.76	90.44	93.06	92.21	95.24	90.62	1.10
Under 1 child survival rate (%)	92.42	94.43	94.15	93.21	92.01	94.19	92.61	95.22	94.69	96.09	93.63	1.03
Aver. vacc. per child (age>=1)	5.19	5.26	5.02	5.17	5.34	5.40	5.74	5.99	5.93	6.43	5.48	1.24
Nutrition												
Stunting z-score	-1.56	-1.48	-1.30	-1.37	-1.17	-1.15	-1.01	-0.90	-0.79	-0.44	-1.06	n.d.

Notes: The explanation for the variables is the following. Income: Real household income per capita in Bolivianos per month (CPI of 1995=100). Education: All variables for education are measured in average single years per household. Respondents and partners are only couples, for which the respondent knows the education of her partner. Health: Under 5 (1) survival rates are estimated with life table estimations taking the sample of children born 10 (5) years prior to the sample. Survival rates are averaged over the household. Vaccinations: Average vaccinations of the children in the household older than 1, where the possible vaccinations are 3 against polio, 3 against DPT, 1 against measles, and 1 BCG. Nutrition: Stunting z-score of the last born child of each respondent (averaged over the household). A a child is defined as stunted if her z-score is below -2.
Source: Demographic and Health Survey (DHS); own calculations.

Table 3.4: Deciles of the Composite Welfare Index (Bolivia, 1989 and 1998)

	1	2	3	4	5	6	7	8	9	10	Mean	100:10	Gini
	Mean of the Deciles (unconditional), 1989												
Composite welfare index													
Small sample	0.29	0.35	0.39	0.43	0.47	0.50	0.54	0.59	0.64	0.74	0.49	2.55	0.15
Big sample	0.11	0.29	0.38	0.45	0.51	0.56	0.61	0.66	0.74	0.86	0.52	7.82	0.23
Composite welfare index (including income)													
Small sample	0.22	0.27	0.30	0.33	0.35	0.38	0.41	0.45	0.50	0.57	0.38	2.64	0.16
Big sample	0.07	0.19	0.26	0.31	0.34	0.38	0.41	0.45	0.51	0.60	0.35	8.57	0.24
	Mean of the Deciles (unconditional), 1998												
Composite welfare index													
Small sample	0.32	0.40	0.44	0.48	0.52	0.55	0.59	0.63	0.67	0.74	0.53	2.31	0.13
Big sample	0.18	0.36	0.43	0.49	0.53	0.58	0.63	0.68	0.74	0.86	0.38	4.78	0.19
Composite welfare index (including income)													
Small sample	0.24	0.30	0.34	0.37	0.39	0.42	0.45	0.48	0.51	0.58	0.41	2.42	0.14
Big sample	0.11	0.23	0.28	0.33	0.37	0.41	0.44	0.48	0.51	0.59	0.55	5.10	0.21
	Mean of the Deciles (conditional), 1989												
Composite welfare index													
Small sample	0.44	0.43	0.45	0.46	0.47	0.50	0.53	0.53	0.58	0.63	0.50	1.43	-
Big sample	0.45	0.45	0.46	0.48	0.51	0.53	0.56	0.59	0.61	0.68	0.53	1.51	-
Composite welfare index (including income)													
Small sample	0.33	0.33	0.34	0.35	0.36	0.38	0.41	0.41	0.45	0.50	0.38	1.52	-
Big sample	0.31	0.31	0.31	0.33	0.34	0.36	0.37	0.39	0.42	0.48	0.36	1.55	-
	Mean of the Deciles (conditional), 1998												
Composite welfare index													
Small sample	0.45	0.48	0.49	0.49	0.52	0.53	0.56	0.58	0.60	0.65	0.53	1.44	-
Big sample	0.46	0.48	0.48	0.50	0.52	0.54	0.58	0.59	0.63	0.69	0.55	1.44	-
Composite welfare index (including income)													
Small sample	0.34	0.36	0.37	0.37	0.39	0.40	0.43	0.44	0.46	0.52	0.41	1.53	-
Big sample	0.32	0.33	0.33	0.34	0.35	0.36	0.39	0.40	0.43	0.49	0.37	1.53	-

*Notes:**The composite welfare index includes average education per household, under five survival rate, average vaccination per child (age>=1) and stunting. *Source:* Demographic and Health Survey (DHS); own calculations.

3.4.2 Pro-Poor Growth

Figure 3.1 shows the relative and absolute GIC for income. The relative GIC plots the annual growth rates in monthly household per capita income for each household of the distribution. The absolute GIC plots absolute increases in real Bolivianos for the whole period 1989-1998 for each percentile. Included are (also in all other figures) the bootstrapped 95% confidence intervals[30] and the moderate and extreme poverty headcounts for 1989 of 77 and 56 percent, respectively. As can be seen from the position and slope of the GIC, income growth was pro-poor in the weak absolute and relative sense since the curve is above 0 for all and negatively sloped for nearly all percentiles. As expected, we do not find strong absolute pro-poor growth since the absolute GIC is positively sloped meaning that absolute increases in income were much higher for the non-poor than for the poor.

Figure 3.1: GIC (absolute and relative)

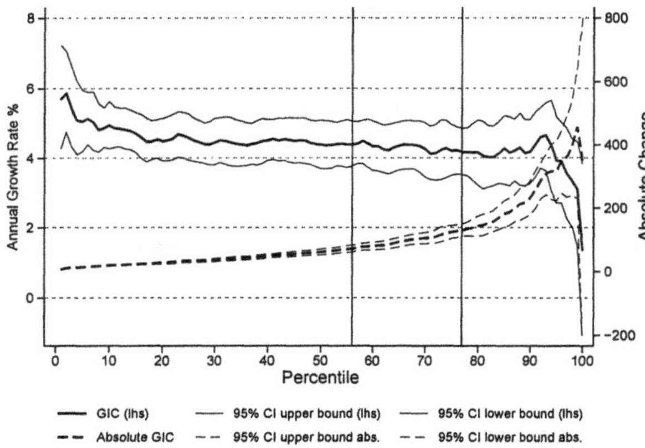

Source : Demographic and Health Survey (DHS); own calculations.

Figure 3.2a shows the relative and absolute unconditional NIGIC for average education per household. Figure 3.2b shows the relative and absolute conditional

[30]In particular, based on the households in both surveys, the bootstrap draws 200 random samples with replacement for each period and calculates the respective percentiles and growth rates (absolute changes) so that we obtain 200 values for each indicator per household. Based on these 200 values, we draw the mean and the standard deviation and calculate based on this the respective lower and upper 95% confidence interval.

(smoothed[31]) NIGIC for this variable. Note that the confidence intervals of the unconditional NIGIC lie very tight around the NIGIC. The reason for this lies in the discrete character of the social indicator. Each percentile contains households with nearly the same level of years of education, which results in low variations within percentiles and which leads to the very tight confidence intervals around the unconditional growth rates (absolute changes).

Whereas for the unconditional NIGIC the growth rates and absolute changes are shown for percentiles (1-100), for the conditional NIGIC the growth rates and absolute changes are shown for vintiles (1-20). The reason for using vintiles instead of percentiles is to get a higher number of observations four each group when households are ranked by income. For example, if a percentile contains only 50 households (ranked by income) and if we assign to these households the respective mean years of education, then it is possible to obtain huge variations within each percentile, which results in very wide confidence intervals between the growth in the two periods, and we will miss to show the income gradient.

For the unconditional NIGIC 3.2b, we find pronounced weak absolute as well as relative pro-poor growth.[32] The relative pro-poorness of average education is reflected comparing the PPGR with the GRIM where the PPGR for moderate poverty is 3.89 percent and the PPGR for extreme poverty 4.88, both much higher than the GRIM of 1.80 percent (Table 3.5).

The conditional NIGIC is more volatile than the unconditional NIGIC and also shows weak absolute and relative pro-poor growth but to a lower extent. Thus, the conditional NIGIC shows that the income-poor have experienced slightly higher educational growth than the average. This is also reflected in the higher PPGR (2.00 percent for moderate and 2.24 percent for extreme poverty) compared to the GRIM (1.80 percent).

[31] As the conditional are very volatile, we only include the smoothed conditional NIGIC in the figures to show the major trend of the curves.

[32] A noteworthy point appears when looking at the upper part of the unconditional NIGIC and their absolute changes. In the range of the 7th and 8th decile, all curves for the education variables fall below 0 and become positively sloped afterward. This reduction might not be a deterioration but might be due to a reform of the schooling system, i.e. in the number of years necessary to complete schooling grades.

Figure 3.2: NIGIC for Average Education

(a)
Unconditional (Relative and Absolute)

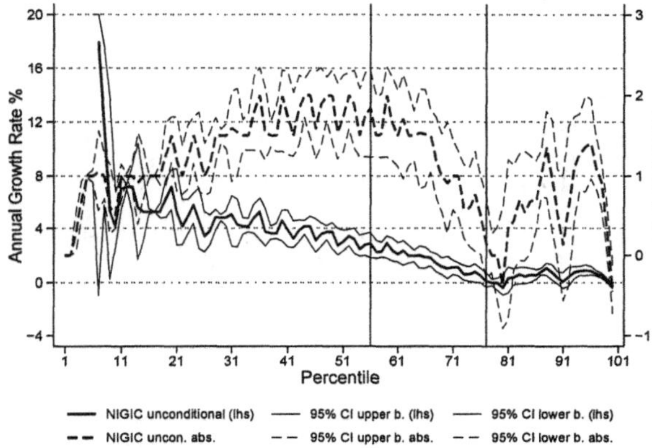

(b)
Unconditional (Relative and Absolute)

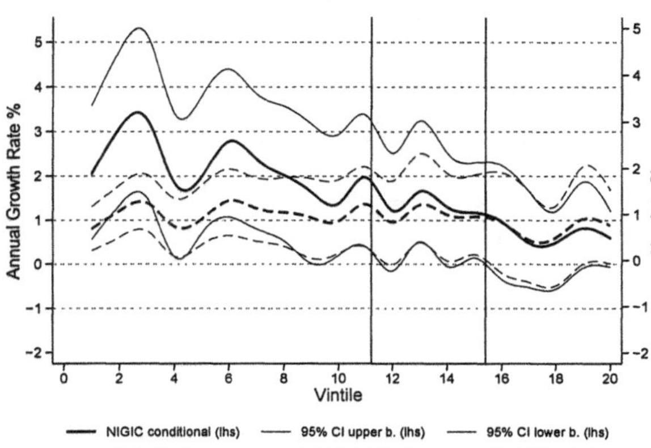

Source: Demographic and Health Survey (DHS); own calculations.

Figure 3.3: NIGIC for Individual Education

(a)
Unconditional (Relative and Absolute)

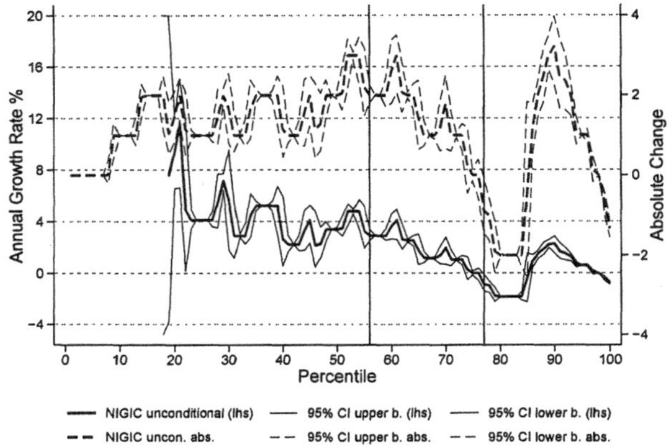

(b)
Unconditional (Relative and Absolute)

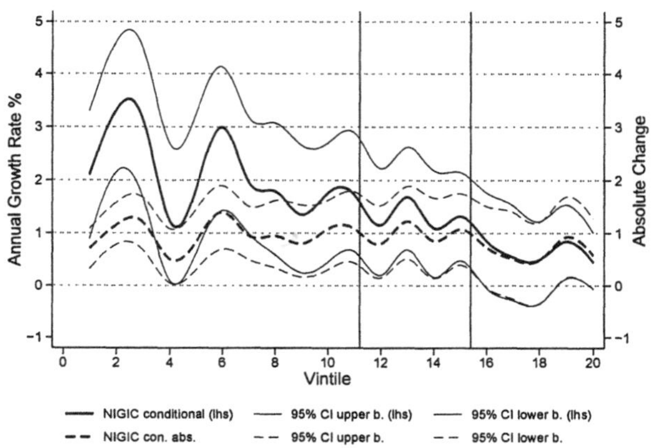

Source: Demographic and Health Survey (DHS); own calculations.

Table 3.5: Pro-Poor Growth Rates (Bolivia, 1989 and 1998)

		NIGIC 1989-1998 (unconditional)		NIGIC 1989-1998 (conditional)			NIGIC 1989-1998 (unconditional)		NIGIC 1989-1998 (conditional)	
	GRIM	PPGR moderate	PPGR extreme	PPGR moderate	PPGR extreme	CHIM	PPCH moderate	PPCH extreme	PPCH moderate	PPCH extreme
Income	3.88	4.54	4.63	4.54	4.63	98.71	53.82	37.02	53.82	37.02
Education										
Ave. educ.	1.80	3.89	4.88	2.00	2.24	1.18	1.30	1.34	1.01	1.01
Ave. educ. respondents	2.30	4.84	6.08	2.48	2.80	1.33	1.59	1.38	1.07	1.06
Ave. educ. respondents (20-30)	1.87	3.47	4.75	1.75	2.02	1.36	1.38	1.74	1.03	1.09
Ave. educ. partners	1.41	2.65	3.61	1.66	1.86	1.03	1.11	1.33	0.95	0.95
Maximal education per household	1.36	2.60	3.74	1.55	1.73	1.10	1.08	1.58	1.01	1.03
Max. educ. household (respondents).	2.24	4.69	5.88	2.37	2.69	1.31	1.52	1.37	1.05	1.04
Max. educ. household (20-30)	1.73	3.42	4.66	1.64	1.89	1.23	1.27	1.58	0.92	0.95
Max. educ. partners	1.35	2.55	3.57	1.57	1.76	1.00	1.05	1.34	0.91	0.92
Health										
Under 5 child survival rate (%)	0.40	0.70	0.96	0.37	0.40	3.57	4.54	6.25	3.19	3.45
Under 1 child survival rate (%)	0.12	0.14	0.19	0.11	0.15	1.07	1.29	1.78	1.00	1.35
Ave. vacc. per child (1-3)	0.34	0.66	0.91	0.15	0.20	0.18	0.21	0.27	0.07	0.09
Nutrition										
Stunting z-score	1.05	1.63	1.87	0.82	0.78	47.71	54.60	55.38	35.12	32.32
Composite welfare index (CWI)										
Small sample	0.82	1.08	1.16	0.72	0.72	0.04	0.05	0.05	0.33	0.34
Big sample	0.58	1.83	2.41	0.35	0.34	0.03	0.04	0.05	0.02	0.02
CWI (including income)										
Small sample	0.83	1.08	1.16	0.72	0.72	0.03	0.04	0.04	0.26	0.72
Big sample	0.63	1.62	2.03	0.44	0.44	0.02	0.03	0.03	0.01	0.01

Notes: Notes: For the explanation of the variables, see Table 3.2. We are using two poverty lines. The moderate poverty line leads to an income headcount of 77 percent and the extreme poverty line to an income headcount of 56 percent, which we also use for the non-income indicators. CHIM: Change in mean. PPCH: Pro-poor change. Changes are for the entire period and not annualized.
Source: Demographic and Health Survey (DHS); own calculations.

To take into account also possible intra-household inequalities, in addition, Figures 3.3a and 3.3b show the unconditional and conditional NIGIC for individual education in single years. Both figures reflect the picture that was found for average education per household showing relative pro-poor growth both for the unconditional and for the conditional case. This indicates that intra-household inequalities have not a substantial impact on the pro-poorness in the improvements in education attainment in Bolivia between the two periods.

Turning to the absolute growth incidence curves, the absolute GIC in Figure 3.1 clearly shows that income growth in Bolivia was strongly anti-poor using the strong absolute definition. The absolute increments of the rich far exceed those of the poor.

We do not find strong absolute pro-poor growth for the absolute unconditional NIGIC for education as the slope of the absolute curves in Figure 3.2 and 3.3 is not negative, but even positive for the poorest deciles. This is quite interesting because it puts the findings of the relative unconditional NIGIC in Figure 3.2a in perspective where we have found high relative pro-poor growth for the first 3 deciles. This seemingly contradictory finding is largely due to the high growth rates for the lower deciles which results from the very low base in 1989. The absolute conditional NIGIC is virtually flat, meaning that the income-poor have not been able to improve their educational attainment by more than the average. These findings are also reflected in comparing the PPCH with the CHIM. As Table 3.5 shows, the unconditional pro-poor change is still larger than the change in mean, however, only slightly: the average years of schooling only increased by 1.18 years in mean and by 1.30 years for the moderately poor and 1.34 for the extremely poor. For the absolute conditional changes and for both poverty lines, the CHIM is higher than the PPCH of 1.01.

Another way to look at intra-household inequalities is to look at the gender gaps in education within households. To remind, we calculate the female minus male education in the households (in years of education). Ranking the households by this gap, we plot in Figure 3.4 the unconditional and conditional absolute change in the gender gap. We find that the intra-household gender gaps were reduced for nearly all households except for those between the 10th and the 20th percentile. Again, especially households in the middle of the distribution showed the strongest reductions (3.4a). When looking at the conditional NIGIC, we find no clear trend meaning that the reduction in gender gaps is equally distributed across all groups (3.4b).

Figure 3.4: NIGIC for Gender Gap in Education

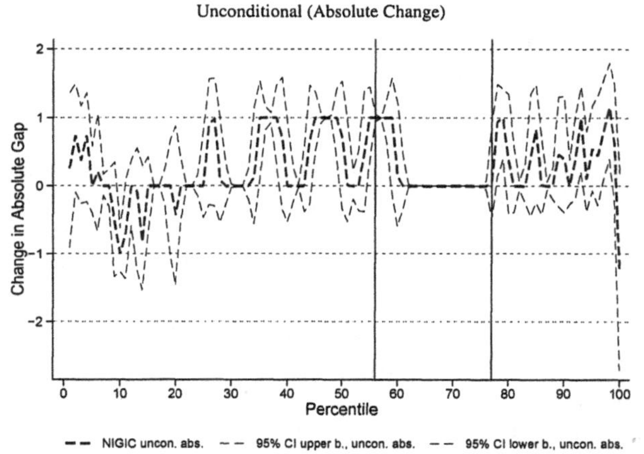

(b)
Conditional (Absolute Change)

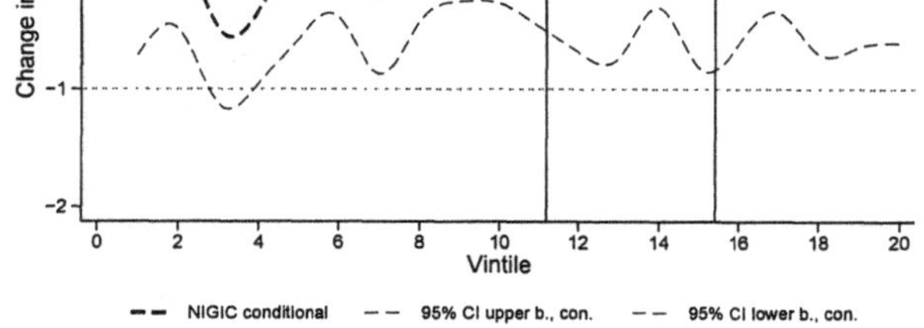

Source: Demographic and Health Survey (DHS); own calculations.

Figures 3.5a and 3.5b show the results for average vaccination. The unconditional NIGIC shows pro-poor growth in the weak absolute and is also slightly negatively sloped. Table 3.5 confirms the pro-poorness in the relative sense. Here, both PPGR exceed the GRIM. However, improvements are relatively low, which was also shown in Table 3.2.[33]

The conditional NIGIC shows no clear pro-poor growth trend, also visible in the wide confidence intervals. In addition, the PPGR are lower than the GRIM and for some deciles we even find a deterioration. The same findings also hold for the absolute curves. This reveals that relative pro-poor growth might not be enough for the poor and that absolute increases (the amount of additional vaccinations) are of particular weight. Finally, it is essential for the health status of children to have all possible vaccinations. The conditional absolute NIGIC shows that the improvements are relatively equally distributed among the income groups.

When examining the high relative growth in the unconditional NIGIC for education and vaccinations, Figures 3.2a and 3.5a do not report growth rates for the very poor deciles. This is due to two reasons. First, the very poor began and ended with no education and no vaccinations (see discussion below). Second, the slightly between off started with no education or no vaccination and ended up having positive levels of education and vaccinations in the second period. But in this case the growth rate is not defined and, thus, not reported. Remember that the very high growth rates that appear on the graphs at the left are, therefore, based on percentiles who had some small amount of education and vaccinations, and even a moderate absolute expansion translates into a very high growth rate.

Examining the absolute unconditional NIGIC for education and vaccinations also reveals an important finding regarding the very low tail of the distribution. As Figures 3.2a, 3.3a, and 3.5a show, the very education-poor and vaccination-poor had no education (vaccinations) in the first period and this continued to be the case in the second period. This is true for the first few deciles in the education indicator and nearly the entire first decile in the vaccination indicator. Thus, whatever expansion has taken place in non-income improvements, it bypassed a core group of very poor.[34]

[33]Interesting to note is the bump around the 70th percentile. Whereas the flat parts of the curves before and after the bump show the percentiles that had 7 and 8 vaccinations in both periods respectively, the bump shows the improvements of those who had vaccinations between 7 and 8 in the initial period.

[34]The findings with the education indicator have to be treated with some caution as they may simply say that adult women that had no education in the first survey continue to have no education in the second survey, which is to be expected in the absence of adult education programmes. This is not the case, however, with the vaccination indicator as it refers to children between ages 1 and 5 and, thus, it is indeed worrying that a new cohort of children has grown up without any vaccinations.

For all the other educational variables, we confirm the findings above. Comparing the results for females with males, we find some signs for gender inequality, which are most obvious in the lower percentiles. But we find that the gender inequality seems to have been reduced because the average and maximal education for females increased by more years than for the other groups, especially for males (Tables 3.2 and 3.5). However, the women in the all respondents sample started from a lower level and are on average still worse educated.

For both survival variables, the unconditional NIGIC and the absolute NIGIC are only interpretable for the first few deciles where they show clear improvements in the sense of weak absolute and relative pro-poor growth, but they become flat from the 4th decile onward in the case of under 5 survival since 100 percent survival is already reached as shown in Figures 3.6a and 3.6b. Also the conditional NIGIC, which oscillate closely to 0 but always above, reflects the moderate and more or less equally distributed mortality risk for the income groups. Also, the deciles of Table 3.3 show only a small income gradient of mortality risk.

Figure 3.5: NIGIC for Vaccinations

(a)
Unconditional (Relative and Absolute)

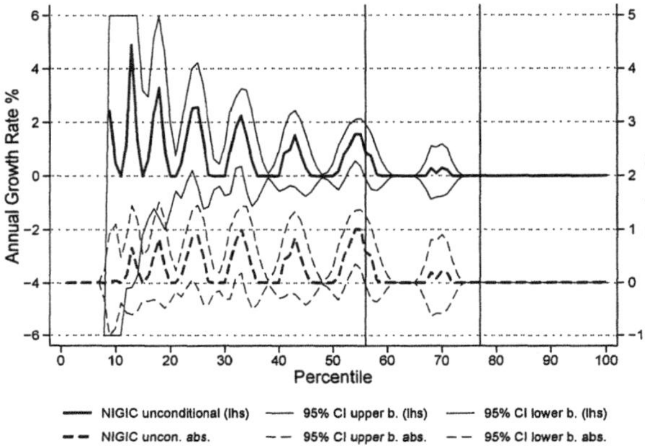

(b)
Conditional (Relative and Absolute)

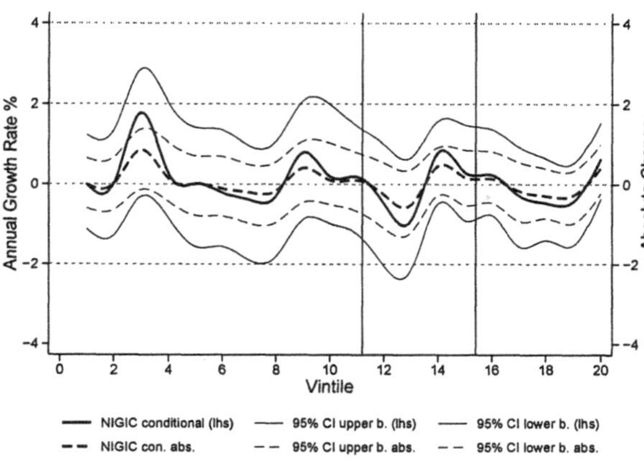

Source: Demographic and Health Survey (DHS); own calculations.

Figure 3.6: NIGIC for Under Five Survival

(a)
Unconditional (Relative and Absolute)

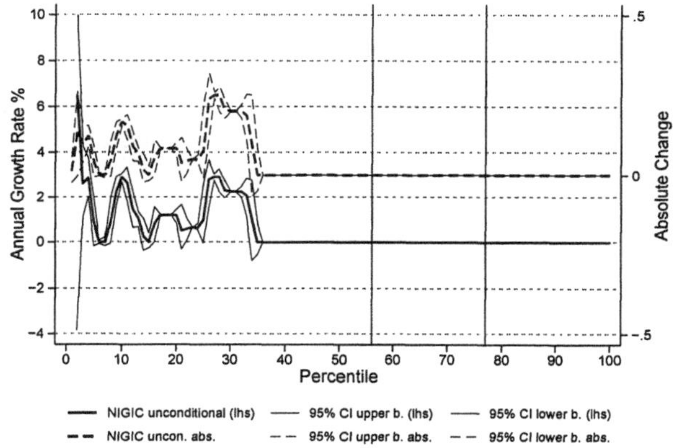

(b)
Conditional (Relative and Absolute)

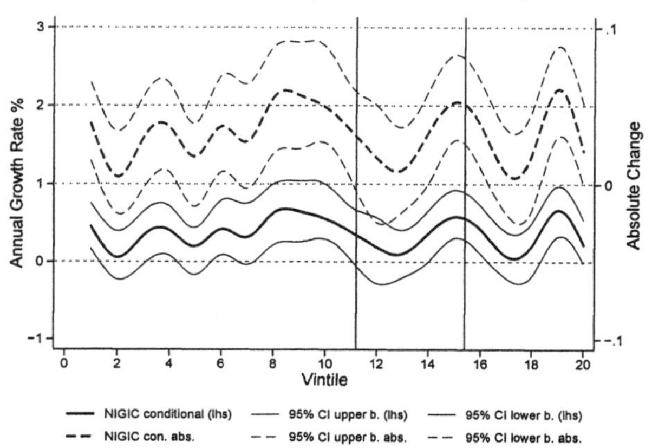

Source: Demographic and Health Survey (DHS); own calculations.

Figures 3.7a and 3.7b show the NIGIC for stunting. The unconditional NIGIC indicates weak absolute and relative pro-poor growth. For the conditional NIGIC, we only find weak absolute but no relative pro-poor growth.[35] These results are also found when looking at the PPGR and the GRIM for the improvements in the stunting z-score. Both absolute NIGIC show that the absolute changes are distributed nearly equally over the sample.

Aggregating the several variables in the CWI, Figures 3.8a and 3.8b summarize the development of the social indicators in one single NIGIC. As expected, we find pro-poor growth in the weak absolute and relative sense for the unconditional NIGIC. Looking at Table 3.5, we find very high relative pro-poor growth as both PPGR clearly exceed the GRIM. As being somewhat more volatile the conditional NIGIC shows also pro-poor growth in the weak absolute but not in the relative sense. Asking for pro-poor growth in the strong absolute sense, we find a anti-poor trend for the lower end of the distribution for the unconditional absolute NIGIC and a more or less equally distributed trend for the conditional absolute NIGIC.

Altogether, for nearly all variables, we find the strongest increases in the unconditional absolute NIGIC for some medium groups and not for the poorest groups. For most of the centiles, we find weak absolute pro-poor growth, but we do not find relative pro-poor growth, especially not for the poorest. These outcomes mirror the findings of previous analysis about poverty in Bolivia (Bolivia, 2001; INE, 2004; World Bank, 2004), which also find improvements in income and non-income poverty but not for the very poor.[36] Nevertheless, Bolivia remains one of the poorest countries in Latin America in the income as well as in the non-income dimension.

However, one should bear in mind that the findings regarding the NIGIC come from a period when there were great improvements made in social indicators, particularly among middle and lower income groups. When translating these measures to other countries (particularly in Africa) it could well be that the NIGIC would show that growth rates were not pro-poor as was found by Günther et al. (2006) for Mali from 1995-2001. To illustrate this, we additionally present the NIGIC for individual education of the household head and partner for Burkina Faso between 1994 and 2003 in Figures 3.9a and 3.9b.[37] Figure 3.9a nicely illustrates that the improvements in education between the two periods have been made only for the upper 30 percentiles, whereas all other groups are bypassed from improvements. This means that no pro-poor growth is found for Burkina Faso

[35] Again, the confidence intervals raise doubts about the statistical significance

[36] Most of the improvement furthermore benefited mainly the urban population with little improvement in the rural areas.

[37] For the calculation of the NIGIC, we use the Enquête Prioritaire sur les Conditions de Vie des Ménages (EPM) household survey data sets from 1994 and 2003.

between 1994 and 2003 and that only the initially educated population group has experienced relative and absolute improvements, which was not found for Bolivia. When looking at Figure 3.9b, we see that the relative and absolute improvements in years of education show no significant income gradient.

Figure 3.7: NIGIC for Stunting

(a)
Unconditional (Absolute and Relative)

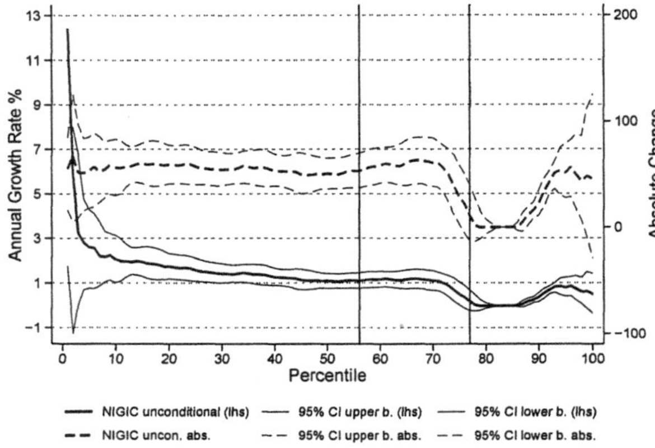

(b)
Conditional (Absolute and Relative)

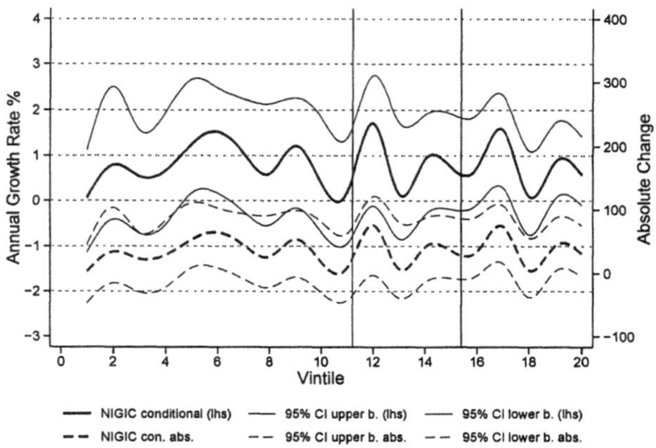

Source: Demographic and Health Survey (DHS); own calculations.

Figure 3.8: NIGIC for the Composite Welfare Index

(a)
Unconditional (Absolute and Relative) (Small Sample)

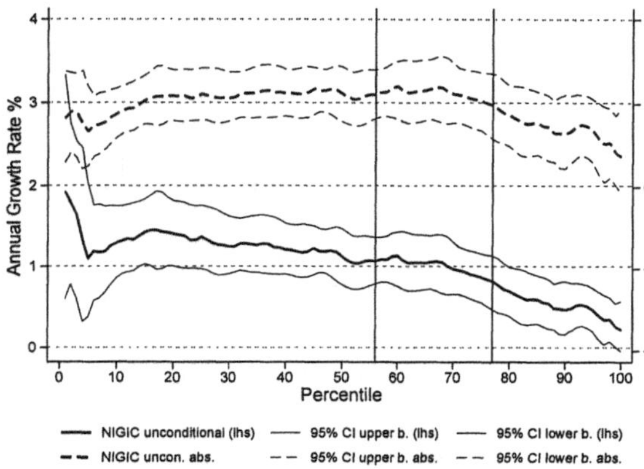

(b)
Conditional (Absolute and Relative) (Small Sample)

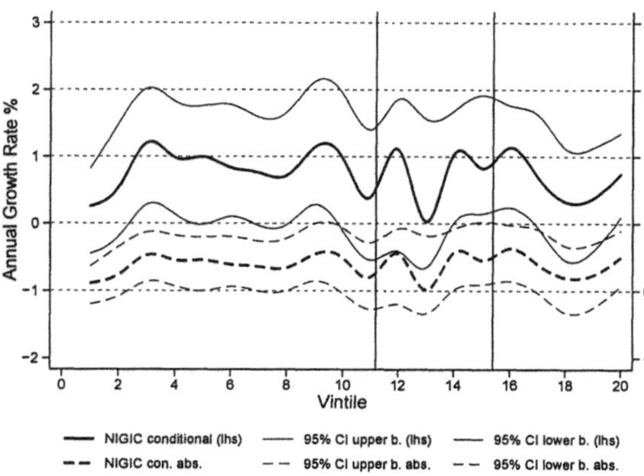

Source: Demographic and Health Survey (DHS); own calculations.

Figure 3.9: NIGIC for Education (Burkina Faso)

(a)
Unconditional (Absolute and Relative)

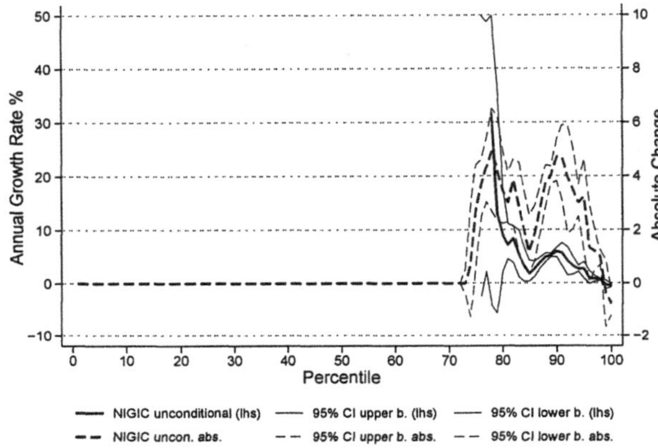

(b)
Conditional (Absolute and Relative)

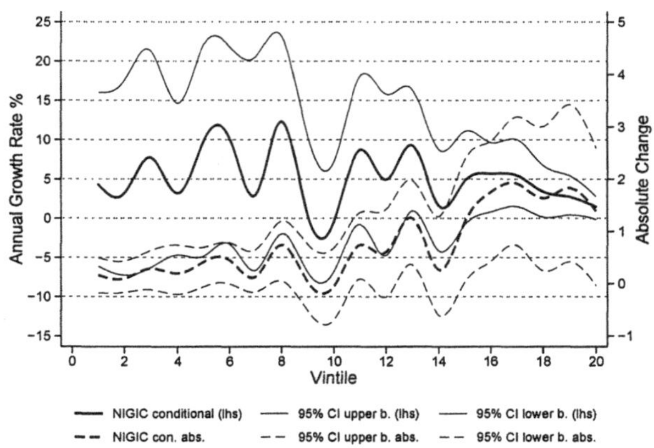

Source: Enquête Prioritaire sur les Conditions de Vie des Ménages (EP); own calculations.

3.5 Conclusion

We introduced the multidimensionality of poverty into pro-poor growth measurement. The purpose is to overcome the major shortcoming of the existing pro-poor growth measurements, which are exclusively focussed on income but give no information on how social indicators changed over time for poor population groups. The aim is to better monitor the MDGs and not only to focus on the income dimension of poverty.

In our approach, we apply the methodology of the GIC to non-income indicators and investigate pro-poor growth of non-income indicators using the NIGIC. We analyze how income and non-income indicators changed in favor of the poor. Also, we analyze how social indicators have developed when they are linked to their position in the income distribution. This is of special interest when evaluating distributional welfare impact of aid and public spending. Furthermore, we take absolute inequality explicitly into account and analyze if absolute improvements are large enough for the poor to catch up. Reducing absolute inequality in social indicators is crucial for sustainable development and for equal choices.

We exemplarily illustrate this approach using data for Bolivia from 1989 to 1998. Using the GIC and the unconditional NIGIC, we find improvements both in the income and non-income dimensions of poverty which is a common finding for Bolivia. Growth was pro-poor in the weak absolute and the relative sense both for income and non-income indicators, whereas we find no pro-poor growth in the strong absolute sense for income and only limited strong absolute pro-poor growth for the middle percentiles for non-income indicators. However, in general this is not the case when using the conditional NIGIC, where the social indicators were sorted by the initial income [38] Thus, there is not at all a perfect overlap of income-poor and of non-income-poor households. These findings suggests that the improvements in non-income dimensions were more focussed on the initially poor in those indicators, whereas they were not focussed on the initially income-poor. The absolute changes show that the poor have not benefited disproportionately more from the improvements. This means that relative pro-poor growth does not automatically mean that the poor catch-up with the non-poor in absolute terms because we find that relative income and non-income inequality have fallen, but not absolute inequality.

When calling for pro-poor growth as the most significant policy measure to achieve the MDGs, policy makers should not only focus on income pro-poor growth rather on multidimensional dimensions of pro-poor growth and, therefore,

[38] One has to note again that the data used is not panel data. Additionally, for the two-dimensional view of the conditional NIGIC it is even more crucial to keep in mind that we do not consider the same households and that the trends of social indicators of the income-poor have nothing of a panel character (Grimm, 2005).

take non-income indicators explicitly into account. We have shown the income-poor are not automatically the ones that benefit most from growth in social indicators, which is an important and new finding. In addition, policy makers should also give attention to pro-poor growth in the strong absolute sense in order to accelerate progress in meeting the MDGs.

Essay 4

Estimating Vulnerability to Covariate and Idiosyncratic Shocks

Abstract: Households in developing countries are frequently hit by severe idiosyncratic and covariate shocks resulting in high consumption volatility. A households' currently observed poverty status might, therefore, not be a good indicator of the households' general poverty risk, or in other words its vulnerability to poverty. Although several measurements to analyze vulnerability to poverty have recently been proposed, empirical studies are still rare as the data requirements are often not met by the surveys that are available for developing countries. In this paper, we propose a simple method to empirically assess the impact of idiosyncratic and covariate shocks on households' vulnerability, which can be used in a wide context as it relies on commonly available living standard measurement surveys. We apply our approach to data from Madagascar and show that whereas covariate and idiosyncratic shocks have both a substantial impact on rural households' vulnerability, urban households' vulnerability is to a larger extent determined by idiosyncratic shocks.

---

based on joint work with Isabel Günther.

4.1 Introduction

Households in developing countries are frequently hit by severe idiosyncratic and covariate shocks resulting in high income volatility.[1] Although (poor) households in risky environments have developed various (*ex-ante* and *ex-post*) risk-coping strategies to reduce income fluctuations or to insure consumption against these income fluctuations, the variance of households' consumption over time remains generally high (see e.g. Townsend, 1994; Udry, 1995). A households' currently observed poverty status is, therefore, in many cases not a very good predictor of a households' vulnerability to poverty, i.e. its general poverty risk. Or in other words, whereas some households are trapped in chronic poverty, others are only temporarily poor, whereas other households, currently non-poor, might still face a high risk to fall into poverty in the future.

Most established welfare measurements, e.g. the FGT poverty measures (Foster et al., 1984), only assess the current poverty status of households, ignoring poverty dynamics. Results from such a static poverty analysis might, therefore, be misleading if high consumption volatility persists within countries. Not only might poverty rates fluctuate from one year to another, but even if aggregate poverty rates are constant over time, the share of the population, which is vulnerable to poverty, i.e. which is poor 'only' from time to time, might be much higher. Moreover, these poverty measures cannot assess whether high poverty rates are caused by structural poverty (i.e. low endowments) or a cause of poverty risk (i.e. high uninsured income fluctuations), which is important to know from a policy perspective.

To overcome the shortcomings of traditional poverty assessments, which can only present a static picture of households' welfare, vulnerability measures estimate the *ex-ante* welfare of households, taking into account the dynamic dimension of poverty. Vulnerability assessments, therefore, try to estimate *ex-ante* both the expected mean as well as the volatility of consumption, with the latter being determined by idiosyncratic and covariate shocks.

Although there has recently been a growing theoretical literature on vulnerability measurement, relevant empirical studies on vulnerability are still rare, largely due to data limitations. Apart from the fact that only past welfare data is and will be available to assess future welfare,[2] vulnerability analysis is so far

[1] In this paper, idiosyncratic shocks refer to household-specific shocks (e.g. injury, birth, death or job loss of a household member) that are either uncorrelated or only weakly correlated across households within a community. Covariate shocks refer to shocks that are correlated across households within communities but uncorrelated (or only weakly correlated) across communities, i.e. they can be defined as community-specific shocks (e.g. natural disasters or epidemics).

[2] Most of the time, we do not even possess data on future welfare perceptions of households.

also severely constrained by missing data on the two most important dimensions of vulnerability.

First, to appropriately examine the dynamic aspects of poverty, lengthy panel data on income and consumption are needed. But for many developing countries, lengthy panel data does not exist and cross-sectional surveys (or sometimes panels with two or three waves), with either income or consumption data, are the only data available. Second, to assess the underlying causes of vulnerability, comprehensive data on shocks and coping strategies would be necessary. However, most household surveys were not designed to provide a full accounting of the impact of shocks on households' income (or consumption) and information on idiosyncratic and covariate shocks is either completely missing or very limited in most data sets. Most existing empirical studies have, therefore, either examined the vulnerability of households, ignoring the causes of the observed vulnerability, or have only studied the impact of selected idiosyncratic or covariate selected shocks on households' consumption, leaving out an analysis of the relative importance of different shocks on households' vulnerability.

The objective of this paper is twofold. The first objective is to assess the relative impact of idiosyncratic and covariate shocks on households' vulnerability to poverty. More precisely, we both estimate how much of a households' variation in consumption is structural and risk induced and estimate the share of consumption volatility that is idiosyncratic and covariate.

The second objective is to propose and illustrate a simple method to assess a households' vulnerability using cross-section or short panel data. Recently, the approach of Chaudhuri (2002) was widely discussed and applied to overcome the problem of missing panel for the analyzes of vulnerability. We propose a simple method, which can be applied to commonly available living standard household measurement surveys (LSMS) without being constrained by the usual data limitations for vulnerability analysis, i.e. the method allows one to assess the impact of idiosyncratic and covariate shocks on households' vulnerability without lengthy panel data and information on a wide range of shocks. We are aware of the fact that several rather strong assumptions have to be made to estimate a households' vulnerability based on data from a single period and that panel data are preferable. However, since lengthy panel data are very rare for developing countries, we argue that the suggested approach can provide quite interesting insights into the relative impact of idiosyncratic and covariate shocks on households' variations in consumption. The suggested approach should not serve as an alternative to the use of lengthy penal data but rather as an attempt to apply the estimation of vulnerability to cross-section data. In particular, the suggested approach is an integration of multilevel analysis (Goldstein, 1999) into the concept of Chaudhuri (2002) to estimate vulnerability from cross-sectional data.

The remaining paper is structured as follows. Section 4.2 briefly discusses the current theoretical and empirical literature on vulnerability to poverty, including its shortcomings. Section 4.5 proposes a methodology that allows assessing the relative importance of idiosyncratic and covariate shocks for households' vulnerability with short panel data or cross-sectional data and discusses some critical issues. Section 4.6 presents an empirical application to Madagascar. Section 4.7 concludes.

4.2 The Concept of Vulnerability

As discussed in the introduction, a households' currently observed poverty status might not be a reliable guide to a households' longer-term well-being. Policy makers and researchers in development economics have, therefore, long emphasized that it is critical to go beyond a static *ex-post* assessment of who is currently poor to a dynamic *ex-ante* assessment of who is vulnerable to poverty. But although there has been an emerging literature on both the theory and empirics of vulnerability, its significance especially for policy makers is still rather low.

The current state of the theoretical literature on vulnerability can be described in the words of Hoddinott and Quisumbing (2003) as a 'let a hundred flowers bloom' phase of research with numerous definitions and measures and seemingly no consensus on how to estimate vulnerability. Several competing measurements have been offered (for an overview see e.g. Hoddinott and Quisumbing, 2003) and the literature has not yet settled on a preferred definition or measure. However, in principal, three main definitions have emerged in the literature.

Combining the literature on imperfect insurance with an assessment of prospective risks, the first approach proposes to measure vulnerability as uninsured exposure to risks, or in other words, the ability of households to insure consumption against income fluctuations (e.g. Glewwe and Hall, 1998). The second concept defines vulnerability as expected poverty, i.e. as the probability that a households' future consumption will lie below a pre-defined poverty line (e.g. Chaudhuri, 2002, 2003; Pritchett et al., 2000). The third definition associates vulnerability with low expected utility (Ligon and Schechter, 2003). Based on the microeconomic theory that utility of risk-averse individuals falls if volatility of consumption rises, vulnerability is measured with reference to the utility derived from some level of certain-equivalent-consumption, i.e. the level of constant consumption that would yield the same utility as the observed volatile consumption. Last, using an axiomatic approach, Calvo and Dercon (2005) have combined the latter two measures and define vulnerability as 1 minus the expected value of the ratio of a households' consumption to the poverty line with an exponent between 0 and 1 to account for risk aversion.[3]

But independent of the applied definition of vulnerability, vulnerability measures are always a function of the estimated expected mean and variance of households' consumption. The mean of expected consumption is determined by household and community characteristics, whereas the variance in households' consumption is determined by the severity and frequency[4] of idiosyncratic and covariate shocks as well as the strength of households' coping mechanisms to insure consumption against these shocks.

For a comprehensive understanding of vulnerability to poverty it is, therefore, important to know both the magnitude of consumption volatility (i.e. the level of vulnerability) as well as the causes of volatility in consumption (i.e. the sources of vulnerability). Currently available data does, however, not even allow for a thorough estimation of either the *ex-ante* vulnerability of households or the *ex-post* impact of shocks on consumption, let alone measure both the level and sources of vulnerability at the same time. The existing empirical literature is, therefore, divided into two strands of literature, which are either concentrating on the measurement of aggregate vulnerability within a population or analyzing the *ex-post* impact of selected shocks on households' consumption.

4.3 Estimates of Vulnerability

The first strand of literature, which intends to estimate the aggregate vulnerability of households, was pioneered by Townsend (1994) and Udry (1995), who were some of the first using panel data to analyze whether households are able to insure their consumption against idiosyncratic income fluctuations over time and space. In this spirit, several studies followed analyzing consumption fluctuations over time (see e.g. Dercon and Krishnan, 2000; Jalan and Ravallion, 1999; Morduch, 2005), concluding that households are partly but not fully capable of insuring consumption against income fluctuations.

A severe drawback of this literature is that it relies on panel data (and often also on the presence of both income and consumption data), which is seldom available for developing countries. The existing studies and drawn conclusions are, therefore, often based on very few rounds (often not more than 2 waves) and/or observations (often not more than 100 households) of rural panel data,

[3]More precisely, the formula is $V = 1 - \sum_{i=1}^{I} p_i(\frac{x_i}{z})^{\alpha}$, where p_i is the probability and x_i the consumption of state i. z is the poverty line and α the risk-aversion factor between 0 and 1. Whenever x_i is greater than z, the ratio is set to 1.

[4]The question of the impact of the frequency of shocks on households consumption is often ignored, as lengthy data on the occurrence of shocks is practical not available.

whereas urban households are mostly ignored (see also Morduch, 2005). A major confounding factor is the problem of measurement error, i.e it is quite difficult to distinguish real consumption changes from measurement error in these relatively short panels (see e.g. Luttmer, 2001; Woolard and Klasen, 2005).[5] However, in many developing countries even short panel data is completely missing and one has to rely on cross-section surveys when one wishes to estimate vulnerability.

The second strand of empirical literature on vulnerability, which estimates the impact of selected shocks on a households' consumption, also has serious (mostly) data-driven limitations. In most household surveys, information on idiosyncratic and covariate shocks is very limited and sometimes even completely missing (see also Günther and Harttgen, 2005). As a consequence, most authors have only been able to focus on the impact of selected shocks on consumption (see e.g. Gertler and Gruber, 2002; Glewwe and Hall, 1998; Kochar, 1995; Paxon, 1992; Woolard and Klasen, 2005).

However, concentrating on specific shocks does not allow for an analysis of the relative impact of other shocks on a households' consumption. It is necessary to assess, which shocks should be given first priority in anti-poverty programs. Moreover, these studies have rarely been able to analyze the impact of these shocks on the vulnerability of households, as a households' vulnerability to shocks is not only a function of the magnitude of shocks on a households' consumption but also of the frequency distribution of these shocks.

In addition, there are severe econometric problems related to this work, which usually rely on standard regression analysis (e.g. OLS) to quantify the impact of shocks on a households' consumption. First, focusing on specific shocks introduces a considerable omitted variable bias as various shocks are often highly correlated (Mills et al., 2003; Tesliuc and Lindert, 2004).[6] The impact of selected shocks on households' consumption is, therefore, likely to be overestimated. On the other hand, the impact of other shocks might be underestimated, if the impact of these shocks depends on the occurrence of other shocks, and, therefore, would only be significant in an interaction term.

Second, it is often assumed that the impact of shocks on consumption is the same across all households, which is a rather strong assumption to make. We should, for example, expect that the marginal effect of shocks on households' consumption is lower for households at the upper end of the income distribution as these households are more likely to posses self-insurance mechanisms. Third, the problem of endogeneity might be severe as a households' welfare has presumably also an impact on the occurrence of certain shocks. For example, poor households normally face higher mortality risks.

[5] See also the discussion in Section 4.5.2.

[6] See also Table 4.2 in the empirical analysis.

Most important, several studies, which have analyzed the impact of covariate community shocks might be biased or miss information by a disregard of the hierarchical data structure underlying these estimates (Goldstein, 1987, 1999).[7] If covariate community shocks are simply assigned to each household within a community, 'multiplying up' data values from a small number of communities to many more household observations, the assumption of independent observations might be violated, leading to estimates that might be statistically insignificant and, therefore, overestimate the impact of covariate shocks on a households' consumption (Hox, 2002; Steenbergen and Jones, 2002).[8]

4.4 Idiosyncratic and Covariate Shocks

We certainly cannot bridge the data gaps that exist with regard to lack of panel data and of data on shocks in developing countries. What we propose is a method, which allows one to study the relative impact of idiosyncratic and covariate shocks on a households' vulnerability if cross-section or short panel data is the only available data source, without facing the discussed econometric problems that usually occur when estimating the impact of certain shocks on household consumption. Furthermore, we estimate the level and sources of vulnerability simultaneously, which has rarely been done. Although we cannot distinguish between the impact of individual shocks, a disaggregation of the impact of covariate community versus idiosyncratic household specific shocks should already be an interesting undertaking.

Since covariate (community) shocks are correlated across households, mutual insurance mechanisms within communities can easily break down during covariate 'crisis'. On the other hand, mutual insurance across communities, which would mitigate the problem of correlated shocks across households, are hypothesized to break down because of information asymmetries and enforcement limitations (Ray, 1998). On the contrary, micro-economic theory claims that households are (imperfectly) able to insure consumption against idiosyncratic shocks, as they are uncorrelated across households even within communities, where information asymmetries and enforcement limitations are assumed to be be less severe than across communities. Hence, analyzing the relative magnitude of covariate and idiosyncratic variance in a households' consumption can, first of all, test the

[7]We speak of hierarchical data structure or multilevel data whenever variables, i.e. economic indicators, are collected at different hierarchical levels with lower hierarchical levels (e.g. households) nested within higher hierarchical levels (e.g. communities) For a detailed discussion, see Section 4.5 and Section 1.2 in Essay 1.

[8]For a more detailed discussion, see Section 4.5.

hypothesis of better functioning (mutual) insurance mechanisms against idiosyncratic shocks than again covariate shocks.

Possible insurance mechanisms for idiosyncratic shocks on the one hand and covariate shocks on the other hand might differ quite significantly. Whereas higher information asymmetries persist for mutual or informal insurance across communities, the opposite is the case for external or formal insurance mechanisms, where higher information asymmetries prevail for shocks and consumption volatility within communities. Moreover, in contrast to idiosyncratic shocks, covariate income (or consumption) fluctuations are much easier to target externally, as they are geographically clustered.

Few studies (e.g. Carter, 1997; Dercon and Krishnan, 2000) have attempted to estimate the relative importance of covariate and idiosyncratic shocks on a households' consumption. Their estimations generally show that covariate shocks have a larger and more significant impact on a households' consumption than idiosyncratic shocks. However, these studies often only analyzed rural households, relied on panel data, which is rarely available for developing countries and also faced the discussed econometric problems of concentrating on some selected idiosyncratic and covariate shocks, without taking into account the hierarchical data structure. Moreover, assessing the relative impact of idiosyncratic and covariate shocks based on a classification of shocks into covariate and idiosyncratic shocks is problematic as several shocks have an idiosyncratic and a covariate component.[9]

It is difficult to assess whether a higher impact of certain types of shocks on a rural or urban households' consumption is the result of a more severe impact of these shocks on households' income or the result of worse insurance mechanisms of households against these shocks. In other words, with the proposed method we can only assess the net (and not gross) impact of shocks on a households' consumption. With these cautionary remarks in mind, we think that our approach, which will be discussed in the following, might contribute to a better understanding of the relative significance of idiosyncratic and covariate shocks on a households' vulnerability.

[9]For example, it is difficult to say whether the death of a household member is an idiosyncratic or a covariate shock, as the death might have occurred because of age - in this case the death were an idiosyncratic shock - or because of an epidemic - in this case the death constituted a covariate shock.

4.5 Methodology

4.5.1 Mean and Variance in Consumption

Our approach is based on the concept proposed by Chaudhuri (2002) to estimate the expected mean and variance in consumption using cross-sectional data or short panel data. This estimation procedure has recently become quite popular, as lengthy panel data is not available for most developing countries.[10]

The approach of Chaudhuri (2002) to estimate the expected mean and variance in consumption is based on the following main hypothesis. The error term in a consumption regression, or the variance in consumption of otherwise equal households, captures the impact of household-specific idiosyncratic and community-specific covariate shocks on households' consumption, and that this variance is correlated, i.e. can be explained, with observable household and community characteristics (Chaudhuri, 2002).[11] This concept can be illustrated in three main steps. First, suppose that the consumption of household i $(i = 1,...,n)$ in period t is determined by a set of variables X_i. Hence, we can write down the following equation:

$$lnc_i = \beta_0 + \beta_1 X_i + e_i \tag{4.1}$$

where $\ln c_i$ is the log of per capita household consumption, X_i a set of covariates, and e_i the unexplained part of a households' consumption, i.e. the impact of shocks on a households' consumption.

Second, as we assume that the impact of shocks on a households' consumption is also correlated with observable household and community characteristics, we can define the variance of the unexplained part of households' consumption e_i as:

$$\sigma_{e_i}^2 = \theta_0 + \theta_1 X_i + \eta_i. \tag{4.2}$$

Whereas standard ordinary least squares (OLS) regression techniques assume homoscedasticity, i.e. the same variance $V(e_i) = \sigma^2$ across all households, Chaudhuri (2002) assumes that the variance of the error term is not equal across households but depends on X_i, i.e. is heteroscedastic,[12] reflecting the impact of shocks on households' consumption. Since we assume heteroscedasticity, simply using

[10] In the following, we only present the estimation procedure for cross-sectional data although the same method can certainly be applied to (short) panel data. For a discussion of implementing the proposed method using panel data with a two-wave panel, see Chaudhuri et al. (2002) who uses a two-wave panel data set from Indonesia between 1998 and 1999, or Ligon and Schlechter (2004). They estimate various vulnerability measures for a two-wave panel data set from Vietnam (1993-1998) and Bulgaria (1994-1995).

[11] See Section 4.5.2 below for a critical discussion of this assumption.

[12] It is still assumed that the conditional distribution of e_i - given X - has a mean of zero.

OLS for an estimation of β and θ would lead to unbiased but inefficient coefficients. To overcome this problem, Equation 4.1 has to be reduced to a model where the residuals e_i have a homogeneous variance.[13]

In a third step, for each household, the expected mean (Equation 4.3) as well as variance (Equation 4.4) of consumption can be estimated using consistent and asymptotically efficient estimators $\hat{\beta}$ and $\hat{\theta}$.

$$\hat{E}[lnc_i|X] = \hat{\beta}X_i \tag{4.3}$$

$$\hat{V}[lnc_i|X] = \hat{\sigma}^2_{e_i} = \hat{\theta}X_i. \tag{4.4}$$

4.5.2 Assumptions and Critical Issues

The above approach to estimate the expected mean and variance in consumption using cross-section data and to draw conclusions about inter-temporal variations in consumption is based on several stringent assumptions. This lead to various substantial issues if one wants to implement the concept of Chaudhuri (2002) in practice and which should be discussed critically.

First, the perhaps most stringent and critical assumption is that present cross-sectional variance can be used to estimate future inter-temporal variance in consumption. To illustrate this substantial issue, suppose there is only a single covariate X_i for household i, and that the log of consumption is determined by $lnc_i = \beta_0 + \beta_1 X_i + e_i$.[14] What one wishes to estimate is the particular households' consumption over time (lnc_{it}), and the respective residuals (e_{it}) to draw conclusions about inter-temporal variations in future consumption. Since the model assumes that $E(e_i) = 0$ and that $Var(e_i) = \sigma^2$, over time, this assumption means that $E(e_{it}) = 0$ and that $Var(e_{it}) = \sigma^2$, i.e. the variance in consumption is constant over time. As a consequence, one assumes that the estimated variance in consumption of household i, based on a single period, is the same in any other period.[15] This is a very critical assumption, because it might lead to misleading conclusions about future variations in consumption of households.

The only argument for justifying this assumption is the non-existence of panel data, and one should really be aware of the limited explanatory power of drawing conclusions about the inter-temporal variance in consumption that is based on

[13] For a detailed discussion, see Maddala (1977).

[14] Since we assume heteroscedasticity, the error term e_i for household i is $e_i = lnc_i - (\beta_0 + \beta_1 X_i)$.

[15] Ligon and Schlechter (2003) also make the assumption using a two-wave panel that, for any particular household, the probability distribution of consumption in one period is identical to the probability distribution of consumption in any other period, and adopt this strategy to estimate vulnerability in Bulgaria.

an estimate from a single period.[16] Even for a short panel, this assumption remains very critical. Only panel data for an extended time period would allow to overcome this problem and would allow to draw conclusions about inter-temporal variations in consumption, since lengthy panel data include information about changes in consumption and covariates over time.

Second, to estimate the variance in consumption (Equation 4.2), which reflects the impact of shocks on a households' consumption, it has to be assumed that the impact of shocks is indeed correlated with observable characteristics X_i. In addition, the above setup also assumes that shocks have no impact on the covariates X_i. For example, a death in the household would have an effect on the household size. Furthermore, if the dead household member was the only income earner, this effect would also other household characteristics, which cannot be considered using cross-section data.

Third, it is assumed that the cross-sectional variance can explain part of inter-temporal variance due to idiosyncratic or covariate community-specific shocks. But the model will miss the impact of inter-temporal shocks on the national level (for example, terms of trade shocks). One could argue that panel estimators use past variance to estimate future variance in consumption, which might not be much better if we assume low unobserved deterministic heterogeneity in household characteristics. However, since even short panel data include information on time-changing covariates and if we assume high unobserved deterministic heterogeneity, even short panel data are preferred to cross-sectional data.

Fourth, it has to be assumed that the error term in Equation 4.1 mainly captures some 'economic' variance and only to a lesser extent measurement error in consumption.[17] This is also a critical issue, since the existence of measurement error, when using information on consumption from household survey data, remains a major concern for the estimation of the mean and variance of consumption.[18] Large measurement errors could lead to a significant overestimation of the variance in consumption, i.e. a general overestimation of the impact of idiosyncratic and covariate shocks on a households' consumption. More precisely, whenever high measurement error is present, the square of the residuals from Equation 4.1 are overestimated by the variance of the measurement error, which is translated into the estimates of Equation 4.2.

---

[16]For example, suppose that that the error term e_i for a particular household i is positive ($e_{it} > 0$) in the given year, i.e. this household consumes more than the average of 'similar' households. This could be due to a positive shock and in the next period, this household could have an error term that is negative ($e_{it+1} < 0$). However, this variations cannot be observed using cross-section data.

[17]This assumption is not only made by Chaudhuri (2002), but is also made in other (panel) estimators of consumption variance over time (see e.g. Townsend, 1994).

[18]Note that measurement error is also a major problem in estimators of vulnerability which are based on panel data.

Fifth, a more general critical issue is the hierarchical data structure of household survey data, which is often ignored in the empirical analysis both of poverty and vulnerability. Households are nested within communities, which means that households are more homogeneous within a community than between communities. This hierarchical data structure has to be considered to avoid inefficient parameter estimates and misleading significance results.[19]

However, the potential advantage of the proposed approach is that it allows an assessment of vulnerability although lengthy panel data and data on shocks are missing.[20] In addition, conducting Monte Carlo experiments, Ligon and Schlechter (2004) argue that the proposed approach of Chaudhuri (2002) is the 'best' so far proposed estimator of a households' mean and variance in consumption whenever expenditure is measured with low error and whenever at least a two-wave panel is at hand. However, Ligon and Schlechter (2004) do not recommend to estimate the mean and variance of a households' consumption from one single cross-sectional data set, as a cross-sectional estimator only considers the part of consumption, which can be predicted by observed characteristics as the base level of consumption. Ligon and Schlechter (2004) argue that a large portion of consumption might, however, not be predicted by observed characteristics. Thus, as already discussed, we also have to assume low unobservable household-specific effects.[21]

Keeping the critical assumption in mind, the proposed approach should be understood as an illustrative attempt of what one could do when one wishes to asses the vulnerability of households, when cross-section (or short panel) data are the only available data. As mentioned before, there is no doubt that lengthy panel data are in any case preferable for the estimation of a households' vulnerability. However, the proposed approach is able to provide some interesting findings about an assessment of vulnerability. Based on the concept of Chaudhuri (2002), we extend this idea by assessing the relative impact of idiosyncratic and covariate shocks on a households' vulnerability and by taking the hierarchical data structure of household survey data explicitly into account.

---

[19]See Section 4.5.3 below for a detailed discussion.

[20]Chaudhuri (2003) demonstrates the robustness of the above described approach using a two-year panel of Indonesia and the Philippines, comparing estimated *ex-ante* poverty rates from the vulnerability estimates in the first year with the actual incidence of poverty in the second year. In the first round, given the estimated expected mean and variance in consumption of households, households were grouped based on their estimated probability to fall below the poverty line. The predicted poverty rates - which must be equal to the estimated mean probability to fall below the poverty line - for each decile of this poverty risk (or vulnerability) distribution matched almost exactly the actual poverty rates in the second round.

[21]In any case, the thereinafter proposed extension of Chaudhuri (2002) in Sections 4.5.2 and 4.5.3 can also easily be applied to short panel-data.

We apply the proposed concept of Chaudhuri (2002) to multilevel analysis (Goldstein, 1999). This first of all allows to differentiate between the unexplained variance on the household level (i.e. the impact of idiosyncratic household specific shocks) and the unexplained variance on the community level (i.e. the impact of covariate community specific shocks). Second, multilevel analysis corrects for inefficient estimators, which might occur whenever the proposed methodology by Chaudhuri (2002) is applied to hierarchical data structures, i.e. whenever variables from various levels are introduced in the regressions.

4.5.3 Multilevel Analysis

Multilevel models are designed to analyze the relationship between variables that are measured at different hierarchical levels (see Section 1.2 in Essay 1 for a more detailed introduction, and for a general description of multilevel, see e.g., Bryk and Raudenbush, 1992; Goldstein, 1999; Hox, 2002). Again, we speak of a hierarchical data structure or multilevel data whenever variables, i.e. economic indicators, are collected at different hierarchical levels with lower hierarchical levels (e.g. households) nested within higher hierarchical levels (e.g. communities).

Using a multilevel model allows one to use both individual observations and groups of observations simultaneously in the same model without violating the assumption of independent observations. Multilevel models include the various dependencies between variables at different levels without violating the assumption of independent observations and provide correct standard errors and significance tests (Goldstein, 1999). If this data structure was ignored, for example, if the same community characteristics were simply assigned to each household living in the community, the assumption of independent observations would be ignored, leading to downward biased standard errors and overestimated *t*-values. As a result, the precision of estimates would be overstated.[22]

Moreover, multilevel models not only account for dependencies between individual observations but also explicitly analyze dependencies at each level and across levels. In a multilevel model, each level is formally represented by its own sub-model, which expresses the relationships among variables within the given level and across different levels. For example, multilevel models would assume

[22] A related problem of dependent individual observations, leading to biased standard errors, also occurs in surveys with cluster sampling. Several methods have been proposed to estimate unbiased standard errors in clustered survey samples (Deaton, 1997) and, in principle, these correction procedures could also be applied to hierarchical data structure. However, and in contrast to multilevel models, most of the proposed procedures for cluster sampling assume intra-class correlations between observations within clusters that are equal for all variables, which is usually not the case for variables of different hierarchical levels (Hox, 2002).

that covariate shocks not only have a direct impact on households[23], but also an indirect impact on the returns to household-specific characteristics.[24]

In addition, and most important for our case, multilevel models decompose the unexplained variance of the dependent variable (e.g. consumption) into a lower-level (e.g. household) and higher-level (e.g. community) component, which we use for an assessment of the impact of idiosyncratic households-specific versus covariate community-specific shocks on households' consumption.

To formally illustrate the basic idea of multilevel modelling, suppose $j = 1,...,J$ level two units (e.g. communities) and $i = 1,...,nj$ level one units (e.g. households) and that the household i is nested within the community j. If lnc_{ij} is (in our case) per capita household log consumption and X_{ij} a set of household characteristics of household i in community j, then we can set up a regression equation as follows:

$$lnc_{ij} = \beta_{0j} + \beta_{1j}X_{ij} + e_{ij} \tag{4.5}$$

where the error term e_{ij} reflects the unexplained variance in the households' consumption. Note that, in contrast to standard regression models and Equation 4.1, the variables in Equation 4.5 are denoted by two subscripts: one referring to the household i and one to the community j, and that coefficients are denoted by a subscript referring to the community j. This means that it is assumed that β_{0j} and β_{1j} vary across communities. Various community characteristics Z_j can then be introduced to estimate the variance of coefficients across communities.

$$\beta_{0j} = \gamma_{00} + \gamma_{01}Z_j + u_{0j} \tag{4.6}$$

$$\beta_{1j} = \gamma_{10} + \gamma_{11}Z_j + u_{1j}. \tag{4.7}$$

where the error terms u_{0j} and u_{1j} represent level two residuals, i.e. the unexplained variance in consumption of communities.[25] Equations 4.6 and 4.7, therefore, reflect the impact of community characteristics Z_j on household consumption, which differs across communities but which is the same for all households within the same community j.

Substituting Equation 4.6 and Equation 4.7 into Equation 4.5 provides the full model, which can be written as

[23]This direct impact is assumed to be the same on all households within the same community.

[24]In contrast, to control for sample clustering, i.e. to compute efficient estimators, usual regression techniques assume constant intra-class correlations for all variables, ignoring the relationship of variables at each level and between variables of different hierarchical levels.

[25]The residuals u_0j and u_{1j} are assumed to have a mean of zero, $E(u_{oj}) = E(u_{uj}) = 0$. The variance of u_0j and u_{1j} is $var(u_{oj}) = \sigma^2_{u0}$ and $var(u_{1j}) = \sigma^2_{u1}$ respectively, and the covariance is $cov(u_{oj}, u_{1j}) = \sigma_{u01}$.

$$lnc_{ij} = \overbrace{\gamma_{00} + \gamma_{10}X_{ij} + \gamma_{01}Z_j + \gamma_{11}X_{ij}Z_j}^{deterministic} + \overbrace{(u_{0j} + u_{1j}X_{ij} + e_{ij})}^{stochastic}. \quad (4.8)$$

and estimated via maximum likelihood (Mason et al., 1983; Goldstein, 1999; Bryk and Raudenbush, 1992). The first part of Equation 4.8 reflects the deterministic part of the equation, including the interaction term $X_{ij}Z_j$, which represents cross-level interactions between variables at the household and variables at the community level. The second part, expressed in brackets, captures the stochastic part of the model.

In contrast to standard OLS regression, the error term in Equation 4.8 contains not only an individual or household component e_{ij} but also a group or community component $u_{0j} + u_{1j}X_{ij}$. The meaning of the different variance components is illustrated in Figure 4.1.

Figure 4.1: Variance Decomposition in Multilevel Models

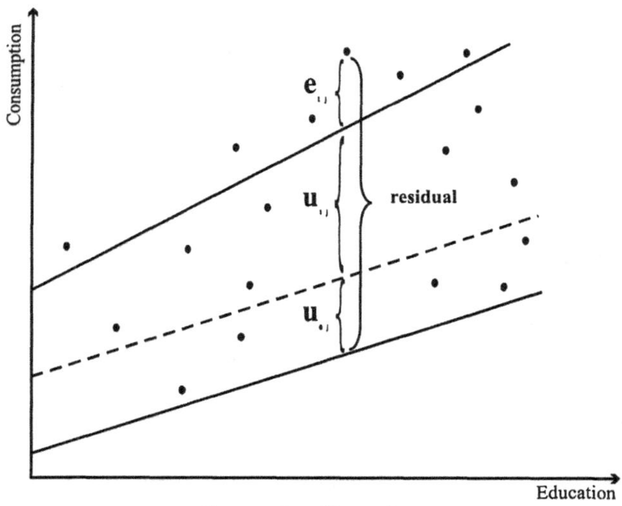

Source: Own illustration.

The error term u_{0j} represents the unexplained variance across communities for the intercept β_{0j}. The error term u_{1j} reflects the unexplained variance across communities for the slopes β_{1j}. The error term e_{ij} captures the remaining unexplained individual or household variance in consumption.

The stochastic part in equation (4.8) demonstrates the problem of dependent errors in multilevel data structure.[26] Whereas the household error component e_{ij} is independent across all households, the community level errors u_{0j} and u_{1j} are independent between communities but dependent, i.e. equal, for every household i within community j. This already leads to heteroscedastic error terms, as the error term of a household depends on u_{0j} and u_{1j}, which vary across communities and on household characteristics X_{ij}, which vary across households. For the case that the individual error term e_{ij} is heteroscedastic - an assumption we make - multilevel modelling also allows to specify heteroscedasticity at the household level.[27]

4.5.4 The Impact of Idiosyncratic and Covariate Shocks

To assess the relative impact of idiosyncratic and covariate shocks on the households' vulnerability with cross-sectional data, we proceed in the following four steps. In the first step, combining Equation 4.1 and Equation 4.8, we estimate the log of consumption of household covariates i in community j on a set of household X_{ij} and community covariates Z_j using the basic two-level model.

$$lnc_{ij} = \gamma_{00} + \gamma_{10}X_{ij} + \gamma_{01}Z_j + (u_j + e_{ij}). \tag{4.9}$$

The difference to Equation 4.8 is that in our model no cross-level interactions are included so that the error part $u_{1j}X_{ij} = 0$, which means that the variance components of the sloped are assumed to be zero and only the regression intercept is assumed to vary across communities expressed by the term u_j.[28]

This model provides us with two variance components. The variance component at the household level $\sigma^2_{e_{ij}}$ captures the idiosyncratic shocks and the variance component at the community level $\sigma^2_{u_j}$ captures the covariate shocks on consumption. This variance decomposition allows us now two assess the relative impact of idiosyncratic and covariate shocks on the mean of consumption, and also on the variance of consumption, since it is assumed that the variance in consumption depends on the household and community characteristics

[26] See also Section 1.2 in Essay 1.

[27] For the estimation of the multilevel model, the GLAMM package for STATA is used. To provide consistent and asymptotically efficient estimators, the Huber/White sandwich estimator of the covariance matrix of the parameter estimates is used (see e.g. Mass and Hox, 2004).

[28] When setting up the multilevel model, we also tried to include cross-level interaction terms but they did not show significant results. As in multilevel models the interaction terms should only be incorporated if they show significant results, they were removed from the model (see e.g. Hox, 2002).

$$\sigma^2_{e_{ij}} = \theta_0 + X_{ij}\theta_1 + Z_j\theta_2 \tag{4.10}$$

$$\sigma^2_{u_j} = \tau_0 + Z_j\tau_1 \tag{4.11}$$

where $\sigma^2_{e_{ij}}$ refer to as the level-1 variance and $\sigma^2_{u_j}$ refers to the level-2 variance.

In the second step, we can now estimate the variance at level 1 ($\sigma^2_{e_{ij}}$) and level 2 ($\sigma^2_{u_j}$) from the predicted residuals in step one using again a multilevel approach that provides us with asymptotically efficient and consistent estimation parameters for each variance component.[29]

In the third step, we then can predict the mean consumption and the variance of consumption for the part that is due to idiosyncratic shocks and the part that is due to covariate shocks

$$\hat{E}[lnc_{ij}|X,Z] = X_{ij}\hat{\beta}_1 + Z_j\hat{\beta}_2 \tag{4.12}$$

$$\hat{V}_{idiosyncratic}[lnc_i|X,Z] = \hat{\sigma}^2_{e_{ij}} = X_{ij}\hat{\theta}_1 + Z_j\hat{\theta}_2 \tag{4.13}$$

$$\hat{V}_{covariate}[lnc_i|Z] = \hat{\sigma}^2_{u_j} = Z_j\hat{\tau}_1. \tag{4.14}$$

In step four, we can now use any measure of vulnerability υ_{ij} to assess the risk of a household i in community j being vulnerable to poverty.

Although all possible vulnerability definitions (or measurements) could be applied to analyze a households' vulnerability to idiosyncratic and covariate shocks, we use the measurement proposed by Chaudhuri et al. (2002), defining vulnerability as the probability of a household to fall below the poverty line in the near future. The focus of this paper clearly lies on the estimation of vulnerability parameters (i.e. the mean and variance in consumption), so that the applied measure of vulnerability only serves for illustrative purposes. Hence, we chose a measure that has, in contrast to most other vulnerability measurements, an intuitive interpretation - although it might have some undesirable axiomatic properties (see Calvo and Dercon, 2005).

Assuming that consumption is log-normally distributed, we can estimate the probability of a household to fall below the poverty line using the estimated expected mean and variance of consumption:

$$\hat{\upsilon}_{ij} = \hat{P}(lnc_{ij} < lnz|X,Z) = \Phi\left(\frac{lnz - ln\hat{c}_{ij}}{\hat{\sigma}^2}\right) \tag{4.15}$$

[29]In this model, it is not guaranteed that the estimates of $\sigma^2_{e_{ij}}$ and $\sigma^2_{u_j}$ will be positive. In our case, we did not face this problem. An alternative way to estimate the variance that guarantees positive values is to estimate the log of the variance so that Equation 4.10 and Equation 4.11 become to $log(\sigma^2_{e_{ij}}) = X_{ij}\theta_1 + Z_j\theta_2$ and $log(\sigma^2_{u_j}) = Z_j\tau_1$.

where $\Phi(.)$ denotes the cumulative density of the standard normal distribution function, z denotes the poverty line, $\hat{lnc}_{ij}$ the expected mean of per capita log consumption and $\hat{\sigma}^2$ the respective estimated variance in consumption. The probability to fall below the poverty line is conducted separately for the estimated idiosyncratic variance $\sigma^2_{e_{ij}}$ and covariate variance $\sigma^2_{u_j}$ in consumption as well as jointly $\sigma^2_{e_{ij}+u_j}$ for the overall variance in consumption.

To assess a households' vulnerability, we have to define a vulnerability threshold υ_{ij} above which we consider a household i in community j as vulnerable to poverty as well as a time horizon, which we consider as the 'near' future. In the empirical literature, often a vulnerability threshold of 50 percent is used and a time horizon of t+2 years (see, e.g. Chaudhuri et al., 2002; Tesliuc and Lindert, 2004). This means that those households are considered as vulnerable, which have a 50 percent or higher probability to fall below the poverty line (at least once) in the next two years, $\upsilon_{ij,t+2} \geq 0.5$, which is equivalent to a 29 percent or higher probability P, i.e. probability threshold, to fall below the poverty line in any given year. However, since we have only cross-sectional data (and not even a two-wave panel) and concerning the critical assumptions that have to be made to draw conclusions about future variations in consumption based on cross-sectional data, we constrain our analysis to a time horizon of t+1 year. In particular, this means that we consider those households as vulnerable, which have a 25 percent or higher probability to fall below the poverty line in the next year, which can be formally written as

$$\upsilon_{ij,t+1} = 1 - [P(\ln c_{ij} > \ln z)] \tag{4.16}$$

where $\upsilon_{ij,t+1}$ is the vulnerability threshold in t to fall below the poverty line in the next year and $P(\ln c_{ij} > \ln z)$ is the probability to have a consumption above the poverty line. Certainly, any vulnerability threshold could be used, and the choice of a threshold of 25 percent is quite arbitrary, but our focus is not on an absolute assessment of vulnerability but rather on the relative impact of idiosyncratic and covariate shocks.

4.6 Empirical Analysis

4.6.1 Data Description and Model Specification

We empirically illustrate our proposed approach for Madagascar. Madagascar is one of the poorest countries in Sub-Saharan Africa with a GDP per capita of 744 USD PPP and an estimated headcount poverty rate of about 70 percent. Its poor economic performance is also reflected in very low social indicators of human well-being. Life expectancy at birth is 55 years and high rates of child mortality (7.6 percent) and child undernutrition (41.9 percent) persist (World Bank, 2005a).

Moreover, Table 4.1 shows that households in Madagascar are frequently hit by various types of shocks, which have an additional severe down-side impact on households' well-being (Mills et al., 2003). Mills et al. (2003) report that households are most notably hit by frequently occurring covariate shocks, in particular epidemics like malaria and climatic shocks like flooding, which also show a quite strong spatial and temporal correlation, which is shown both in Table 4.1 and Table 4.2.

Table 4.1: Households with Exposure to Different Shocks

Shock	Persons in cummunes with exposure (percent)	Commune correlation across years (1999/2000)*
Human diseases		
Malaria	73.93	0.88
Tuberculosis	54.19	0.81
Typhoid	32.53	0.81
Cholera	33.64	0.44
Agricultural and livestock diseases		
Rice pest	22.72	0.84
Swineflu	39.46	0.63
Newcastle	75.91	0.85
Climate shocks		
Flooding	24.69	0.52
Impassible bridge or road	21.00	0.70
Drought	17.97	0.57
Cyclones	7.37	0.25

Source: 2001 Enquete Aupres Des Menages (EPM) and 2001 ILO/Cornell Commune Levels census; own calculations. *Mills et al., 2003.

Table 4.2: Correlations of Shocks

	Malaria	Tuberculosis	Typhoid	Cholera	Rice pest	Swineflu	Newcastle	Flooding	Impassible bridge or road	Drought	Cyclones
Malaria	1.00										
Tuberculosis	0.60	1.00									
Typhoid	0.40	0.44	1.00								
Cholera	0.39	0.36	0.34	1.00							
Rice pest	0.25	0.21	0.18	0.03	1.00						
Swineflu	0.35	0.25	0.07	0.21	0.19	1.00					
Newcastle	0.63	0.49	0.29	0.34	0.15	0.41	1.00				
Flooding	0.15	0.15	0.24	0.17	0.00	-0.05	0.20	1.00			
Impassible bridge or road	0.29	0.18	0.26	0.15	0.14	-0.09	0.19	0.36	1.00		
Drought	0.26	0.24	0.28	0.06	0.20	-0.06	0.18	0.09	-0.02	1.00	
Cyclones	0.07	0.14	0.15	0.11	0.07	0.07	0.03	0.43	0.34	-0.09	1.00

Source: 2001 Enquete Aupres Des Menages (EPM) and 2001 ILO/Cornell Commune Levels census; own calculations.

The data, which we use for our analysis is derived from a cross-sectional household survey and a cross-sectional community census. The community census is the 2001 ILO/Cornell Commune Levels census, which provides information on community characteristics like social and economic infrastructure as well as data on the occurrence of covariate shocks. It covers 1,385 out of the 1,395 communities in Madagascar. Data on household characteristics is taken from the national representative household survey of 2001 (Enquete Aupres Des Menages (EPM)), covering 5,080 households (1,778 urban and 3,302 rural households) in 186 communities.

Table 4.3: Summary Statistics
for Household and Community Characteristics

	Urban	Rural	National
Household characteristics			
Age of household head (in years)	42.60	41.71	42.25
Sex of household head (1=male)	76.70	78.07	77.60
Education of household head (in years)	7.80	4.15	6.35
Household size	4.42	4.78	4.56
Total no. children	1.70	2.16	1.88
Number of cattle	0.93	4.88	2.50
Number of chicken	2.63	8.70	5.04
Head works in informal sector (%)	22.88	7.04	16.59
Head works in formal sector (%)	21.74	5.80	15.41
Head works in agricultural sector (%)	41.02	83.00	57.68
Head is employed (%)	43.86	57.27	49.19
Households having an enterprize in the non-agricultural sector (%)	30.22	20.24	26.26
Community characteristics			
Telephone (%)	83.16	18.75	57.60
Sanitation (%)	75.26	20.54	53.54
Save water (%)	98.43	50.00	79.21
Electricity (%)	98.43	42.00	76.02
Secondary education (%)	100	67.86	87.16
Tertiary education (%)	97.89	10.71	63.07
Hospital (%)	93.01	7.14	58.53
National road (%)	93.67	53.75	77.65

Source: 2001 Enquete Aupres Des Menages (EPM) and 2001 ILO/Cornell Commune Levels census; own calculations.
Note: Unfortunately, we do not have information on graveled or paved roads.

To estimate households' expected mean and variance of consumption, we include a set of household and community characteristics in our model (Table 4.3). In addition to the household characteristics listed in Table 4.3, we consider an agricultural asset index estimated via a principal component analysis (Filmer and Pritchett, 2001). For the calculation of the agricultural asset index, various production assets such as tractor, plough, other agricultural equipment, etc. are included. At the community, level we include population density and the mean educational level of the community as well as several variables reflecting the infrastructure of the community. For the calculation of the infrastructure index the following community dummies are included: Bus stop, community road, provincial road, national road, secondary and tertiary school, water, electricity, veterinary, fertilizer, market, bank. The left our category for the working activity of the household head is whether the head works in the agricultural sector. Also, community infrastructure characteristics do not enter separately into the model but as an infrastructure index based again on a principal component analysis. Using an aggregate index instead of individual variables has two main reason. First, the two chosen indices provide a proxy of the overall agricultural productivity of households and of the infrastructure within communities, respectively. Second, as the individual characteristics are highly correlated, their coefficients are likely to provide no significant effects if they are included separately into the regression.[30]

4.6.2 Estimation Results

As described in Section 4.5, we first estimate the expected mean and variance of log per capita consumption using multilevel modelling. Furthermore, we decompose unexplained consumption variance into an idiosyncratic (household-level) and covariate (community-level) component. To remind, we assume that the estimated variance in consumption on the household level reflects the impact of idiosyncratic shocks on household consumption, whereas the estimated variance in consumption on the community level reflects the impact of covariate shocks on a households' consumption.

The regression results of the estimation of log of consumption are shown in Table 4.4. All coefficients show the expected signs. The amount of variance that is explained at each level is shown by R_0^2 and R_1^2, where R_0^2=0.38 refers to the explained variance at the household level and R_1^2=0.66 refers to the explained variance at the community level, respectively. The R^2s did not improve when other than the reported household and community characteristics were added.

[30]See also Section 1.3.1 in Essay 1 and Section 2.4.1 in Essay 2.

Table 4.4: Regression Results of Per Capita Consumption
(Two Level Model)

	Coefficient	Standard error
Household demographic characteristics		
Age (head)	0.007**	(0.003)
Age^2/100 (head)	0.000	(0.000)
Number of children	-0.073**	(0.016)
Female headed household	0.008	(0.024)
Household Size	-0.087**	(0.008)
Household head socio-economic characteristics		
Years of schooling (head)	0.053**	(0.001)
Head works in informal sector (=1)	0.081*	(0.032)
Head works in formal sector (=1)	0.119**	(0.026)
Head works in public sector (=1)	0.205**	(0.051)
Head is employed (=1)	0.228**	(0.046)
Enterprize owner (=1)	0.041*	(0.024)
Land owner (=1)	0.006	(0.008)
Number of cattle	0.004**	(0.001)
Number of chicken	0.001	(0.001)
Agricultural asset index	0.024*	(0.012)
Geographic characteristics		
Infrastructure index	0.035*	(0.020)
Population density	0.002	(0.001)
Mean years of schooling per community	0.049**	(0.014)
Household with WC per community (%)	0.052	(0.057)
Head works in formal sector (% per community)	0.616**	(0.227)
Enterprize owner per community (%)	0.313**	(0.113)
σ_e^2	0.250	(0.010)
σ_u^2	0.092	(0.011)
R_0^2	0.376	
R_1^2	0.664	
Obs. level 1 (household)	4694	
Obs. level 2 (community)	180	

Source: 2001 Enquete Aupres Des Menages (EPM) and 2001 ILO/ Cornell Commune Levels census; own calculations.
Notes: *P-value<0.1. **P-value<0.01. Values are household weighted. σ_e^2 refers to the unexplained variance at the household level and σ_u^2 to the unexplained variance at the community level. R_0^2 refers to the explained variance at the household level, R_1^2 refers to the explained variance at the community level. The agricultural asset index and the infrastructure index are based on a principle component analysis. For the calculation of the agricultural asset index, various production assets such as tractor, plough, other agricultural equipment, etc. are included. For the calculation of the infrastructure index the following community dummies are included: Bus stop, community road, provincial road, national road, secondary and tertiary school, water, electricity, veterinary, fertilizer, market, bank. The left our category for the working activity of the household head is whether the head works in the agricultural sector.

We then applied a White-test to verify that the variance of both the error term e_{ij} and u_j is indeed heteroscedastic.[31] Last, we regressed the squared error terms, $(e_{ij}+u_j)^2$, e_{ij}^2, and u_j^2 on several household and community characteristics to estimate the total, idiosyncratic, and covariate variance in consumption for each household in our sample. Again, we use a multilevel model.

Based on the regression results, Table 4.5 shows the results for the estimated mean and variance in consumption, separately for rural and urban households, representing 65 percent and 35 percent of national households respectively. The expected per capita (log) consumption of rural households is considerably below the (log) poverty line, whereas the expected per capita (log) consumption of urban households lies considerably above the poverty line. This already indicates that low mean consumption is the main cause for rural vulnerability, whereas consumption volatility might be relatively more important for urban households.

Table 4.5: Estimated Mean and Standard Deviation of Per Capita log Consumption

	Urban	Rural	National
Poverty line	13.81	13.81	13.81
Mean (estimated)	14.26	13.54	13.77
Standard deviation (estimated)			
Total	0.60	0.58	0.58
Idiosyncratic	0.51	0.47	0.49
Covariate	0.29	0.28	0.28
Idiosyncratic / covariate	1.76	1.67	1.75

Source: 2001 Enquete Aupres Des Menages (EPM) and 2001 ILO/ Cornell Commune Levels census; own calculations.
Note: Estimates are household weighted and refer to per capita log consumption, adjusted for regional price differences.

With regard to the estimated mean variance in consumption, Table 4.5 shows that the estimated variance is slightly higher for rural households than for urban households, with a standard deviation of 0.60 compared to 0.58. Interesting to

[31] For the White-test, it is assumes that the variance of u_i (in our case e_{ij} and u_j) depends on (at least one) value of the covariates X_i (in our case X_{ij} and Z_j, respectively) and can be expressed by $V(u_i)=\theta^2+\eta(\beta_1+\beta_2X_{2i}+...+\beta_nX_{ni})^2$. If $\eta\neq 0$, heteroscedasticity exists. The White-test regresses the squared residuals u_i^2 from a regression model $Y_i=\beta_0+\beta_1X_{1i}+\beta_2X_{2i}+...+\beta_nX_{ni}+u_i$ on the regressors $X_1, X_2...X_n$ (as well as on the squares and the cross-products of the regressors to allow for non-linearities). An F-statistic is used to test the joint null hypothesis of all coefficients of the equation $u_i^2=\delta_0+\delta_1X_{1i}+\delta_2X_{2i}+...+\delta_nX_{ni}+v_i$ being equal to zero: $H_0=\hat{\delta}_1=\hat{\delta}_2=...=\hat{\delta}_n=0$. If H_0 is rejected, the error term u_i is heteroscedastic, i.e. $\eta\neq 0$. The test shows that $H_0:\eta=0(P>F)=0.000$, i.e. heteroscedasticity exists.

note is that idiosyncratic variance is higher than covariate variance both for urban and rural households. However, the relative importance of idiosyncratic variance is slightly higher for urban than for rural households, this is also shown in Figure 4.2, which presents the density distribution of estimated standard deviation of consumption. More precisely, whereas among urban households the idiosyncratic standard deviation of consumption is 1.76 as high as the covariate standard deviation, the respective ratio is only 1.67 for rural households.[32] Note that in many studies the village has been used as the 'natural' covariate level, but there is no necessity to do so (Genicot and Ray, 2003; Morduch, 2005), and using communities instead, as we do in this analysis, does not seem less useful.[33]

In Section 4.5.1, we stated that in Chaudhuri's approach (2002) measurement error and unobserved but deterministic components of consumption might lead to an overall overestimation of the variance in households' consumption. Thus, higher idiosyncratic variance in consumption could be caused by higher measurement error on the individual level. However, even if that were the case, we could still assess the relative importance of idiosyncratic and covariate shocks for rural and urban households, with idiosyncratic shocks having a relatively higher impact on urban consumption and with covariate shocks having a relatively higher impact on rural consumption.

In this section, we analyzed the expected mean and variance of households' consumption separately but aggregated over all households. To obtain a full assessment of the level and sources of vulnerability, we, however, have to assess expected mean and variance of households' consumption jointly but separately for each household, which will be done in the next section.

4.6.3 Vulnerability to Poverty

Utilizing the stated vulnerability threshold and time horizon, we estimate that 75 percent of households in Madagascar are vulnerable to poverty, i.e. 75 percent of households have a 25 percent or higher probability to fall below the poverty line in the next year (Table 4.6). The figures for urban and rural households are 43 and 89 percent respectively, indicating that rural households are much more vulnerable to poverty than urban households. Besides the vulnerability rate, we also state the

[32]Recall that we assumed, that the estimated variance in consumption on the household level reflects the impact of idiosyncratic shocks on household consumption whereas the estimated variance in consumption on the community level reflects the impact of covariate shocks on households' consumption.

[33]A community can consist of several villages, which means that community might represent a higher level than the village. Depending on the size of villages and communities, insurance mechanisms might differ between communities and villages, but empirical evidence of risk-sharing exist for villages (see e.g. Morduch, 2005) as well as for communities (see e.g. Grimard, 1997).

mean vulnerability, or in other words the average probability to fall below the poverty line.[34] The estimated average probability to fall below the poverty line should approximately be equal to the observed poverty rate, i.e. the number of households which have fallen below the poverty line, and can, therefore, serve to test whether the estimated mean vulnerability across all households is feasible. As shown in Table 4.6, both figures match to a very large extent.

Table 4.6: Vulnerability Decomposition

	Urban	Rural	National
Poverty rate	0.21	0.64	0.49
Mean vulnerability	0.26	0.64	0.49
Vulnerability rate	0.43	0.89	0.75
Structural vulnerability	0.11	0.66	0.47
Transitory vulnerability	0.33	0.23	0.28
Idiosyncratic vulnerability	0.38	0.85	0.71
Covariate vulnerability	0.24	0.78	0.61
Idiosyncratic / covariate	1.58	1.09	1.16

Source: 2001 Enquete Aupres Des Menages (EPM) and 2001 ILO/ Cornell Commune Levels census; own calculations.
Notes: Estimates are household weighted. National Poverty Line: 990404 Madagascar Franc.

Furthermore, we decompose vulnerability estimates into sources of vulnerability. First, we analyze whether vulnerability is mainly driven by permanent low consumption prospects (i.e. structural vulnerability) or by high consumption volatility (i.e. transitory or risk-induced vulnerability).[35] In other words, if the (estimated) expected consumption $\ln \hat{c}_i$ of a household i already lies below the poverty line $\ln z$, then the household is referred to as structurally vulnerable. If the (estimated) expected consumption $\ln \hat{c}_i$ of a household i lies above the poverty line $\ln z$, but a high estimated variance in consumption $\hat{\sigma}^2_{e_i}$ still leads to an estimated vulnerability $\hat{v}_{i,t+1} \geq 0.25$, then the household is said to face risk induced or transitory vulnerability.[36]

[34]Note that the estimated mean vulnerability is in contrast to the vulnerability rate independent of any vulnerability threshold and/or time-horizon.

[35]We implicitly assume that low expected mean consumption only reflects structural poverty and is not risk induced, although this does not necessarily have to be the case. Low consumption prospects can also be risk induced through behavioral responses of households, e.g. engaging in low risk but also low return activities (Morduch, 1994; Elbers et al., 2003).

[36]Note that with the assumption that consumption is log-normally distributed and with vulnerability defined as poverty risk, the estimated vulnerability of households with an expected mean consumption above the poverty line is an increasing function of consumption variance, whereas the estimated vulnerability of households with an expected mean consumption below the poverty

We see that rural vulnerability is mainly a cause of low expected mean in consumption, whereas urban vulnerability is mainly driven by high consumption volatility (Table 4.6). More precisely, 66 percent of rural households have an expected per capita consumption that already lies below the poverty line, and 'only' 23 percent of rural households are vulnerable because of high consumption volatility. In contrast, only 11 percent of urban households face structural induced vulnerability, whereas 33 percent face risk induced vulnerability (i.e. high consumption fluctuations). In absolute terms, as expected, slightly more rural households are vulnerable to consumption fluctuations than urban households.

We further analyze the impact of idiosyncratic and covariate shocks on vulnerability to poverty. Table 4.6 shows, that idiosyncratic shocks have a slightly higher influence than covariate shocks on consumption volatility among rural households and a much higher influence than covariate shocks on households' consumption volatility in urban areas. 85 percent of rural and 38 percent of urban households are vulnerable to idiosyncratic shocks, whereas 'only' 78 percent of rural and 24 percent of urban households are vulnerable to covariate shocks.

To check the robustness of our results to the poverty line, we show the fraction of households, which have a 0.25 or higher probability to fall below the (ln) poverty line for poverty lines across the entire income distribution in Figure 4.2, for all households and separately for urban and rural households. The official poverty line is indicated at $\ln(990404) = 13.81$ Madagascar Franc, which yields the same vulnerability rates as shown in Table 4.6. For all other poverty lines, we obtain the same idiosyncratic and covariate vulnerability trends but, as expected, on different levels.

However, an assessment of vulnerability to poverty depends not only on the poverty line but also highly on the chosen probability threshold above which we consider households as being vulnerable to poverty. Hence, we also show the percentage of vulnerable households for a given threshold between 0 and 1 in Figure 4.3 (now keeping the poverty line of ln(990404) Madagascar Franc constant). At a threshold of 0, every household is vulnerable to poverty while no household is vulnerable to poverty at a threshold of 1. Again, estimates are also provided for urban and rural households.

We marked the probability threshold of 25 percent, which we used for our vulnerability analysis, providing us with the same estimates as presented in Table

line is a decreasing function of consumption variance. In other words, households with a mean consumption above the poverty line and high variance in consumption face a high poverty-risk, whereas households with mean consumption below the poverty line and a high variance in consumption face a high probability escaping poverty. Hence, it might be useful to not only distinguish between 'structural' and 'risk induced'/'transitory' vulnerability but to add a third category of the 'mobile poor', referring to poor households with a mean consumption below the poverty line but with high up-side potential. However, this is left for further research.

4.6. Vulnerability to poverty is always higher in rural than in urban areas irrespective of the probability threshold chosen. What is now interesting to see is that the relative importance of covariate and idiosyncratic shocks for rural and urban households' consumption depends on the vulnerability threshold chosen.[37] However, independent of the probability threshold, the difference between the share of households vulnerable to idiosyncratic and covariate shocks is almost always much higher for urban households than for rural households.

[37]The main reason for this result is that (i) vulnerability is an increasing (decreasing) function of consumption variance for a vulnerability threshold below (above) 0.25 and that (ii) for most households - irrespective of their mean consumption - idiosyncratic variance is higher than covariate variance in consumption.

Figure 4.2: Cumulative Densities of Vulnerability - Poverty Lines

(a)
National

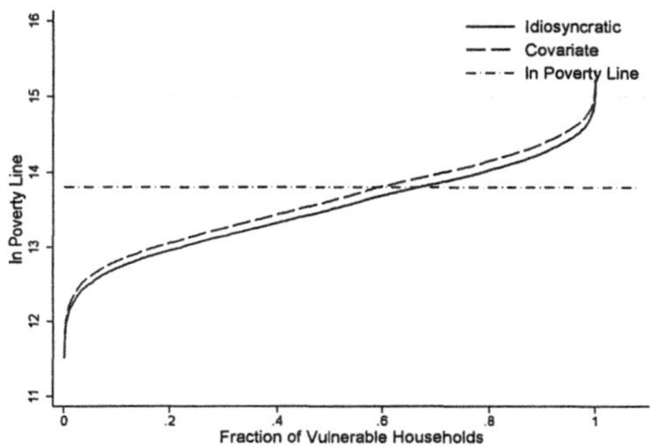

(b)
Urban

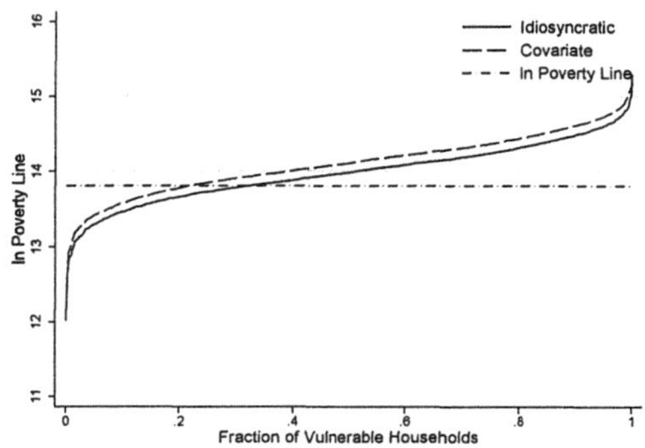

(c)
Rural

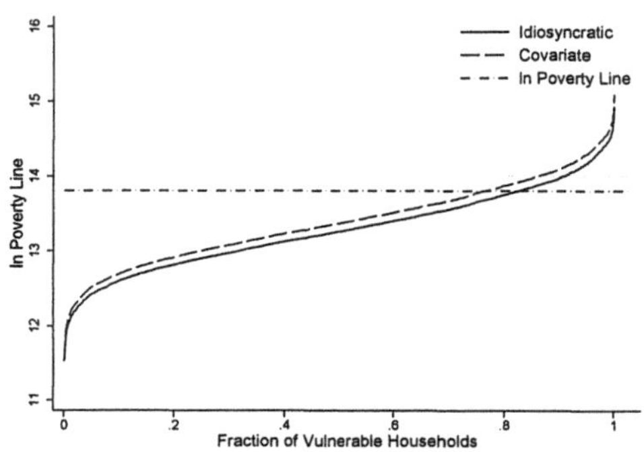

Source: 2001 EPM and 2001 ILO; own calculations.

Figure 4.3: Cumulative Densities of Vulnerability - Probability Thresholds

(a)
National

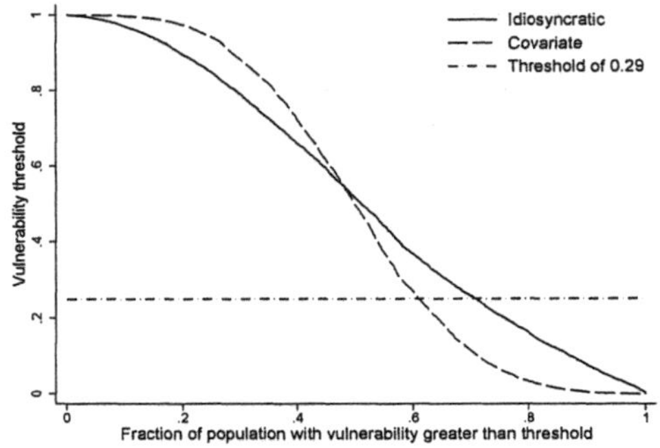

(b)
Urban

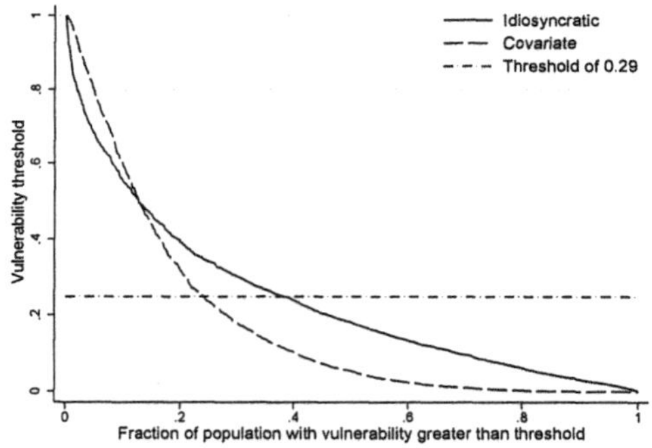

(c)
Rural

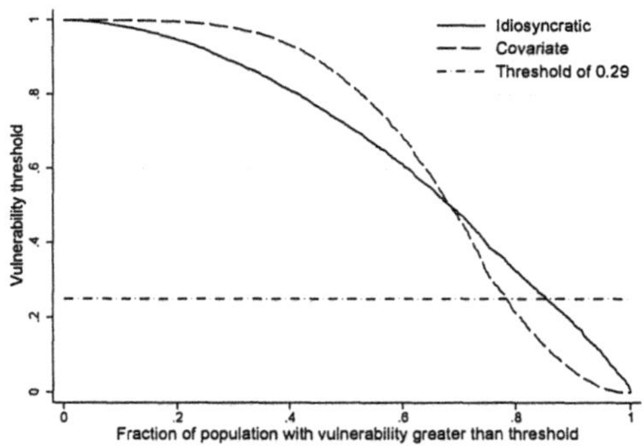

Source: 2001 EPM and 2001 ILO; own calculations.

4.7 Conclusion

We propose a simple method to assess the level and sources of vulnerability using currently available standard cross-sectional household surveys without any explicit information on idiosyncratic and covariate shocks. We are aware of the fact that some rather stringent assumptions have to be made to estimate future variations in consumption based on data of only one single year, which makes it very questionable to draw any policy implications from the results. Therefore, the proposed approach should not be seen as an alternative to estimate vulnerability based on lengthy panel data. In fact, we argue that if only cross-sectional data are available and comprehensive information on idiosyncratic and covariate shocks is missing, the suggested approach is an illustrative attempt to apply the analyzes of vulnerability to cross-section data and can provide quite interesting insights about the relative impact of idiosyncratic and covariate shocks on a households' vulnerability. Moreover, we recommend that any study, which analyzes the influence of covariate shocks on households' consumption - no matter if cross-sectional or panel-data is used and independent of the extent of shock data available - should apply multilevel modeling as it appropriately takes into account the hierarchical structure of the data that is used for such analysis.

Applying the concept of Chaudhuri (2002), defining vulnerability as the probability of a household to fall below the poverty line, we found that both covariate and idiosyncratic shocks have a considerable impact on both urban and rural vulnerability. Furthermore, our results indicate that idiosyncratic shocks have an even higher impact on a households' consumption volatility than covariate shocks and that idiosyncratic shocks seem to have a relatively higher impact on urban households and covariate shocks a relatively higher impact on rural households vulnerability.

The suggested overall higher impact of idiosyncratic shocks on consumption volatility might imply that either insurance mechanisms within communities do not function any better than insurance mechanisms across communities. This would stand in contrast to micro-economic theory and some early empirical papers on consumption smoothing of idiosyncratic income fluctuations (e.g. Townsend, 1994, 1995). Or, and this fact has rarely been tested in the literature yet, idiosyncratic shocks might have a much higher impact on a households' income than covariate shocks and even if mutual (but imperfect) insurance mechanisms are in place, still leading to higher consumption fluctuations than covariate shocks. An alternative explanation could be that some covariate shocks are more anticipated than idiosyncratic shocks - because of a higher frequency and a higher correlation across years - so that *ex-ante* coping strategies take place. Both theories might be worthwhile to be tested empirically in further research.

The relatively higher impact of covariate shocks on a rural households' consumption might be explained by the fact that there are certainly many more covariate shocks (such as climatic shocks), which have a higher impact on rural (agricultural) households than on urban (non-agricultural) households. It is further possible that urban households face higher information and enforcement limitations even within communities and that, therefore, informal insurance mechanisms against idiosyncratic shocks work better among rural than among urban households.

We also noted that the relative importance of consumption fluctuations (versus low mean consumption) seems to be even higher for the welfare of urban households than for the welfare of rural households. Hence, urban households should - if possible - be included into vulnerability studies, which have so far mostly focused on rural villages and households, ignoring the (increasing) urban population in developing countries.

Last, given that lengthy penal data are rarely available for developing countries and given the rather stringent assumption that have to be made when applying the analysis of vulnerability to cross-section data, it might be questioned whether *ex-ante* poverty dynamics can feasibly be estimated, given the fact they have to be estimated with past data, which is often not even able to estimate *ex-post* poverty dynamics properly. However, both from a policy and even more from a welfare perspective future poverty dynamics should have a higher relevance than past poverty dynamics.

From a policy perspective, future poverty estimates are especially for targeting more important than past poverty estimates, as the households, which are[38] or will be poor and not those, which have been poor should be aided. From a welfare perspective, whereas both past as well as future poverty is important from a lifetime welfare perspective, future consumption prospects (or risks) might also have an impact on the current welfare of households, which are risk-averse. How much weight future poverty dynamics should receive in present welfare estimates is open to discussion. Nevertheless, one should be very cautious when drawing any policy implications from vulnerability estimates based on past data, especially if these estimates are based on cross-section data.

If we conclude that it is worthwhile to estimate *ex-ante* welfare dynamics, first, only lengthy panel data would allow a reliable estimate of future variations in households income or consumption, which means that current living standard measurement surveys have to be improved to include (a better) time dimension, i.e. more precise data on past income, consumption, and asset fluctuations (as well as their causes) and possibly also (subjective) information on welfare prospects.

[38]Poverty estimates are in general not available in the same year of the respective household survey, but because of data cleaning and processing in general with a one year delay.

Appendix A

Table A.1: Scoring Coefficients
for Asset Index and Access to Health Facilities Index
(Principal Component Analysis)

	Bangla-desh 2000	India 1999	Mali 2001	Uganda 1995	Zim-babwe 1994	Global value
Asset index						
Radio	0.191	0.173	0.135	0.173	0.141	0.221
TV	0.284	0.270	0.272	0.245	0.195	0.332
Fridge	–	0.239	0.249	0.182	0.167	–
Bike	0.093	0.077	0.021	-0.002	0.036	0.095
Motorized transport	0.143	0.229	0.205	0.177	0.128	0.263
Low floor material	-0.300	–	-0.255	-0.274	-0.184	–
No toilet facility	-0.125	-0.265	-0.144	-0.118	-0.172	-0.220
Flush toilet	0.273	0.282	0.105	0.195	0.221	0.308
Piped drinking water	0.192	0.196	0.206	0.243	0.203	0.268
Surface drinking water	-0.048	-0.070	-0.085	-0.143	-0.086	-0.142
Access to health facility index						
Tetanus vaccination	0.393	0.349	0.344	0.480	0.403	0.358
Prenatal care	0.450	0.367	0.347	0.487	0.442	0.376
Born w/o assistance	-0.357	-0.312	-0.335	-0.252	-0.307	-0.286

Source: Demographic and Health Surveys (DHS); own calculations.

Table A.2: Regression Results of Infant Mortality (Logistic Regression)

	Bangladesh 2000	India 1999	Mali 2001	Uganda 1995	Zimbabwe 1994
Constant	-3.098**	-2.479**	-2.042**	-2.140**	-2.544**
	(0.099)	(0.028)	(0.053)	(0.104)	(0.167)
Age (mother)	-0.119*	-0.214**	-0.145**	-0.080*	-0.176
	(0.061)	(0.030)	(0.033)	(0.065)	(0.150)
Age^2 (mother)	0.178*	0.337**	0.231**	0.110	-0.337
	(0.104)	(0.032)	(0.052)	(0.107)	(0.248)
Sex of child (1=female)	-0.156	0.060	-0.107*	-0.077	-0.414*
	(0.104)	(0.046)	(0.059)	(0.107)	(0.219)
Immediate breastfeeding (=1)	-0.413**	-0.473**	-0.176**	-0.040	-0.499*
	(0.121)	(0.062)	(0.062)	(0.110)	(0.219)
Complete vaccination (=1)	-2.396**	-2.453**	-1.961**	-1.928**	-3.454**
	(0.219)	(0.066)	(0.126)	(0.187)	(0.344)
First born (=1)	0.273	-0.076	-0.116	0.134	-0.317
	(0.185)	(0.081)	(0.114)	(0.195)	(0.382)
Preceding birth interval	-0.006*	-0.007**	-0.015**	-0.003*	0.012*
	(0.003)	(0.001)	(0.002)	(0.004)	(0.005)
Household size (IV)	0.181**	0.068**	0.014**	0.064*	0.035
	(0.049)	(0.016)	(0.004)	(0.042)	(0.073)
Female headed household (=1)	0.028	0.037	-0.107	-0.088	-0.002
	(0.254)	(0.097)	(0.108)	(0.142)	(0.235)
Asset index	-0.132	-0.086**	-0.066	-0.160	-0.013
	(0.111)	(0.026)	(0.042)	(0.103)	(0.128)
BMI of mother	-0.039*	0.048**	0.026*	-0.041*	-0.003
	(0.024)	(0.010)	(0.012)	(0.022)	(0.037)
$BMI^2/100$ of mother	0.469	0.459	-0.253	0.265	-0.370
	(0.271)	(0.120)	(0.155)	(0.310)	(0.366)
Mother has sec. education (=1)	-0.180	-0.210*	-0.305**	-0.507	0.053
	(0.160)	(0.063)	(0.218)	(0.306)	(0.293)
Health facility index	-0.630**	-0.301**	-0.384**	-0.284**	-0.394**
	(0.088)	(0.028)	(0.046)	(0.084)	(0.135)
Community characteristics					
Distance to health facility***	-0.003*	0.001	0.000	-0.018	-0.033
	(0.001)	(0.002)	(0.000)	(0.049)	(0.095)
Secondary education (%)	-0.587	-0.614*	-0.319	-0.006	-1.525*
	(0.418)	(0.204)	(0.463)	(0.431)	(0.595)
Children had fever (%)	0.753*	-0.297	0.062	0.479*	0.333
	(0.418)	(0.255)	(0.181)	(0.252)	(0.480)
Public infrastruct. index	0.041*	-0.014	0.003	0.129*	0.261*
	(0.065)	(0.025)	(0.039)	(0.067)	(0.127)
Pseudo R^2	0.099	0.128	0.068	0.068	0.159
Obs.	5381	28539	9852	4232	1568

Source: Demographic and Health Surveys (DHS); own calculations.

Notes: *P-value<0.1. **P-value<0.01. For details about the variables, see Section 1.3.1. ***In the case of Bangladesh distance is measured in time (hours). The household size enters via an instrumental variable into the model. As instrument the mean household size per cluster is used.

Table A.3: Regression Results of Stunting (Logistic Regression) (Old Reference Standard)

	Bangladesh 2000	India 1999	Mali 2001	Uganda 1995	Zimbabwe 1994
Constant	-0.594**	-0.301**	-0.619**	-0.749**	-1.144**
	(0.046)	(0.014)	(0.035)	(0.168)	(0.097)
Age (child)	0.105**	0.235**	0.146**	0.165**	0.304**
	(0.007)	(0.005)	(0.006)	(0.012)	(0.031)
Age^2 (child)	-0.001**	-0.006**	0.002**	-0.003**	-0.006**
	(0.000)	(0.000)	(0.000)	(0.000)	(0.001)
Sex of child (1=female)	0.029	0.008	-0.055	-0.235**	-0.051
	(0.060)	(0.024)	(0.046)	(0.067)	(0.114)
Immediate breastfeeding (=1)	-0.110*	-0.070*	-0.123*	-0.053*	-0.063
	(0.097)	(0.028)	(0.048)	(0.115)	(0.115)
Complete vaccination (=1)	-0.371*	-0.101*	0.134	-0.051	0.168
	(0.136)	(0.421)	(0.100)	(0.068)	(0.293)
First born (=1)	-0.248*	-0.293**	-0.300**	-0.193*	-0.244
	(0.097)	(0.389)	(0.083)	(0.115)	(0.193)
Preceding birth interval	-0.008**	-0.005**	-0.009**	-0.008	-0.004
	(0.001)	(0.001)	(0.001)	(0.002)	(0.003)
Household size (IV)	0.038	0.069*	-0.005	-0.034	0.056
	(0.026)	(0.009)	(0.003)	(0.024)	(0.037)
Female headed household (=1)	-0.143	-0.141**	-0.102	0.036	-0.122
	(0.133)	(0.050)	(0.082)	(0.086)	(0.123)
Asset index	-0.430**	-0.172**	-0.085**	-0.213**	-0.195**
	(0.061)	(0.013)	(0.033)	(0.064)	(0.071)
BMI of mother	-0.091**	-0.066**	-0.074**	-0.070**	-0.060**
	(0.014)	(0.005)	(0.009)	(0.014)	(0.019)
$BMI^2/100$ of mother	0.332	-0.091	-0.253	-0.117	0.241
	(0.212)	(0.081)	(0.155)	(0.252)	(0.248)
Mother has sec. education (=1)	-0.344**	-0.229**	-0.483**	0.281*	-0.351*
	(0.085)	(0.030)	(0.156)	(0.114)	(0.155)
Health facility index	-0.249**	-0.252**	-0.070**	-0.065**	-0.238**
	(0.047)	(0.015)	(0.032)	(0.056)	(0.084)
Community characteristics					
Distance to health facility***	0.001	-0.001	0.000	0.037	0.043
	(0.001)	(0.001)	(0.002)	(0.003)	(0.052)
Secondary education (%)	-0.167	-1.244**	-2.400**	-1.302**	-0.176
	(0.226)	(0.100)	(0.375)	(0.265)	(0.324)
Children had fever (%)	0.253	-0.602**	0.114	-0.454**	-0.260
	(0.186)	(0.121)	(0.143)	(0.155)	(0.253)
Public infrastruct. index	0.056	-0.007	-0.092**	-0.067	-0.025
	(0.036)	(0.012)	(0.030)	(0.045)	(0.077)
Pseudo R^2	0.109	0.140	0.118	0.108	0.121
Obs.	5284	34797	9258	4518	2057

Source: Demographic and Health Surveys (DHS); own calculations.
Notes: *P-value<0.1. **P-value<0.01. For details about the variables, see Section 1.3.1. ***In the case of Bangladesh distance is measured in time (hours). The household size enters via an instrumental variable into the model. As instrument the mean household size per cluster is used.

Table A.4: Regression Results of Stunting (Logistic Regression) (New Reference Standard)

	Bangladesh 2000	India 1999	Mali 2001	Uganda 1995	Zimbabwe 1994
Constant	-0.245**	-0.093**	-0.327**	-0.344**	-0.885**
	(0.090)	(0.013)	(0.033)	(0.063)	(0.082)
Age (child)	0.104**	0.142**	0.125**	0.125**	0.172**
	(0.007)	(0.005)	(0.005)	(0.010)	(0.023)
Age^2 (child)	-0.001**	-0.002**	-0.002**	-0.002**	-0.003**
	(0.000)	(0.000)	(0.000)	(0.000)	(0.001)
Sex of child (1=female)	-0.059	-0.125**	-0.136**	-0.337**	-0.196*
	(0.058)	(0.022)	(0.044)	(0.063)	(0.101)
Immediate breastfeeding (=1)	-0.113*	-0.084**	-0.128*	-0.092**	-0.298*
	(0.061)	(0.026)	(0.045)	(0.064)	(0.171)
Complete vaccination (=1)	0.102	0.025	0.226	0.007	0.145
	(0.127)	(0.037)	(0.088)	(0.145)	(0.237)
First born (=1)	-0.168*	-0.219**	-0.167**	-0.171	-0.298*
	(0.094)	(0.036)	(0.078)	(0.107)	(0.171)
Preceding birth interval	-0.007**	-0.004**	-0.007**	-0.007	-0.005
	(0.001)	(0.001)	(0.001)	(0.002)	(0.003)
Household size (IV)	0.021	0.059**	-0.008**	-0.034	0.032
	(0.025)	(0.008)	(0.003)	(0.022)	(0.033)
Female headed household (=1)	-0.084	-0.103*	-0.171*	-0.091	-0.125
	(0.128)	(0.046)	(0.078)	(0.081)	(0.110)
Asset index	-0.388**	-0.159**	-0.114**	-0.227**	-0.150**
	(0.058)	(0.012)	(0.031)	(0.060)	(0.062)
BMI of mother	-0.073**	-0.056**	-0.059**	-0.061**	-0.048**
	(0.014)	(0.005)	(0.008)	(0.013)	(0.018)
$BMI^2/100$ of mother	0.379*	-0.075	-0.165	-0.405*	0.126
	(0.150)	(0.070)	(0.121)	(0.238)	(0.208)
Mother has sec. education (=1)	-0.285**	-0.199**	-0.412**	-0.159	-0.249*
	(0.080)	(0.028)	(0.137)	(0.105)	(0.135)
Health facility index	-0.216**	-0.231**	-0.087*	-0.099*	-0.172*
	(0.044)	(0.014)	(0.030)	(0.051)	(0.077)
Community characteristics					
Distance to health facility***	0.001	-0.004*	0.000	0.029	0.017
	(0.001)	(0.001)	(0.000)	(0.028)	(0.047)
Secondary education (%)	-0.246**	-1.118**	-1.850**	-1.122**	-0.304
	(0.218)	(0.093)	(0.330)	(0.244)	(0.287)
Children had fever (%)	0.294	-0.586**	0.120	-0.514**	-0.189
	(0.181)	(0.113)	(0.136)	(0.146)	(0.236)
Public infrastruct. index	-0.001*	-0.001	-0.062**	-0.120**	-0.049
	(0.034)	(0.012)	(0.028)	(0.042)	(0.068)
Pseudo R^2	0.100	0.114	0.100	0.094	0.097
Obs.	5503	37880	9750	4771	2114

Source: Demographic and Health Surveys (DHS); own calculations.

Notes: *P-value<0.1. **P-value<0.01. For details about the variables, see Section 1.3.1. ***In the case of Bangladesh distance is measured in time (hours). The household size enters via an instrumental variable into the model. As instrument the mean household size per cluster is used.

Table A.5: Regression Results of Stunting (OLS Regression)
(Old Reference Standard)

	Bangladesh 2000	India 1999	Mali 2001	Uganda 1995	Zimbabwe 1994
Constant	-1.643**	-1.769**	-1.482**	-1.421**	-1.065**
	(0.024)	(0.009)	(0.024)	(0.040)	(0.042)
Age (child)	-0.065**	-0.167**	-0.110**	-0.111**	-0.139**
	(0.004)	(0.003)	(0.004)	(0.006)	(0.010)
Age^2 (child)	0.001**	0.003**	0.001**	0.002**	0.003**
	(0.000)	(0.000)	(0.000)	(0.000)	(0.000)
Sex of child (1=female)	-0.037	-0.004	0.077**	0.189**	0.073
	(0.034)	(0.016)	(0.033)	(0.041)	(0.053)
Immediate breastfeeding (=1)	0.104**	0.089**	0.089**	0.102*	-0.041
	(0.035)	(0.019)	(0.034)	(0.042)	(0.054)
Complete vaccination (=1)	0.334	0.112	0.134*	0.124	0.202*
	(0.354)	(0.027)	(0.625)	(0.072)	(0.199)
First born (=1)	0.152**	0.207**	0.228**	0.115**	0.174*
	(0.054)	(0.026)	(0.059)	(0.068)	(0.088)
Preceding birth interval	0.005**	0.004**	0.007**	0.007**	0.004
	(0.001)	(0.000)	(0.000)	(0.001)	(0.001)
Household size (IV)	-0.028**	-0.056**	0.004*	0.038*	-0.017
	(0.015)	(0.006)	(0.002)	(0.015)	(0.018)
Female headed household (=1)	0.088	0.025	0.039	-0.007	0.011
	(0.074)	(0.033)	(0.059)	(0.052)	(0.058)
Asset index	0.240**	0.121**	0.056**	0.189**	0.145**
	(0.033)	(0.008)	(0.023)	(0.037)	(0.032)
BMI of mother	0.070**	0.060**	0.065**	0.051**	0.042**
	(0.008)	(0.003)	(0.006)	(0.009)	(0.009)
BMI^2/100 of mother	-0.252*	-0.052	0.020	0.159	-0.107
	(0.110)	(0.046)	(0.076)	(0.127)	(0.103)
Mother has sec. education (=1)	0.188**	0.127**	0.402**	0.118*	0.162*
	(0.046)	(0.020)	(0.090)	(0.065)	(0.070)
Health facility index	0.146**	0.187**	0.047*	0.010	0.064
	(0.026)	(0.010)	(0.023)	(0.034)	(0.042)
Community characteristics					
Distance to health facility***	0.000	0.002**	0.000	-0.046*	0.002
	(0.000)	(0.001)	(0.000)	(0.019)	(0.026)
Secondary education (%)	0.276*	0.850**	1.256**	0.596**	0.313*
	(0.127)	(0.066)	(0.214)	(0.151)	(0.151)
Children had fever (%)	-0.221*	0.380**	-0.178*	0.221*	0.085
	(0.105)	(0.081)	(0.103)	(0.095)	(0.123)
Public infrastruct. index	-0.011	0.008	0.059**	0.030	0.021
	(0.020)	(0.008)	(0.021)	(0.026)	(0.035)
R^2	0.184	0.214	0.174	0.161	0.193
Obs.	5284	34797	9258	4518	2057

Source: Demographic and Health Surveys (DHS); own calculations.
Notes: *P-value<0.1. **P-value<0.01. For details about the variables, see Section 1.3.1. ***In the case of Bangladesh distance is measured in time (hours). The household size enters via an instrumental variable into the model. As instrument the mean household size per cluster is used.

Table A.6: Regression Results of Stunting Z-Scores (OLS Regression) (New Reference Standard)

	Bangladesh 2000	India 1999	Mali 2001	Uganda 1995	Zimbabwe 1994
Constant	-1.925**	-2.152**	-1.610**	-1.826**	-1.253**
	(0.120)	(0.018)	(0.062)	(0.069)	(0.063)
Age (child)	-0.068**	-0.152**	-0.136**	-0.127**	-0.157**
	(0.019)	(0.006)	(0.009)	(0.010)	(0.015)
Age^2 (child)	0.001*	0.002**	0.002**	0.002**	0.003**
	(0.000)	(0.000)	(0.000)	(0.000)	(0.000)
Sex of child (1=female)	-0.230	0.177**	0.001	0.217**	0.194*
	(0.171)	(0.032)	(0.085)	(0.071)	(0.079)
Immediate breastfeeding (=1)	0.020*	0.059	0.084	0.266**	-0.009
	(0.180)	(0.038)	(0.088)	(0.073)	(0.080)
Complete vaccination (=1)	0.285	-0.008	0.056	0.272	0.267*
	(0.375)	(0.544)	(0.160)	(0.126)	(0.159)
First born (=1)	0.188	0.138**	0.332*	-0.115	0.244*
	(0.276)	(0.052)	(0.151)	(0.119)	(0.130)
Preceding birth interval	0.010	0.004**	0.008	0.006*	0.005
	(0.004)	(0.001)	(0.003)	(0.002)	(0.002)
Household size (IV)	0.037	-0.085**	0.002	0.033	0.010
	(0.074)	(0.011)	(0.005)	(0.025)	(0.027)
Female headed household (=1)	1.170**	0.025	-0.013	0.106	0.077
	(0.380)	(0.066)	(0.151)	(0.091)	(0.085)
Asset index	0.056	0.159**	0.127**	0.187**	0.131**
	(0.167)	(0.017)	(0.059)	(0.065)	(0.047)
BMI of mother	0.097*	0.047**	0.070**	0.028**	0.039**
	(0.040)	(0.007)	(0.016)	(0.015)	(0.014)
$BMI^2/100$ of mother	-0.356	-0.091	0.196	0.201*	-0.167
	(0.449)	(0.091)	(0.196)	(0.201)	(0.149)
Mother has sec. education (=1)	0.112	0.170**	0.281	0.083	0.183*
	(0.233)	(0.040)	(0.235)	(0.115)	(0.102)
Health facility index	0.131	0.234**	0.042	0.049	0.070
	(0.132)	(0.020)	(0.058)	(0.059)	(0.060)
Community characteristics					
Distance to health facility***	-0.004*	0.006**	0.000	-0.004	0.021
	(0.002)	(0.002)	(0.000)	(0.033)	(0.038)
Secondary education (%)	0.071	0.944**	1.309*	0.684*	0.506*
	(0.643)	(0.132)	(0.550)	(0.265)	(0.222)
Children had fever (%)	0.362	0.319**	-0.369	0.286*	0.157
	(0.534)	(0.161)	(0.264)	(0.166)	(0.182)
Public infrastruct. index	0.002	0.014	0.020	0.096*	-0.024
	(0.101)	(0.016)	(0.053)	(0.046)	(0.051)
R^2	0.018	0.080	0.038	0.073	0.157
Obs.	5517	37943	9755	3383	2117

Source: Demographic and Health Surveys (DHS); own calculations.

Notes: *P-value<0.1. **P-value<0.01. For details about the variables, see Section 1.3.1. ***In the case of Bangladesh distance is measured in time (hours). The household size enters via an instrumental variable into the model. As instrument the mean household size per cluster is used.

Table A.7: Regression Results of Stunting Z-Scores (Multilevel Regression) (New Reference Standard)

	Bangladesh 2000	India 1999	Mali 2001	Uganda 1995	Zimbabwe 1994
Constant	-0.702**	-0.155**	0.720**	-0.162**	0.229**
	(0.051)	(0.030)	(0.045)	(0.071)	(0.083)
Age (child)	-0.065**	-0.169**	-0.114**	-0.108**	-0.142**
	(0.004)	(0.003)	(0.004)	(0.006)	(0.010)
Age^2 (child)	0.001**	0.003**	0.002**	0.002**	0.003**
	(0.000)	(0.000)	(0.000)	(0.000)	(0.000)
Sex of child (1=female)	0.034	0.003	0.091**	0.188**	0.069
	(0.171)	(0.032)	(0.085)	(0.071)	(0.079)
Immediate breastfeeding (=1)	0.109**	0.032	0.063	0.100*	-0.035
	(0.036)	(0.020)	(0.035)	(0.042)	(0.054)
Complete vaccination (=1)	0.358	-0.002	-0.095	0.124	-0.205*
	(0.746)	(0.027)	(0.061)	(0.072)	(0.109)
First born (=1)	0.146**	0.203**	0.241**	0.120	0.177*
	(0.054)	(0.026)	(0.058)	(0.068)	(0.088)
Preceding birth interval	0.005**	0.004**	0.008**	0.007**	0.004**
	(0.001)	(0.000)	(0.001)	(0.001)	(0.001)
Household size (IV)	-0.023	-0.043**	0.003	0.046**	-0.017
	(0.017)	(0.011)	(0.004)	(0.017)	(0.019)
Female headed household (=1)	0.098	0.036	-0.009	-0.022	0.004
	(0.075)	(0.032)	(0.059)	(0.052)	(0.058)
Asset index	0.232**	0.117**	0.059*	0.166**	0.119**
	(0.034)	(0.008)	(0.026)	(0.040)	(0.033)
BMI of mother	0.068**	0.057**	0.059**	0.051**	0.041**
	(0.008)	(0.003)	(0.006)	(0.009)	(0.009)
$BMI^2/100$ of mother	-0.250*	0.048	0.027	0.154	-0.110
	(0.110)	(0.058)	(0.074)	(0.130)	(0.103)
Mother has sec. education (=1)	0.193**	0.136**	0.123**	0.123*	0.160*
	(0.046)	(0.020)	(0.087)	(0.064)	(0.069)
Health facility index	0.139**	0.176**	-0.004	0.018	0.063
	(0.026)	(0.011)	(0.024)	(0.036)	(0.040)
Community characteristics					
Distance to health facility***	0.000	0.004	-0.002	-0.005*	0.001
	(0.001)	(0.002)	(0.003)	(0.002)	(0.002)
Secondary education (%)	0.277*	0.935**	1.744**	0.622**	0.321*
	(0.149)	(0.138)	(0.303)	(0.172)	(0.158)
Children had fever (%)	-0.208*	0.329*	-0.236	0.181	0.078*
	(0.126)	(0.183)	(0.169)	(0.116)	(0.131)
Public infrastruct. index	-0.011	0.019	0.054*	0.030	0.016
	(0.024)	(0.016)	(0.033)	(0.032)	(0.036)
R^2	0.184	0.214	0.174	0.160	0.191
Obs. (level 1)	5284	34797	9258	4518	2057
Obs. (level 2)	339	424	368	359	229

Source: Demographic and Health Surveys (DHS); own calculations.

Notes: *P-value<0.1. **P-value<0.01. For details about the variables, see Section 1.3.1. ***In the case of Bangladesh distance is measured in time (hours). The household size enters via an instrumental variable into the model. As instrument the mean household size per cluster is used.

Table A.8: Regression Results of Stunting Z-Scores (Multilevel Regression) (New Reference Standard)

	Bangladesh 2000	India 1999	Mali 2001	Uganda 1995	Zimbabwe 1994
Constant	-0.807**	-0.459**	-1.600**	-0.288**	0.362**
	(0.246)	(0.057)	(0.071)	(0.121)	(0.121)
Age (child)	-0.069**	-0.155**	-0.139**	-0.126**	-0.157**
	(0.019)	(0.006)	(0.010)	(0.010)	(0.015)
Age^2 (child)	0.001*	0.002**	0.002**	0.002**	0.003**
	(0.000)	(0.000)	(0.000)	(0.000)	(0.000)
Sex of child (1=female)	-0.230	0.178**	0.005	0.213	0.193*
	(0.171)	(0.032)	(0.085)	(0.071)	(0.079)
Immediate breastfeeding (=1)	0.008	0.056	0.089	0.262**	0.002
	(0.180)	(0.039)	(0.090)	(0.073)	(0.080)
Complete vaccination (=1)	0.280	-0.025	0.863	0.277	0.279*
	(0.375)	(0.054)	(0.159)	(0.123)	(0.159)
First born (=1)	0.191	0.135**	0.340*	-0.110	0.239
	(0.276)	(0.052)	(0.151)	(0.119)	(0.130)
Preceding birth interval	0.010*	0.005**	0.009**	0.006**	0.005
	(0.004)	(0.001)	(0.003)	(0.002)	(0.002)
Household size (IV)	0.039	-0.085**	0.003	0.028	0.011
	(0.075)	(0.019)	(0.007)	(0.028)	(0.028)
Female headed household (=1)	1.170	0.012**	-0.049	0.084	0.076
	(0.380)	(0.066)	(0.154)	(0.092)	(0.085)
Asset index	0.157**	0.151**	0.131**	0.166*	0.132**
	(0.067)	(0.017)	(0.063)	(0.068)	(0.049)
BMI of mother	0.097*	0.049**	0.068**	0.029*	0.038*
	(0.040)	(0.007)	(0.017)	(0.015)	(0.014)
$BMI^2/100$ of mother	-0.354	-0.147	0.008	0.379*	-0.167
	(0.446)	(0.091)	(0.196)	(0.201)	(0.149)
Mother has sec. education (=1)	0.110	0.184**	0.278	0.094	0.185*
	(0.133)	(0.040)	(0.233)	(0.114)	(0.102)
Health facility index	0.130	0.221**	0.043	0.038	0.098
	(0.132)	(0.021)	(0.061)	(0.062)	(0.062)
Community characteristics					
Distance to health facility***	-0.004*	0.008*	0.000	-0.005	0.000
	(0.002)	(0.004)	(0.005)	(0.004)	(0.002)
Secondary education (%)	0.068	0.840**	1.289*	0.644*	0.467*
	(0.651)	(0.246)	(0.641)	(0.288)	(0.233)
Children had fever (%)	0.364	0.234	-0.379	0.259	0.153
	(0.541)	(0.324)	(0.326)	(0.190)	(0.193)
Public infrastruct. index	0.002	0.045	0.015	0.082	-0.028
	(0.102)	(0.030)	(0.064)	(0.052)	(0.054)
R^2	0.018	0.080	0.040	0.080	0.156
Obs. (level 1)	5517	37943	9755	4777	2117
Obs. (level 2)	339	424	368	359	229

Source: Demographic and Health Surveys (DHS); own calculations.

Notes: *P-value<0.1. **P-value<0.01. For details about the variables, see Section 1.3.1. ***In the case of Bangladesh distance is measured in time (hours). The household size enters via an instrumental variable into the model. As instrument the mean household size per cluster is used.

Appendix B

Figure B.1: Survival Rates by Age
and Country

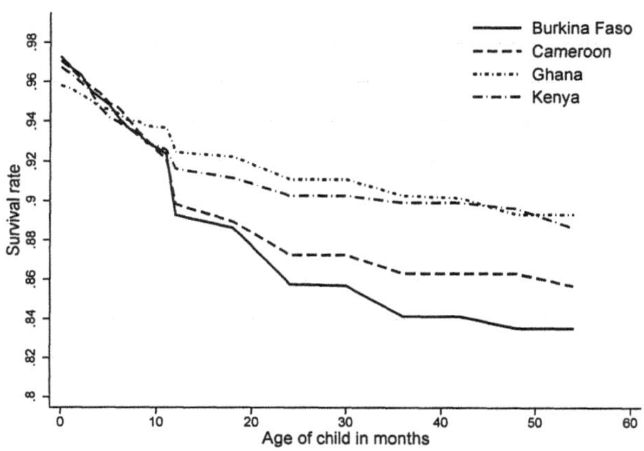

Source: Demographic and Health Surveys (DHS); own calculation.

Table B.1: Sample Comparison
(Logistic Regression)

	Burkina Faso 2003	Cameroon 2004	Ghana 2003	Kenya 2003
Age (child)	0.000	0.005	-0.001	-0.002
	(0.001)	(0.008)	(0.005)	(0.002)
Age (mother)	0.000	0.000	-0.005	-0.001
	(0.004)	(0.026)	(0.016)	(0.005)
Urban	0.182*	1.143*	0.106	0.215*
	(0.069)	(0.303)	(0.230)	(0.069)
Household size	0.005	-0.131*	0.023	0.029*
	(0.004)	(0.045)	(0.032)	(0.012)
Female headed household (=1)	-0.307*	-0.237	0.079	0.103
	(0.101)	(0.346)	(0.236)	(0.069)
Head has prim. education (=1)	-0.038	0.000	-0.356*	0.151*
	(0.085)	(0.297)	(0.210)	(0.065)
Head has sec. education (=1)	0.216	0.440	-0.100	0.065
	(0.196)	(0.451)	(0.361)	(0.079)
Mothers' BMI	0.001	0.021	0.033	0.011
	(0.008)	(0.031)	(0.022)	(0.008)
Mother works for cash (=1)	0.099	0.274	-0.127	-0.029
	(0.080)	(0.279)	(0.276)	(0.058)
Married (=1)	-0.127	-0.260	0.455	0.059
	(0.063)	(0.301)	(0.298)	(0.073)
Sex of child (1=female)	-0.045	-0.316	-0.089	-0.019
	(0.042)	(0.255)	(0.175)	(0.054)
First born (=1)	0.043	0.486	0.092	0.031
	(0.078)	(0.370)	(0.298)	(0.087)
Preceding birth interval	0.002	0.006	0.003	0.000
	(0.001)	(0.005)	(0.004)	(0.001)
Immediate breastfeeding (=1)	-0.028	0.151	-0.247	0.079
	(0.043)	(0.261)	(0.176)	(0.055)
Complete vaccination (=1)	0.029	0.002	-0.732*	-0.059
	(0.045)	(0.300)	(0.187)	(0.063)
Prenatal care (=1)	0.062	0.604	-0.016	-0.081
	(0.046)	(0.307)	(0.198)	(0.062)
Constant	0.504*	-5.048**	-3.614**	-0.148
	(0.217)	(0.976)	(0.755)	(0.224)
R^2	0.001	0.000	0.002	0.004
Obs. (full sample)	10313	8125	3952	5575
Obs. (HIV sub-sample)	3578	3952	3627	2447

Source: Demographic and Health Surveys (DHS); own calculations.
Notes: *P-value<0.1. **P-value<0.01.

Table B.2: Regression Results of Mortality (Global Data Set)
(Cox Proportional Hazard Model)

	(1)		(2)	
	Coefficient	Std. error	Coefficient	Std. error
Age (mother)	0.023*	(0.012)	0.024*	(0.012)
$Age^2/100$ (mother)	-0.026	(0.019)	-0.026	(0.019)
Sex of child (1=female)	-0.098*	(0.056)	-0.093*	(0.056)
Urban (=1)	0.040	(0.084)	0.044	(0.084)
Asset index	0.052	(0.056)	0.068	(0.056)
Household size (adults) (IV)	-0.005	(0.008)	-0.005	(0.008)
Female headed household (=1)	-0.050	(0.083)	-0.006	(0.082)
First born (=1)	-0.099	(0.100)	-0.093	(0.099)
Preceding birth interval	-0.006**	(0.002)	-0.006**	(0.002)
Prenatal care (=1)	-0.546**	(0.063)	-0.533**	(0.063)
Immediate breastfeeding (=1)	-0.419**	(0.061)	-0.423**	(0.061)
Mother has sec. education (=1)	-0.162*	(0.092)	-0.146*	(0.092)
Mothers' BMI	0.014	(0.048)	0.020	(0.048)
Mothers' $BMI^2/100$	0.030	(0.092)	0.015	(0.094)
Complete vaccination (=1)	-0.836**	(0.061)	-0.850**	(0.061)
Vitamin A (=1)	0.063	(0.056)	0.061	(0.056)
Recently had fever in cluster (%)	0.472**	(0.136)	0.497**	(0.136)
Sec. schooling (head) in cluster (%)	-0.500*	(0.252)	-0.486*	(0.251)
Piped water in cluster (%)	-0.321	(0.212)	-0.311	(0.214)
Burkina Faso (=1)	0.350*	(0.184)	0.297	(0.185)
Cameroon (=1)	0.254	(0.183)	0.248	(0.184)
Ghana (=1)	0.304	(0.188)	0.256	(0.189)
HIV positive (mother) (=1)	0.747**	(0.112)		
HIV positive (partner) (=1)			-0.071	(0.200)
Obs.	12688		12688	

Source: Demographic and Health Surveys (DHS); own calculations.
Notes: *P-value<0.1. **P-value<0.01. The household size enters via an instrumental variable into the model. As instrument the mean household size per cluster is used. The left out country for the country dummies is Kenya.

Table B.3: Regression Results of Stunting (OLS Regression)

	Burkina Faso 2003	Cameroon 2004	Ghana 2003	Kenya 2003
Age (child)	-0.131**	-0.094**	-0.102**	-0.096**
	(0.007)	(0.007)	(0.006)	(0.008)
$Age^2/100$ (child)	0.175**	0.131**	0.142**	0.136**
	(0.012)	(0.011)	(0.010)	(0.013)
Sex of child (1=female)	0.140*	0.028	0.213**	0.242**
	(0.062)	(0.056)	(0.049)	(0.066)
Urban (=1)	0.244*	0.081	0.058	0.131
	(0.118)	(0.070)	(0.069)	(0.097)
Asset index	0.179**	0.333**	0.291**	0.246**
	(0.057)	(0.044)	(0.041)	(0.057)
Household size (adults) (IV)	0.006	-0.023	-0.025	0.053*
	(0.011)	(0.015)	(0.021)	(0.030)
Female headed household (=1)	0.261*	0.089	-0.127	0.131
	(0.139)	(0.077)	(0.064)	(0.079)
First born (=1)	0.143	0.262**	0.264**	0.127
	(0.116)	(0.089)	(0.081)	(0.102)
Preceding birth interval	0.007**	0.007**	0.004**	0.002
	(0.002)	(0.001)	(0.001)	(0.002)
Prenatal care (=1)	0.047	-0.030	0.204**	-0.121
	(0.074)	(0.065)	(0.061)	(0.080)
Immediate breastfeeding (=1)	0.053	0.066	0.179**	0.005
	(0.064)	(0.070)	(0.058)	(0.092)
Mother has sec. education (=1)	0.335**	0.186**	0.124**	0.188**
	(0.192)	(0.069)	(0.058)	(0.091)
BMI of mother	0.130**	0.124**	0.148**	0.104*
	(0.071)	(0.057)	(0.041)	(0.065)
BMI of $mother^2/100$	0.011	-0.004	-0.233**	0.067
	(0.150)	(0.110)	(0.077)	(0.132)
Age of first birth	0.014	0.007	-0.007	0.025*
	(0.011)	(0.009)	(0.007)	(0.011)
Complete vaccination (=1)	0.014	0.007	-0.007	0.024
	(0.011)	(0.009)	(0.007)	(0.011)
Vitamin A (=1)	0.070	0.006	0.080	0.011
	(0.069)	(0.066)	(0.062)	(0.080)
HIV positive (partner)(=1)	-0.064	0.005	0.024	0.054
	(0.288)	(0.155)	(0.238)	(0.175)
Constant	-1.153	-0.911	-2.296**	-1.335
	(0.864)	(0.740)	(0.576)	(0.844)
R^2	0.195	0.146	0.193	0.140
Obs.	2538	2844	2828	1856

Source: Demographic and Health Surveys (DHS); own calculations.
Notes: *P-value<0.1. **P-value<0.01.

Table B.4: Regression Results of Stunting (Global Data Set) (OLS Regression)

	(1)		(2)	
	Coefficient	Std. error	Coefficient	Std. error
Age	-0.107**	(0.003)	-0.107**	(0.003)
$Age^2/100$	0.147**	(0.006)	0.147**	(0.006)
Sex of child (1=female)	0.148**	(0.029)	0.148**	(0.029)
Urban (=1)	0.113**	(0.042)	0.111**	(0.042)
Asset index	0.283**	(0.027)	0.281**	(0.027)
Household size (adults) (IV)	-0.003	(0.007)	-0.003	(0.007)
Female headed household (=1)	0.046	(0.040)	0.050	(0.040)
First born (=1)	0.201**	(0.047)	0.201**	(0.047)
Preceding birth interval	0.005**	(0.001)	0.005**	(0.001)
Prenatal care (=1)	0.028	(0.034)	0.027	(0.034)
Immediate breastfeeding (=1)	0.059*	(0.030)	0.060*	(0.030)
Mother has sec. education (=1)	0.081*	(0.040)	0.082*	(0.040)
Mothers' BMI	0.076**	(0.027)	0.075**	(0.027)
Mothers' $BMI^2/100$	-0.094*	(0.053)	-0.091*	(0.053)
Age of first birth	0.006	(0.005)	0.006	(0.005)
Complete vaccination (=1)	0.044	(0.034)	0.044	(0.034)
Vitamin A (=1)	0.041	(0.029)	0.041	(0.029)
Recently had fever in cluster (%)	-0.074	(0.072)	-0.078	(0.072)
Sec. schooling (head) in cluster (%)	0.406**	(0.104)	0.409**	(0.103)
Piped water in cluster (%)	-0.270**	(0.090)	-0.271**	(0.090)
Burkina Faso (=1)	-0.213**	(0.054)	-0.204**	(0.054)
Cameroon (=1)	-0.084*	(0.051)	-0.082*	(0.051)
Ghana (=1)	-0.119*	(0.050)	-0.113*	(0.050)
Constant (=1)	-1.474**	(0.358)	-1.474**	(0.358)
HIV positive (mother)(=1)	-0.011	(0.079)		
HIV positive (partner) (=1)			-1.474	(0.358)
R^2	0.172		0.172	
Obs.	10066		10066	

Source: Demographic and Health Surveys (DHS); own calculations.
Notes: *P-value<0.1. **P-value<0.01. The household size enters via an instrumental variable into the model. As instrument the mean household size per cluster is used. The left out country for the country dummies is Kenya.

Table B.5: Regression Results of School Enrollment (Logistic Regression)

	Burkina Faso 2003	Cameroon 2004	Ghana 2003	Kenya 2003
Age (child)	0.014	0.000	-0.019*	0.004
	(0.016)	(0.008)	(0.009)	(0.010)
$Age^2/100$ (child)	-0.009	0.008**	0.044	0.003
	(0.027)	(0.014)	(0.015)	(0.017)
Age (mother)	0.003	0.017*	0.034**	0.055**
	(0.008)	(0.004)	(0.007)	(0.010)
Urban (=1)	1.056**	0.171*	0.075	-0.416**
	(0.206)	(0.090)	(0.114)	(0.137)
Household size (adults) (IV)	-0.122**	0.055**	0.051	0.276**
	(0.031)	(0.021)	(0.039)	(0.050)
Female children in household (%)	-0.376	-0.444**	-0.016	-0.680**
	(0.268)	(0.131)	(0.148)	(0.175)
Asset index	0.513**	0.286**	0.226**	0.198**
	(0.104)	(0.062)	(0.066)	(0.081)
Head has no education (=1)	0.407	-1.049**	-0.622**	-0.635**
	(0.427)	(0.196)	(0.179)	(0.148)
Head has prim. education (=1)	0.615	-0.177	-0.107	-0.152
	(0.429)	(0.187)	(0.159)	(0.146)
Mother has sec. education (=1)	0.368*	0.594**	0.269**	1.085**
	(0.194)	(0.074)	(0.100)	(0.103)
Complete vaccination (=1)	0.796**	0.218**	0.311**	0.454**
	(0.174)	(0.079)	(0.107)	(0.108)
Female headed household (=1)	0.690**	0.480**	0.380**	0.573**
	(0.241)	(0.098)	(0.109)	(0.117)
Mother works for cash (=1)	-0.227	0.164*	-0.008	0.345**
	(0.205)	(0.082)	(0.136)	(0.097)
HIV positive (partner) (=1)	-0.776*	0.095	-0.284*	0.146
	(0.539)	(0.202)	(0.437)	(0.249)
Constant	-3.426**	-0.994**	-2.388**	-3.295**
	(0.569)	(0.246)	(0.296)	(0.323)
Pseudo R^2	0.171	0.094	0.049	0.146
Obs.	3323	3575	3421	2261

Source: Demographic and Health Surveys (DHS); own calculations.
Notes: *P-value<0.1. **P-value<0.01. The household size enters via an instrumental variable into the model. As instrument the mean household size per cluster is used.

Table B.6: Regression Results of Enrollment (Global Data Set) (Logistic Regression)

	(1)		(2)	
	Coefficient	Std. error	Coefficient	Std. error
Age (child)	-0.002	(0.005)	-0.002	(0.005)
$Age^2/100$ (child)	0.016*	(0.008)	0.016*	(0.008)
Age (mother)	0.019**	(0.002)	0.019**	(0.002)
Urban (=1)	0.125	(0.060)	0.124	(0.060)
Household size (adults) (IV)	0.044*	(0.012)	0.044*	(0.012)
Female children in household (%)	-0.546**	(0.081)	-0.546**	(0.081)
Asset index	0.410**	(0.041)	0.409**	(0.041)
Head has no education (=1)	-0.099**	(0.100)	-0.093**	(0.099)
Head has prim. education (=1)	0.076	0.103)	0.076	(0.103)
Mother has sec. education (=1)	0.635**	(0.048)	0.635**	(0.048)
Complete vaccination (=1)	0.359**	(0.051)	0.359**	(0.051)
Female headed household (=1)	0.521**	(0.059)	0.521**	(0.058)
Mother works for cash (=1)	0.225**	(0.055)	0.225**	(0.055)
Sec. schooling (head) in cluster (%)	-0.077	(0.173)	-0.076	(0.173)
Piped water in cluster (%)	-0.566**	(0.128)	-0.566**	(0.128)
Burkina Faso (=1)	-2.585**	(0.104)	-2.583**	(0.104)
Cameroon (=1)	-0.261**	(0.067)	-0.260**	(0.067)
Ghana (=1)	-1.408**	(0.072)	-1.406**	(0.071)
Constant	-1.149**	(0.158)	-1.151**	(0.158)
HIV positive (mother) (=1)	-0.016	(0.105)		
HIV positive (partner) (=1)			0.022	(0.142)
Pseudo R^2	0.210		0.210	
Obs.	12336		12336	

Source: Demographic and Health Surveys (DHS); own calculations.
Notes: *P-value<0.1. **P-value<0.01. The household size enters via an instrumental variable into the model. As instrument the mean household size per cluster is used. The left out country for the country dummies is Kenya.

Bibliography

Adebayo, S., L Fahrmeir and S. Klasen (2004), Analyzing Infant Mortality with Geoadditive Categorial Regression Models: A Case Study for Nigeria, *Economics and Human Biology*, 2: 229-244.

Adetunji, J. (2000), Trend in under-5 mortality rates and the HIV epidemic, *Bulletin of the World Health Organization*, 78: 1200-1206.

Ahmed, S.M., A. Adams, A.M.R. Chowdhuri, and A. Bhuiya (1998), Chronic Energy Deficiency in Women from Rural Bangladesh: Some Socioeconomic Determinants, *Journal of Biosocial Science*, 30: 349-358.

Ainsworth, M and I. Semali (2000), The impact of Adult Deaths on Childrens' Health in Northwestern Tanzania, World Bank Policy Research Working Paper No. 2266, Washington, World Bank.

Alderman, H., J.R. Berhmann, S. Khan, D.R. Ross, and R. Sabot (1996), Public Schooling Expenditures in Pakistan, in K. van der Walle and D. Nead (eds) *Public Spending and the Poor: Theory and Evidence*, Baltimore: Johns Hopkins University Press.

Arndt, C. and J.D. Lewis (2000), The macro implications of HIV/AIDS in South Africa: a preliminary assessment, Mimeo, Washington, World Bank.

Atkin, M, D. Anderson, and J. Hinde (1981), Statistical modelling of data on teaching styles (with discussion), *Journal of the Royal Statistical Society*, 144: 148-161.

Atkinson, A. and A. Brandolini (2004), Global World Inequality: Absolute, relative or Intermediate, presented at the 28th General Conference of the International Association in Income and Wealth, August 22-28, Cork, Ireland.

Barker, M., G. Chorghade, S. Crozier, S. Leary, and C. Fall (2006), Gender Differences in Body Mass Index in Rural India are Determined by Socio-Economic Factors and Lifestyle, *The Journal of Nutrition*, 136: 3062-3068.

Basu, K. and J. Foster (1998), On Measuring Literacy, *Economic Journal*, 108 (451): 1733-1749.

Béchu, N. (1998), The impact of AIDS on economy of families in Côte d'Ivoire: changes in consumption among AIDS affected households, in M. Ainsworth, L. Fransen, and M. Over (eds) *Confronting AIDS: Evidence from the Developing World*, Brussels: European Commission and Washington: World Bank.

Becker G.S., T.J. Philipson, and R.R. Soares (2005), The Quantity and Quality of Life and the Evolution of World Inequality, *American Economic Review*, 95: 277-291.

Bell, C., S. Devarajan, and H. Gersbach (2003), The Long-run Economic Costs of AIDS: Theory and an Application to South Africa, World Bank Policy Research Working Paper Series No. 3152, Washington, World Bank.

Bennett, N. (1976), *Teaching Style and Pupil Progress*, London: Open Books.

Berthélemy, J.C. (2005), To what Extent are African Education Policies Pro-Poor?, *Journal of African Economies*, 15 (3): 434-469.

Bicego, G., S. Rutstein, and K. Johnson (2003), Dimensions of the emerging orphan crisis in Sub-saharan Africa, *Social Choice and Medicine*, 56 (6): 1235-1247.

Blackorby C., W. Bossert, and D. Donaldson (2005), *Population Issues in Social Choice Theory, Welfare Economics, and Ethics*, Econometric Society Monographs, Cambridge: Cambridge University Press.

Bloom, D.E. and A.S. Mahal (1997), Does the AIDS Epidemic Threaten Economic Growth?, *Journal of Econometrics*, 77: 105-124.

Bolivia (2001), Bolivia: Poverty Reduction Strategy, República de Bolivia, La Paz.

Bonnel, R. (2000), HIV/AIDS: Does it Increase or Decrease Growth in Africa?, Mimeo, Washington, World Bank.

Booysen, F. (2003), Poverty Dynamics and HIV/AIDS-related morbidity and mortality in South Africa, Paper presented at the scientific meeting on empirical evidence for the demographic and socio-economic impact of AIDS, hosted by HEARD, Durban, South Africa, 26-28 March 2003.

Bourguignon, F. and S. Chakravarty (2003), The Measurement of Multidimensional Poverty, *Journal of Economic Inequality*, 1: 25-49.

Bryk, A.S. and S.W. Raudenbush (1992), *Hierarchical Linear Models: Applications and Data Analysis*, Newbury Park: Sage.

Carter, M.R. (1997), Environment, Technology, and the Social Articulation of Risk in West African Agriculture, *Economic Development and Cultural Change*, 45 (3): 557-590.

Calvo, C. and S. Dercon (2005), Measuring Individual Vulnerability, Discussion Paper No. 229, Oxford, University of Oxford.

Case, A., C. Paxson, and J. Ableidinger (2004), Orphans in Africa: Parental Death, Poverty and School Enrollment, Center for Health and Wellbeing, Research Program in Developing Studies, Princeton, Princeton University.

Chaudhuri, S. (2002), Empirical methods for assessing household vulnerability to poverty, Mimeo, Department of Economics, New York, Columbia University.

Chaudhuri, S., J. Jalan, and A. Suryahadi (2002), Assessing Household Vulnerability to Poverty from Cross-sectional Data: A Methodology and Estimates from Indonesia, Discussion Paper No. 0102-52, New York, Columbia University.

Chaudhuri, S. (2003), Assessing vulnerability to poverty: concepts, empirical methods and illustrative examples, Mimeo, Department of Economics, New York, Columbia University.

Cogneau, D. and M. Grimm (2006), Socio-economic status, sexual behavior and differential AIDS mortality - Evidence from Côte d'Ivoire, *Population Research and Policy Review*, 25 (4): 393-407.

Cox, D.R. (1972), Regression Models and Life Tables (with Discussion), *Journal of the Royal Statistical Society*, Series B 34: 187-220.

Cornia, G.A. and L. Menchini (2007), Health Improvements and Health Inequality during the Laset 40 Years, in G. Mavrokas and A. Shorrocks (eds) *Advancing Development - Core Themes in Global Economics*, Helsinki: Wider.

Cuddington, J.T. (1993), Modelling the Macroeconomic Effects of AIDS, with Application to Tanzania, *World Bank Economic Review*, 7 (2): 173-189.

Deaton, A. (1997), *The Analysis of Household Surveys. A Microeconomic Approach to Development Policy*, published for the World Bank, Baltimore and London: John Hopkins University Press.

De Cock, K.M., M.G. Fowler, E. Mercier, I. de Vincenzi, J. Saba, E. Hoff, D.J. Alnwick, M. Rogers, and N. Shaffer (2000), Prevention of mother-to-child transmission in resource poor countries: translating research in policy and practice, *Jama*, 283 (9): 1175-1182.

Dercon, S. and P. Krishnan (2000), Vulnerability, seasonality and poverty in Ethiopia, *Journal of Development Studies*, 36 (6): 25-53.

Dietz, W.H. (1998), Health consequences of obesity in youth: childhood predictors of adult disease, *Pediatrics*, 101 (supplement): 518-525.

De Onis, M. and M. Blössner (2000), Prevalence and trends of overweight among preschool children in developing countries, *American Journal of Clinical Nutrition*, 72: 1032-1039.

Dreyfuss, M.L., G.I. Msamanga, D. Spiegelman, D.J. Hunter, E.J.N. Urassa, E. Hertzmark, and W.W. Fawzi (2001), Determinants of low birth weight among HIV-infected pregnant women in Tanzania, *The American Journal of Clinical Nutrition*, 74: 814-826.

Duclos, J. and Q. Wodon (2004), What is Pro Poor?, CIPREE Working Paper No. 04-25, CIPREE.

Ehrlich, I. and F.T. Lui (1997), The Problem of Population and Growth: a Review of the Literature from Malthus to Contemporary Models of Endogenous Population and Endogenous Growth, *Journal of Economic Dynamics and Control*, 21 (1): 205-242.

Elbers, C., J.W. Gunning, and B. Kinsey (2003), Growth and Risk: Methodology and Micro Evidence, *Tinbergen Institute Discussion Paper* TI 2003-068/2.

Eliason, S.R. (1993), *Maximum Likelihood Estimation*, Newbury Park: Sage.

Engle, P., P. Menon, and C. Haddad (1999), Care and Nutrition: Concepts and Measurement, *World Development*, 27 (8): 1309-1337.

Eveleth, P.E. and J.M. Tanner (1990), *Worldwide Variations in Human Growth*, Cambridge: Cambridge University Press.

Filmer, D. and L.H. Pritchett (2001), Estimating Wealth Effects without Expenditure Data - or Tears: An Application to Educational Enrollments in States of India, *Demography*, 38 (1): 115-132.

Foster, J., Greer, J., and E. Thorbecke (1984), A class of decomposable poverty measures, *Econometrica*, 52: 761-5.

Genicot, G. and D. Ray (2003), Endogenous Group Formation in Risk-Sharing Arrangements, *Review of Economic Studies*, 70 (1): 87-113.

Gertler, P. and J. Gruber (2002), Insuring Consumption Against Illness, *American Economic Review*, 92 (1): 55-70.

Gillespie, S., J. Mason, and R. Martorell (1996), How Nutrition Improves, ACC / SCN Nutrition Policy Discussion Paper 15, United Nations Administrative Committee on Coordination / Sub-Committee on Nutrition, Geneva.

Glewwe, P. and G. Hall (1998), Are some groups more vulnerable to macroeconomic shocks than others, Hypothesis tests based on panel data from Peru, *Journal of Development Economics*, 56 (1): 181-206.

Glynn, J.R., M. Carael, A. Burve, S. Anagonou, L. Zekeng, M. Kahindo, and R. Musonda (2004), Does increased general schooling protect against HIV infection? A study in four African cities, *Tropical Medicine and International Health*, 9 (1): 4-14.

Goldstein, H. (1999), *Multilevel Statistical Models*, London: Arnold.

Goldstein, H. (1987), *Multilevel Models in Educational and Social Research*, London: Griffin.

Gopalan, C. (1992), Undernutrition: Measurement and Poverty, in S.R. Osmani (ed) *Undernutrition and Poverty*, Oxford: Oxford University Press.

Graff Zivin, J.S., H. Thirumurthy, and M. Goldstein (2006), AIDS treatment and Intrahousehold Resource Allocations: Childrens' Nutrition and Schooling in Kenya, NBER Working Paper No. 12689, NBER.

Gray, R.H., M.J. Wawer, D. Servadda, N. Sewankambo, C. Li, F. Wabwire-Mangen, L. Paxton, N. Kiwanuka, and G. Kigozi (1998), Population-based study of fertility in women with HIV-1 in Uganda, *Lancet*, 351: 98-103.

Grimard, F. (1997), Household Consumption Smoothing through Ehtnic Ties: Evidence from Côte d'Ivoire, *Journal of Development Economics*, 53: 391-422.

Grimm, M. (2007), Removing the anonymity axiom in assessing pro-poor growth. With an application to Indonesia and Peru, *Journal of Economic Inequality*, forthcoming.

Grimm, M., C. Guénard, and S. Mesplé-Somps (2002), What has happened to the urban population in Côte d'Ivoire since the eighties? An analysis of monetary poverty and deprivation over 15 years of household data, *World Development*, 30 (6): 1073-1095.

Grimm, M. and K. Harttgen (2007), Longer Life, Higher Welfare?, *Oxford Economic Papers*, forthcoming.

Grosse, M., S. Klasen, and J. Spatz (2005), Creating National Poverty Profiles and Growth Incidence Curves with Incomplete Income or Consumption Expenditure Data, Background Paper for the Study: Operationalizing Pro-Poor Growth - Country Case Study Bolivia, Ibero-America Institute for Economic Research (IAI) Discussion Paper No. 129, University of Göttingen.

Grosskurth, H., F. Mosha, and J. Todd (1995), A community trial of the impact of improved sexually transmitted disease treatment on the HIV epidemic in Rural Tanzania: 2. Baseline Survey Results, *AIDS*, 9: 927-934.

Günther, I., M.A. Marouani, and M. Raffinot (2006), La croissance est-elle propauvres au Mali?, Document De Travial DT/2006-15, Paris, DIAL.

Günther, I. and K. Harttgen (2005), Vulnerability to Poverty in Madagascar. Background Paper prepared for the World Bank Social Protection Unit, Mimeo, University of Göttingen.

Haddad, L. and S. Gillespie (2001), Effective Food and Nutrition Policy Responses to HIV/AIDS: What We Know and Need to Know, FCND Discussion paper No. 112, International Food Policy Research Institute (IFPRI), Washington.

Hanmer, L. and D. Booth (2001), Pro-Poor Growth: Why do we need it?, Mimeo, London, ODI.

Hargreaves, J.R., L.A. Morison, J. Chege, N. Rutenberg, M. Kahindo, H.A. Weiss, R. Hayes, and A. Burve (2002), Socioeconomic status and risk of HIV infection in an urban population in Kenya, *Tropical Medicine and International Health*, 7 (9): 793-802.

Hasin, A., R. Bequm, M.R. Khan, and F. Ahmed (1996), Relationship between birth weight and biochemical measures of maternal nutritional status at delivery in Bangladeshi urban poors, *International Journal of Food Sciences and Nutrition*, 43(3): 273-279.

Hellinger, F. (1993), The Lifetime Cost of Treating a Person with HIV, *Journal of the American Medical Association*, 270: 474-748.

Hill, K., G. Bicego, and M. Mahy (2001), Childhood Mortality in Kenya: An Examination of Trends and Determinants in the Late 1980 to Mid 1990s, Hopkins Population Center Working Paper No. WP 01-01, Johns Hopkins University.

Hoddinott J. and A. Quisumbing (2003), Methods for Microeconometric Risk and Vulnerability Assessments, Social Protection Discussion Paper, No. 0324, Washington, World Bank.

Hox, J. (2002), *Multilevel Analysis - Techniques and Applications*, Mahwah: Erlbaum.

INE (2004), Encuesta Nacional de Demografia y Salud 2003, Informe Preliminar, La Paz.

Jalan, J. and M. Ravallion (1999), Are the poor less well insured? Evidence on vulnerability to income risk in rural China, *Journal of Development Economics*, 58 (1): 61-81.

Jamison, D.T., J.D. Sachs, and J. Wang (2001), The Effect of the AIDS Epidemic on Economic Welfare in Sub-Saharan Africa, Commission on Macroeconomics and Health (CMH) Working Paper Series No. WG1: 13.

Kanbur R. and D. Mukherjee (2003), Premature Mortality and Poverty Measurement, ISER Working Papers No. 2003-6, ISER, University of Essex.

Kandala, N.B., S. Lang, L. Fahrmeir, and S. KLasen (2001), Semiparametric Analysis of the Socio-Demographic and Spatial Determinants of Chronic Undernutrition in Two African Countries, *Research in Official Statistics*, 4 (1): 81-100.

Kakwani, N. and E. Pernia (2000), What is Pro-Poor Growth?, *Asian Development Review*, 18 (1): 1-16.

Kakwani, N. and H. Son (2006), Pro-Poor Growth: The Asian Experience, WIDER Research Paper No. 2006/56, Helsinki, WIDER.

Kakwani, N. and H. Son (2002), Pro-Poor Growth: Concept, Measurement, and Application, Mimeo, University of New South Wales, Sidney, Australia.

Kakwani, N. (1993), Performance in living standards - An international comparison, *Journal of Development Economics*, 41: 307-336.

Klasen, S. (2007), Poverty, undernutrition, and child mortality; some inter-regional puzzles and their implications for research and policy, *Journal of Economic Inequality*, forthcoming.

Klasen, S. (2005), Economic Growth and Poverty Recuction: Measurement and Policy Issues, OECD Development Center Working Paper No. 246, OECD.

Klasen, S. (2004), In Search of the Holy Grail: How to Achieve Pro Poor Growth?, in Tungodden, B., N. Stern, and I. Kolstad (eds) *Toward Pro Poor Policies-Aid, Institutions, and Globalization*, New York: Oxford University Press.

Klasen, S. (2003), Malnourished and Surviving in South Asia, better Nourished and Dying Young in Africa: What can Explain this Puzzle? in FAO (eds) *Measurement and Assessment of Food Deprivation and Undernutrition*, Rome: FAO.

Klasen, S. (2000), Measuring Poverty and Deprivation in South Africa, *Review of Income and Wealth*, 46 (1): 33-58.

Klasen, S. (1996), Nutrition, Health, and Mortality in Sub-Saharan Africa: Is there a Gender Bias?, *Journal of Development Studies*, 32: 913-933.

Klasen, S., R. Thiele, M. Grosse, J. Lay, J. Spatz, and M. Wiebelt (2004), Operationalizing Pro-Poor Growth - Country Case Study Bolivia, Ibero-America Institute for Economic Research (IAI) Discussion Paper No. 101, University of Göttingen.

Kochar, A. (1995), Explaining Household Vulnerability to Idiosyncratic Income Shocks, *The American Economic Review*, 85 (2): 159-164.

Kremer, M. (1996), Integrating Behavioral Choice into Epidemiological Models of Aids, *The Quarterly Journal of Economics*, 112 (1): 115-139.

Lanjouw, P. and M. Ravallion (1998), Benefit Incidence and the Timing of Program Capture, Washington, World Bank.

Lee, E.T. (1992), *Statistical Methods for Survival Data Analysis*, 2nd edition, Oklahoma: University of Oklahoma.

Ligon, E. and S. Schechter (2003), Measuring vulnerability, *Economic Journal*, 113 (486): C95-C102.

Ligon, E. and S. Schechter (2004), Evaluating Different Approaches to Estimating Vulnerability, Social Protection Discussion Paper Series, No. 0410, Washington, World Bank.

Luttmer, E.F.P. (2001), Measuring Poverty Dynamics and Inequality in Transition Economies: Disentangling Real Events from Noisy Data, World Bank Policy Research Paper No. 2549, Washington, World Bank.

Maas, C.J.M. and J. Hox (2004), Robustness issues in multilevel regression analysis, *Statistica Neerlandica*, 58 (2): 127-137.

MacFarlan, M. and S. Sgherri (2001), The macroeconomic impact of HIV/AIDS in Botswana, IMF Working Paper WP/01/80, Washington, IMF.

Madalla, G.S. (1977), *Econometrics*, Tokyo: McGraw-Hill.

McCulloch, N. and B. Baulch (2000), Tracking Pro-Poor Growth, ID21 insights No. 31, Sussex, Institute of Development Studies.

Marcoux, A. (2002), Sex Differentials in Undernutrition: A look at Survey Evidence, *Population and Development Review*, 28 (2): 275-284.

Martorell, R., K.L. Kettel, M.L. Hughes, and L.M. Grummer-Strawn (1998), Obesity in Latin American women and children, *Journal of Nutrition*, 128: 1464-1473.

Mason, W.M., G.M. Wong, and B. Entwistle (1983), Contextual analysis through the multilevel linear model, *Sociological Methodology*, 13: 72-103.

Menon, R., M.J. Wawer, J.K. Konde-Lule, N.K. Sewanlambo, and C. Li (1998), The economic impact of adult mortality on households in Rakai district, Uganda, in M. Ainsworth, L. Fransen and M.Over (eds) *Confronting AIDS: Evidence from the Developing World*, Brussels: European Commission and Washington: World Bank.

Messer, E. (1986), The 'Small but Healthy' Hypothesis: Historical, Political and Ecological Influences on Nutritional Standards, *Human Ecology*, 14 (1): 57-75.

Mills, B., Ninno, C., and H. Rajemison (2003), Commune Shocks, Household Assets and Economic Well-Being in Madagascar, Mimeo, Washington, World Bank.

Montes, C. (2003), Results-Based Public Management in Bolivia, Overseas Development Institute Working Paper 202, ODI, London.

Morgan, D., C. Mahe, B. Mayanja, J. Okongo, R. Lubega, and J. Whitworth (2002), HIV-1 infection in rural Africa: is there a difference in median time to AIDS and survival compared with that in industrial countries?, *AIDS*, 16(4): 587-603.

Morduch, J. (1994), Poverty and Vulnerability, *The American Economic Review*, 84 (2): 221-225.

Morduch, J. (2005), Consumption smoothing across space: Testing theories of risk-sharing in the ICRISAT study region of South India, in S. Dercon (ed) *Insurance against Poverty*, Oxford: Oxford University Press.

Mosley, W.H. and L.C. Chen (1984), An Analytical Framework for the Study of Child Survival in Developing Countries, *Population and Development Review*, 10: 25-45.

Mukherjee, D. (2001), Measuring multidimensional deprivation, *Mathematical Social Sciences*, 42: 233-251.

Mutangadura, G.B. (2000), Household welfare impacts of mortality of adult females in Zimbabwe: implications for policy and program development, Paper presented at the AIDS and economics symposium organized by IAEN, Durban, South Africa, 7-8 July 2000.

Nduati, R., B.A. Richardson, G. John, D. Mbori-Ngasha, A. Muratha, J. Ndinya-Achola, J. Burano, F.E. Onyango, and J. Kreis (2001), Effect of breastfeeding on mortality among HIV-1 infected women: a randomized trial, *Lancet*, 357: 1651-1655.

Osmani, S.R. (1997), Poverty and Nutrition in South Asia, in *Nutrition and Poverty: papers from the ACC/SCN 24th Session Symposium*, Kathmandu, March 1997, United Nations Administrative Committee on Coordination, Sub-Committee on Nutrition.

OECD (2006), *Promoting Pro-Poor Growth: Key Policy Messages*, Paris: OECD.

OECD (2001), Rising to the Global Challenge: Partnership for Reducing World Poverty, Statement by the DAC High Level Meeting. April 25- 26, 2001, OECD, Paris.

Osberg, L. (2000), Schooling, Literacy and Individual Earnings, Statistics Canada, Ottawa, Canada.

Oster, E. (2006), Measuring the Magnitude of HIV in Africa, Mimeo, University of Chicago and NBER.

Over, M. (1992), The macroeconomic impact of AIDS in Sub-Saharan Africa, Washington, World Bank.

Paxon, C.H. (1992), Using Weather Variability to Estimate the Response of Savings to Transitory Income in Thailand, *The American Economic Review*, 82 (1): 15-33.

Pebley, A.R., N. Goldman, and G. Rodriguez (1996), Prenatal and delivery care and Childhood immunization in Guatemala: do family and community matter?, *Demography*, 33: 231-247.

Pelletier, D.L. and E.A. Frongillo (2002), Changes in Child Survival are strongly Associated with Changes in Malnutrition in Developing Countries, *The Journal of Nutrition*, 133: 107-119.

Pelletier, D.L., E.A. Frongillo, Jr., D.G. Schroeder, and J.P. Habicht (1995), The effects of malnutrition on child mortality in developing countries, *Bulletin of the World Health Organization*, 73 (4): 443-448.

Pelletier, D. (1994), The relationship between child anthropometry and mortality in developing countries, *Journal of Nutrition*, (Supplement) 124: 2047S-2081S.

Piwoz, E.G. and E.A. Prebele (2000), HIV/AIDS and Nutrition: A Review of the Literature and Recommendations for Nutritional Care and Support in Sub-Saharan Africa, Support for Analysis and Research in Africa (SARA) Project, Washington, USAID.

Pritchett, L., Suryahadi, A., and S. Sumarto (2000), Quantifying Vulnerability to Poverty: A Proposed Measure, with Application to Indonesia. *SMERU Working Paper*, Social Monitoring and Early Response Unit (SMERU), Washington, World Bank.

Pritchett, L. and L.H. Summers (1996), Wealthier is healthier, *Journal of Human Ressources*, 31 (4): 841-868.

Ramalingaswami, V., U. Johsnon, and J. Rohde (1996), The Asian enigma, in *Progress of Nations*, New York: United Nations Childrens' Fund.

Rao, S., C.S. Yajuik, A. Kanade, C.H.D. Fall, B.M. Margetts, A.A. Jackson, R. Shier, S. Joshi, S. Rege, H. Lubree, and B. Desai (2001), Intake of

Micronutrient-Rich Foods in Rural Indian Mothers is Associated with the Size of their Babies at Birth: Pune Maternal Nutrition Study, *Journal of Nutrition*, 131: 1217-1224.

Ravallion M. (2005), On the Contribution of Demographic Change to Aggregate Poverty Measures for the Developing World, World Bank Policy Research Working Paper No. 3580, Washington, World Bank.

Ravallion M. (2005a), A Poverty-Inequality Trade-Off?, *Journal of Economic Inequality*, 3 (2): 169-181.

Ravallion, M. and S. Chen (2003), Measuring Pro-Poor Growth, *Economics Letters*, 78 (1): 93-99.

Ravallion, M. and G. Datt. (2002), Why has economic growth been more pro-poor in some states of India than others?, *Journal of Development Economics*, 68: 381-400.

Ray, D. (1998), *Development Economics*, Princeton: Princeton University Press.

Ridder, G. and I. Tunali (1999), Stratified partial likelihood estimation, *Journal of Econometrics*, 92: 193-232.

Roberts, J. (2003), Poverty Reduction Outcomes in Education and Health: Public Expenditure and Aid, Overseas Development Institute Working Paper 210, ODI, London.

Ryder, R.W., M. Kamenga, M. Knusu, V. Batter, and W. Heyward (1994), AIDS orphans in Kinshasa, Zaire: Incidence and socioeconomic consequences, *AIDS*, 8 (5): 673-679.

Sahn, D.E. and D. Stiefel (2003), Exploring Alternative Measures of Welfare in the Absense of Expenditure Data, *Review of Income and Wealth*, 49 (4): 463-489.

Schultz, T.P. (1999), Health and Schooling Investments in Africa, *Journal of Economic Perspectives*, 13 (3): 67-88.

Seckler, D. (1982), Small but healthy: a basic hypothesis in the theory, measurement and policy of malnutrition, in: D. Sukhatme (ed) *Newer Concepts in Nutrition and their Implication for Policy*, Maharashtra Association for the Cultivation of Science, Pune.

Sen, A.K. (1988), The Concept of Development, in H. Chenery and T. Srinivasan (eds) *Handbook of Development Economics*, Vol. 1, 9-26.

Sen, A.K. (1987), *Standard of Living*, New York: Cambridge University Press.

Sen, A.K. (1981), Public action and the quality of live in developing countries, *Oxford Bulletin of Economics and Statistics*, 43: 287-319.

Smith, J., F. Nalagoda, and M.J. Wawer (1999), Education attainment as a predictor of HIV risk in rural Uganda: results from a population-based study, *International Journal of STD and AIDS*, 10: 452-459.

Smith, L.C. and L. Haddad (2000), Explaining Child Malnutrition in Developing Countries, International Food Policy Research Institute (IFPRI), Washington.

Son, H. (2003), Approaches to Defining and Measuring Pro-Poor Growth, Mimeo, Washington, World Bank.

Spira, R., P. Lepage, P. Msellati, P. Van de Perre, V. Leroy, A. Simonon, E. Karita, and F. Dabis (1999), Natural History of Human Immunodefiency Virus Type 1 Infection in Children: A Five-Year Prospective Study in Rwanda, *PEDIATRICS*, 104 (5).

Ssewanyana, S. and S. Younger (2004), Infant Mortality in Uganda: Determinants, Trends, and the Millennium Development Goals, Development Policy Research Unit (DPRU), University of Cape Town, South Africa.

Steenbergen, M.R. and B.S. Jones (2002), Modelling Multilevel Data Structures, *American Journal of Political Science*, 46 (1): 218-237.

Strauss, J. and D. Duncan (1998), Health, Nutrition and Development, *Journal of Economic Literature*, 36 (2): 766-817.

Subbaro, K. and L. Rany (1995), Social gains from female education: A cross-national study, *Economic development and cultural change*, 44 (1): 105-128.

Summer, A. (2003), Economic and Non-Economic Well-Being: A Review of Progress on the Meaning and Measurement of Poverty, Paper Prepared for WIDER Conference: Inequality, Poverty and Human Well-Being, May 30-31, 2003, Helsinki.

Svedberg, P. (2002), Hunger in India - Facts and Challenges, Institute for International Economic Studies Seminar Paper No. 699, Stockholm.

Svedberg, P. (2000), *Poverty and Undernutrition: Theory, Measurement and Policy*, Oxford: Oxford University Press.

Svedberg, P. (1999), 841 Million Undernourished? On the Tyranny of Deriving a Number, *World Development*, 27 (12): 2081-2098.

Taha, T.E., G.A. Dallabeta, J.K. Canner, J.D. Chphangwi, G. Liomba, D.R. Hoover, and P.G. Miotti (1995), The effect of immunodeficiency virus infection on birthweight and infant and child mortality in urban Mali, *International Journal of Epidemiology*, 24 (5): 1022-1029.

Tesliuc, E. and K. Lindert (2004), Risk and Vulnerability in Guatemala: A Quantitative and Qualitative Assessment, Social Protection Discussion Paper No. 0404, Washington, World Bank.

Thomas, V., Y. Wang, and X. Fan. (2000), Measuring Educational Inequality: Gini Coefficients of Education, World Bank Policy Research Working Paper 2525, World Bank.

Topouzis, D. (1994), The socio-economic impact of HIV/AIDS on rural families with an emphasis on youth, Rome, FAO.

Townsend, R.M. (1994), Risk and Insurance in Village India, *Econometrica*, 62 (3): 539-591.

Udry, C. (1995), Risk and Saving in Northern Nigeria, *The American Economic Review*, 85 (5): 1287-1300.

UN (2006), *The Human Development Report 2006*, New York: United Nations.

UN (2005), *The Millennium Development Goals Report 2005*, New York: United Nations.

UN (2005a), Population, Development and HIV/AIDS with Particular Emphasis on Poverty - The Concise Report, New York, United Nations.

UN (2005b), *The Human Development Report 2005*, New York: United Nations.

UN (2004), The Impact of AIDS, Department of Economic and Social Affairs, New York: United Nations.

UN (2000), *A Better World for All*, New York: United Nations.

UN (2000a), United Nations Millennium Declaration, A/RES55/2, New York, United Nations.

UN (1996), *Human Development Report 1996*, New York: United Nations.

UN (1991), *Human Development Report 1991*, New York: United Nations.

UNAIDS (2006), *2006 Report on the global AIDS epidemic*, New York: UNAIDS.

UNDP (2000), Human Development Report 2000 Technical Report, pp. 269-273, New York, United Nations.

UNICEF (2004), Progress for Children - A Child Survival Report Card Vol 1, New York, UNICEF.

UNICEF (1998), The State of the Worlds' Children 1998, New York, UNICEF.

UNICEF (1990), Strategy for improved nutrition of children and women in developing countries, New York, UNICEF.

Van der Klaauw, B. and L. Wang (2004), Child mortality in Rural India, Mimeo, Washington, World Bank.

Van de Walle, D. (1998), Assessing the Welfare Impacts of Public Spending, *World Development*, 26 (3): 365-379.

Van de Walle, D., and K. Nead (eds) (1995), *Public Spending and the Poor - Theory and Evidence*, published for the World Bank, Baltimore and London: John Hopkins University Press.

White, H. and E. Anderson (2000), Growth versus Distribution: Does the Pattern of Growth Matter?, *Development Policy Review*, 19 (3): 267-289.

WHO (2005), *Health and the Millennium Development Goals*, World Health Organization: Geneva.

WHO (2006), *WHO Child Growth Standards - Length/ height-for-age, weight-for-age, weight-for-length and body mass index for age - Methods and Development*, Geneva: WHO.

WHO (2006a), WHO/UNAIDS Global HIV/AIDS Online Database.

WHO (2002), *World Health Report 2001*, Geneva: World Health Organization.

WHO (1995), Physical Status: The Use and Interpretation of Anthropometry, WHO Technical Report Series No. 854, Geneva, World Health Organization.

Woolard, I. and S. Klasen (2005), Income Mobility and Household Poverty Dynamics in South Africa, *Journal of Development Studies*, 41: 865-897.

World Bank (1997), *Confronting AIDS: Public priorities in a global epidemic*, Oxford: Oxford University Press.

World Bank (2005), World Development Indicators 2005, World Bank.

World Bank (2005a), *World Development Report 2005*, Washington: World Bank.

World Bank (2004), Bolivia Poverty Assessment: Establishing the Basis for more Pro-Poor Growth, Report No. 28068-Bo, Washington, World Bank.

World Bank (2000), *World Development Report 2000 - Attacking Poverty*, Washington: World Bank.

Yamaguchi, K. (1991), Event History Analysis, Applied Social Research Series No. 28, Sage.

Young, A. (2005), The Gift of the Dying: The Tragedy of AIDS and the Welfare of Future African Generations, *Quarterly Journal of Economics*, CXX (2): 423-466.

Göttinger Studien zur Entwicklungsökonomik
Göttingen Studies in Development Economics

Herausgegeben von/Edited by Hermann Sautter
und/and Stephan Klasen

Die Bände 1-8 sind über die Vervuert Verlagsgesellschaft (Frankfurt/M.) zu beziehen.

Bd./Vol. 9 Hermann Sautter / Rolf Schinke (eds.): Social Justice in a Market Economy. 2001.

Bd./Vol.10 Philipp Albert Theodor Kircher: Poverty Reduction Strategies. A comparative study applied to empirical research. 2002.

Bd./Vol.11 Matthias Blum: Weltmarktintegration, Wachstum und Innovationsverhalten in Schwellen ländern. Eine theoretische Diskussion mit einer Fallstudie über „Argentinien 1990-1999". 2003.

Bd./Vol.12 Jan Müller-Scheeßel: Die Privatisierung und Regulierung des Wassersektors. Das Beispiel Buenos Aires/Argentinien. 2003.

Bd./Vol.13 Ludger J. Löning: Economic Growth, Biodiversity Conservation, and the Formation of Human Capital in a Developing Country. 2004.

Bd./Vol.14 Silke Woltermann: Transitions in Segmented Labor Markets. The Case of Brazil. 2004.

Bd./Vol.15 Jörg Stosberg: Political Risk and the Institutional Environment for Foreign Direct Investment in Latin America. An Empirical Analysis with a Case Study on Mexico. 2005.

Bd./Vol.16 Derk Bienen: Die politische Ökonomie von Arbeitsmarktreformen in Argentinien. 2005.

Bd./Vol.17 Dierk Herzer: Exportdiversifizierung und Wirtschaftswachstum. Das Fallbeispiel Chile. 2006.

Bd./Vol.18 Jann Lay: Poverty and Distributional Impact of Economic Policies and External Shocks. Three Case Studies from Latin America Combining Macro and Micro Approaches. 2007.

Bd./Vol.19 Kenneth Harttgen: Empirical Analysis of Determinants, Distribution and Dynamics of Poverty. 2007.

www.peterlang.de

Peter Lang · Internationaler Verlag der Wissenschaften

Clemens Breisinger

Modelling Infrastructure Investments, Growth and Poverty Impact

A Two-Region Computable General Equilibrium Perspective on Vietnam

Frankfurt am Main, Berlin, Bern, Bruxelles, New York, Oxford, Wien, 2006.
XIX, 174 pp., num. tab. and graphs
Development Economics and Policy. Edited by Franz Heidhues and Joachim von Braun. Vol. 56
ISBN 978-3-631-55557-6 · pb. € 39.–*

Evaluation pro-poor growth enhancing investments in infrastructure and rural development requires comprehensive appraisal tools. Traditional methods have taken a project or sector perspective that did not capture economy-wide effects. However, in addition to inter-sectoral effects, large-scale investments can also have long-term impacts on national capital formation, the government budget and the foreign trade balance. This study builds a computable general equilibrium model and links it to a micro-accounting module for poverty analysis in Vietnam. The spatial dimension is captured by incorporating two regions into the model: the lagging mountainous province of Son La is compared to the rest of Vietnam. This model is applied to several infrastructure investments and identifies economic growth rates that would be needed to achieve the first Millennium Development Goal.

Contents: Reviewing Growth, Poverty and Infrastructure: Theory and Empirical Evidence · Understanding Socio-Economic Development in Vietnam · Modelling Spatial Impacts of Infrastructure Investments · Analysing Regional and National Impacts of Infrastructure Investments

FSC
www.fsc.org
MIX
Papier | Fördert gute Waldnutzung
FSC® C083411

Kolibri 360 GmbH
Ferdinand-Jühlke-Straße 7
99095 Erfurt, Deutschland
produktsicherheit@kolibri360.de

Druck:
CPI Druckdienstleistungen GmbH
im Auftrag der
Kolibri 360 GmbH
Ferdinand-Jühlke-Str. 7
99095 Erfurt